THE STUFFED GRIFFIN

presented by

The Utility Club
Griffin, Georgia

Celebrating
Fifty Years
Of Volunteer Service To The Community
1927 - 1977

ii

ISBN No. 0-9607584-0-2

First Printing	October, 1976
Second Printing	November, 1976
Third Printing	October, 1977
Fourth Printing	December, 1978
Fifth Printing	February, 1980
Sixth Printing	September, 1981
Seventh Printing	October, 1982
Eighth Printing	October, 1984
Ninth Printing	October, 1986
Tenth Printing	June, 1989
Eleventh Printing	June, 1992
Twelfth Printing	May, 1996
Thirteenth Printing	March, 2002

For additional copies, please use order blanks in the back of the book or write:

The Stuffed Griffin
P.O. Box 711
Griffin, Georgia 30224

THE STUFFED GRIFFIN may be obtained by retail outlets or organizations for fund raising at special rates. For further information, write the above address.

The Utility Club of Griffin has been serving the community for over 60 years through volunteer projects and community improvement efforts. Proceeds from the sale of THE STUFFED GRIFFIN will be used for community service projects sponsored by the Utility Club.

WIMMER
COOKBOOKS
ConsolidatedGraphics

1-800-548-2537

FOREWORD

The Griffin is a mythical animal, half eagle, half lion, but there is nothing mythical about our recipe collection, "stuffed" cover to cover with parties, tips, and recipes ranging from easy to elegant. Griffin, Georgia mingles the gracious traditions of our Southern heritage with the cosmopolitan flair of our neighboring metropolis, Atlanta.

Each section in The Stuffed Griffin has been tested, edited, and evaluated to give you, the discerning cook, the best recipes of middle Georgia, where gracious "dining in" is a practiced art.

The Utility Club
Cookbook Committee

Mrs. William S. Colvin
Editor

Mrs. H. Alfred Bolton III
Associate Editor

Section Editors:

Mrs. John R. Carlisle
Mrs. Lutie C. Johnston
Mrs. Lester L. Luttrell
Mrs. Taylor B. Manley, Jr.
Mrs. Eugene F. Robbins, Jr.
Mrs. James E. Scharnhorst

Mrs. Warren K. Wells
Publicity

Mrs. Donald L. Hutcheson
Cover Design and Illustrations

The ten months from conception to publication of The Stuffed Griffin have been busy, hectic and exhilarating. What a memorable way to celebrate our 50th year! We are deeply appreciative to each member of The Utility Club and to our many friends for their imaginative contributions, their interest and their enthusiasm. A special thanks to our husbands who gave up their old favorites to test new creations and to our patient children for whom the words "cookbook" and "recipe" have become synonymous with "mommy".

TABLE OF CONTENTS

ABBREVIATIONS

tsp.	-	teaspoon(s)
T.	-	tablespoon(s)
c.	-	cup
pt.(s)	-	pint(s)
qt.(s)	-	quart(s)
gal.	-	gallon
oz.	-	ounce(s)
lb.(s)	-	pound(s)
lge.	-	large
med.	-	medium
sm.	-	small
pkg.	-	packages
†	-	means will freeze
*	-	designation by a recipe means that it was submitted by 3 or more people
**	-	(menu section) indicates recipe is included in book

Trade names of products are given
only when necessary.

Oven temperatures are pre-heated
unless otherwise stated.

MENUS and PARTIES

BRUNCH

NEW ORLEANS BRUNCH

Ambrosia (Beverage)**

Grilled Grapefruit**

Eggs Bourguignonne**

French Bread**

Wine - Piesporter Riesling

Crepes Fitzgerald**

Cafe au Lait

NEW YEAR'S MORNING BRUNCH

Bloody Marys   Milk Punch**

Eggs Rachel**

with

Maple Flavored Ham**

Cheese Grits**   Seasonal Fruit Salad

Honey & Sour Cream Dressing

Blueberry Muffins**

Coffee Cake

Coffee

SEASONAL LUNCHES FOR TEN

SPRING

Chicken Salad** on nest bed of
Chow Mein Noodles

Baked Cheese-Stuffed Tomatoes**

Asparagus With Hollandaise**

Yeast Rolls**

Chocolate Velvet Pie**

SUMMER

Aspic ring** filled with Crabmeat and
Homemade Mayonnaise**

Artichoke Hearts and Hearts of Palm
Marinated

Fresh Fruit with Cointreau

Cheese Biscuits**

Crustless Coconut Pie**

WINTER

Hot Chicken Salad**

Green Beans (French-Style)**
with Mushrooms

Tart Congealed Salad
(not creamy)

Mother's Date Muffins**

Rum Cream Pie**

TAILGATE PICNICS

I

Sliced Sirloin Tip Roast
(cook pinker than usual)

Sour Cream Dressing
for Meat
(add horseradish and lemon juice
to sour cream - to taste)

Loaf of Pre-buttered French Bread
for Sandwiches

Artichokes
Mayonnaise for Dipping

Frozen Cheese Cake

Wine - Barbera or Hearty Burgundy

II

Pork Picnic Rolls**

Assorted Raw Vegetables
Onion or Garlic Flavored Bottled Salad Dressing
for Vegetable Dip

Cookies

Fruit

Wine - Gamay Beaujolais

AFTERNOON TEA FOR "MISS KITTY"

Sandwiches

Rolled-Up Deviled Ham**   Chicken Salad

Fig Conserve**   Carrot**

Cucumber**

*   *

Graham Bread Slices with Cream Cheese

Concord Butter Mints**

Nanaemo Bars**

Apricot Balls**

Pound Cake**

Assorted Cookies

*   *

Cheese Straws**

Nuts

*   *

Fruit Punch

SOUTHERN SUMMER BARBECUE

Brunswick Stew**

Barbecued Ribs**   Barbecued Chicken**

Cole Slaw**

Corn on the Cob

French Bread**

Iced Tea

Cakes, Pies

COME FOR COCKTAILS

Country Ham with Homemade Mayonnaise**

Use Two:

Hot Sausage in Sour Cream**
Broccoli Dip**
Chafing Dish Oysters with Mushrooms**

Serve from Crock:
Sardine Pate** or Liver Pate**
with Toast Points

Celery Sticks with Quick Vegetable Dip**

Olive Cheese Balls**

For Set-ups see Helpful Hints

DINNER

FOR TWO

Jellied Consomme in Avocado Halves

Beef Wellington**

Celery au Gratin**

Baked Tomato

Wilted Lettuce Salad**

Lemon Ice**

FOR TEN

Steak Tartare on Melba Toast**

Iced Tomato Soup

Leg of Lamb**
with
Horseradish and Currant Jelly**

Bibb Lettuce Salad
with Oil and Vinegar

Potatoes au Gratin**

Biscuits**

Baked Custard with Fresh Fruit**

DINNER

FOR TWENTY-FIVE

Hot Hors D'oeuvres

Cheese Wafers**

Artichokes Marinated in Parmesan Cheese, Oil and Vinegar

French Chicken**   Sliced Tenderloin

Fruit Bowl

Broccoli Casserole**

Spinach Salad**

Hot Rolls**

Pecan Tarts**

Queen Ann's Lace & fresh strawberries

INTERNATIONAL DINNERS

MEXICAN DINNER PARTY

Sangria**

Avocado and Shrimp Cocktail**

Beef and Bean Enchiladas**

Chicken Mexicaine**

Three Bean Salad**

Honeydew Melon Slices with Lime Garnish

Bread Sticks or Rolls

Vanilla Ice Cream with Kahlua**

Use brightly colored or striped tablecloth, large paper flowers, Mexican clay birds and black wrought-iron candle holders.

ITALIAN DINNER PARTY

Antipasto Tray

Salami

Melon Wrapped with Prosciutto

Assorted Raw Vegetables with Dip

Filetti di Pollo Parmigiana**

Fettuccini

Spinach Salad**

Hard Rolls

Strawberries Capri**

Chianti

FAMILY CAROLING PARTY

Hot Buttered Rum**   Instant Hot Chocolate**

Scrambled Eggs

Baked Grits

Fruit Bake**

Biscuits   Sweet Rolls

Fruit Cake Drops**

Pecan Tarts**

Pecan Crescents**

A versatile menu for a cold holiday evening - perfect for all the hungry carolers, young and old.

COFFEE TASTING

A great mixer for large groups or an elegant finale for a dinner party.

Have a large 30-cup coffee maker available to guests or 2-3 coffee makers for a crowd. Figure 2 or 3 cups per person. Disposable cups encourage guests to try several creations.

Make several "stations" around the table with spoons and garnishments, plus cards with the name of the coffee creations and what to mix (no proportions).

Serve assorted sweets and nuts and enjoy this relaxed gathering.

Brazilian Coffee
Creme de Cacao
Cinnamon Sticks
Cream
Grated Sweet Chocolate

Caribbean Coffee
Rum
Cream
Fresh Grated Nutmeg

Irish Coffee
Whipped Cream
Irish Whiskey

Mexican Coffee
Cinnamon Sticks
Cream
Grated Chocolate
Kahlua

Tuscano Cafe
Sugar
Lemon Peel
Brandy

BIRTHDAY TIPS FOR YOUNG CHILDREN

Do not plan too long a party for young children. The longest list of games will take a short time with little ones.

*   *   *

Have whistle handy - saves voice.

*   *   *

Have prizes for everyone if the age group is 5 or under.

*   *   *

If you plan to give balloons as favors, blow up twice as many as you think you'll need. Tie on individual strings or yarn.

*   *   *

Serve small portions. Ice Cream spooned into small plastic cups and stored in freezer ahead of time helps in serving a young group.

*   *   *

Plan not only your activities, but space your time as well. Have games initially to help include shy, reluctant guests, eat and then have a few games after the refreshments.

*   *   *

Paper bags, pre-labeled with the name of each child, will help you keep up with which favor belongs to whom!

*   *   *

Have plenty of help - not onlookers.

*   *   *

Have a good time - parties for any age group should be fun for everyone!

CELEBRATIONS FOR THE VERY YOUNG
THEME PARTIES

OLD MacDONALD (Ages 3-5)

Invitations: Farm Animal Stationery   **Time:** 1 hour without lunch
1½ hours with lunch

Decorations: Bale of Hay, Farm Animal Pictures, and
Lots of Balloons

Beginning Games (Need 3 Helpers)
Choose all and play simultaneously, so that no one has to wait long or create your own theme games.

1. Drop The Beans in the Bottle
   Large mouth bottle - drop string beans (or dry beans) from appropriate height above.

2. Throw Pumpkins in Basket
   Balls, laundry basket - throw ball from appropriate distance.

3. Toss Rings over Rabbit Ears (or Pole-Cornstalk)
   Toy rabbit, plastic rings.

Go Fishing
Need:
1. Wooden dowels cut 14-15" (or paper dowel from hangers), string tied on end with small magnet attached.

2. 10 or more fish per child cut from paper with paper clip attached.

Fishing game can go on for 15-20 minutes if you have a lot of fish and encourage youngsters to "throw back" their catch.

Food
Lunch: Corn dogs
Potato Chips
Punch

Ice Cream
Cake

For the cake there are many possibilities - animal shapes, barn shape, or Old MacDonald himself. (Wilton's "Raggedy Ann" cake pan can easily be adapted to a boy farmer.)

More Games:
Play and sing Old MacDonald. Give each child an animal picture to imitate. ("Farmer in the Dell" is usually a disaster under 4 or 5 years.)

If you are inside, read "The Little Red Hen", or listen to the record. This story also lends itself well to a puppet show if one is available.

Favors:
Tie small treats in red and blue bandannas - hobo style and send home on the fishing poles.

Inexpensive farm books or cowboy hats add an extra touch.

CIRCUS PARTY (Ages 2-5)

Invitations:
1. Shape of circus tent.
2. Note tied to a balloon.
3. Clown's face

Time:
1 hour without lunch
1½ hours with lunch

Decorations: Lots of balloons, clown posters or pictures, streamers to give feeling of "Big Top", clown costumes if available.

Beginning Games (3 Helpers)
Play simultaneously

1. Lion Act - jump through hoop.
   Need hula-hoop, held a few inches above ground.
   Children jump through.

2. Bean Bag Toss
   Draw picture or paste picture of clown on heavy paper. Cut 2 or 3 large circles to throw bean bags through.

3. Put Nose on Clown
   Need: Picture of clown, red circles cut from paper, mask, or have children close eyes. (Very young children 4 and under will probably not wear mask).

Group Game
Balloon play - keep balloons in air, pop balloons, bounce on nose, bounce with friend. (Whatever is appropriate for age.)

Musical Clowns - cut clown faces from heavy paper - 1 per child. March to circus music and jump on face when music stops.

Food:
Lunch: Hot dogs
           Popcorn
           Punch

           Cake
           Ice Cream

Make clown ice cream by putting scoop on plate and putting a pointed cone on top for hat. Add gum drops for eyes and mouth.

Clown cake shapes can be readily purchased or convert Wilton's "Raggedy Ann" pan to a clown.

More Games
Balloon blowing contest

Hula-Hoop contest

"Tricks" from individuals with other children for audience.

Favors:
Clown party hats
Small plastic circus animals
Neck ruffles (clown attire)
Whistles

STORYBOOK PARTY (Ages 4-7)

Time: 1½ hours

Invitations: Fold construction paper like a book - ask guests to come dressed as their favorite characters.

Decorations:
Signs on sticks
"Magic Mushroom Field"
"Humpty Dumpty's Wall"
"Pirates' Treasure"
"Fishing Hole"
"Jack's Candlestick"

Games: (3 helpers)
1. Humpty Dumpty
Need: Toy Humpty Dumpty or large plastic egg, or paper bag stuffed with newspaper. Place on bench. Players have 3 throws with ball to knock Humpty off wall.

2. Jack's Candlestick
Need: Broomstick and bricks
Players jump over broomstick which is set at appropriate height. Can raise higher if group responds well.

3. Fishing Hole
Need: Pole with string and clothespin and small prizes.
Use large box or open window or curtain to hide helper for go fishing.

Group Game
Pirates' Treasure
Hide small prizes in yard or house and let players find. If group can read, give a series of clues for a few of the prizes.

Food:
Mary Poppins Punch
Freeze small prizes or candies in ice cubes and float in cups.

Mary's Lamb Cake (Wilton's cake mold)
or any whimsical shape that appeals to your child.

Story Book Hour
When everyone is eating and seated announce that you want to meet all the story book characters who came to the party. Have each child come up and either tell, or let their friends guess, who they are. Some will be reluctant - don't push.

Magic Mushroom Field
Lead everyone to the mushroom field where you have large circles of heavy paper in bright colors - one for each child. Play musical mushrooms (chairs).

Favors:
Provide paper bag for prizes won during party.

INDIAN PARTY (Ages 4-7)

Time: 1½ - 2 hours to fall in evening if possible.

Invitations: Make tepees from construction paper triangles, fold in sides to form door. Decorate with Indian signs. Ask guests to wear Indian attire.

Decorations: Outside in woodsy setting if possible, have pit fire laid and tepees (blankets) close by.

Games:

Animal Hunt
Give each player a color sign (or written clue, if they can read). Have colored disks spaced on trail to hidden animals (paper pictures cut into puzzles or stuffed animals.)

War Paint
Provide guests with theatrical makeup crayons (lipstick is hard to get off) and let them make each other up in war paint.

Dances
Light campfire and have a war dance around campfire at a safe distance.

Food:

Cooking sticks for:
Hot dogs
Marshmallows

"Some-Mores"
Graham crackers
Chocolate bars
Marshmallows

(Cake is optional at this party.)

To make "Some-Mores":
First toast marshmallows. Make "sandwich" by placing marshmallows and squares of chocolate between graham crackers.

While guests are eating around campfire have a Big Chief sit in tepee and tell Indian stories (library is excellent source).

Favors:
Indian headdresses
Drums

"MOTHERS" DRESS-UP PARTY" (Ages 4-6 for small group of 6-8)

Invitations: Cut purse shapes (on fold so they will open up) from construction paper. Have guests come dressed as "mothers" and bring a favorite doll (if ages 4 or 5).

Decorations: Balloons, card tables with bright cloths - set with "tea party" equipment. Flowers in center of each table.

Entertainment:

1. Sewing Game
   Need: large eye needles and lengths of thread cut - one per child. See who can thread needle first.

2. Sock Game
   Have large pile of socks - men's and children's multicolored. Give each child several socks and see who can find matches first.

3. Measuring Game
   Have saucer and cup for each child.
   Pour small candy pieces or miniature marshmallows or dry beans into saucer. Give each a spoon (or straw if pieces are large enough not to be "sucked up" and with one hand (or mouth only with straw) have them move all pieces from saucer to cup.

Food - Luncheon
Individual Raggedy Ann salads
½ boiled egg cut lengthwise for head (cloves for eyes, cherry mouth), lettuce leaf "dress" over small serving of tuna fish salad, carrot stick arms and legs.

Punch (in cups and saucers)

Crackers or small sandwiches

Cake - Give individual cakes or 2 cupcakes to each child to decorate - one for herself and one for her doll. Provide canned frosting and plenty of "sprinkles".

More Entertainment
"Make up" each child. Take pictures for mail-home favors (or use a Polaroid camera).

Favors:
Sewing cards - bought or home-made from poster paper and yarn
Small mirrors
"Make your own" necklace sets

AIRPLANE PARTY (Ages 6-10)

Invitations: Paper airplane instructing guests to bring their best flier. (Have rain date.)

Decorations: Airfield "sock" on poles - signs "runway" marked off or "helicopter landing pad".

Entertainment:
Air Show
Demonstration of planes brought by guests. Prizes or ribbons for highest flight, longest, shortest, etc.

Food:
Lunch bags
Canned or bottled soft drinks
Cake - airplane shape - cut from rectangular cake pan
Ice Cream

More Entertainment
Provide each guest with several sheets of paper, 1 or 2 balsa plane kits or paper plane kits. Have magic markers, paper clips, etc. for decorations and flying equipment.

Stage flying contests and "on the ground" judging for cleverness of design and flying ability.

BIRTHDAYS FOR OLDER CHILDREN

Older children enjoy doing and making things. The following ideas may spark some original party themes of your own.

HAT PARTY

Provide a "findings" box of material, flowers, feathers, etc. Make poster paper circles or provide "thrift shop" hats. Let the girls create their own "original". Have hat-shaped cake, play throw hat in ring.

CAKE PARTY

Make 3 small cakes per child (use "tea-party" size cake pans). Have cake decorating tools, canned colored icing and a variety of sprinkles. Also great for children's Christmas party - can substitute large cookies for cakes.

BLOCK PARTY

Gather small wood pieces from building lot trash piles (ask first). Provide wood glue, nails, hammers and a pile of wood to each guest. See what turns up.

WHO AM I PARTY

As each guest arrives, pin name card on back - can be story book, history hero, athlete, etc. Guest must guess who he is by asking questions of the other guests. Good ice-breaker for early teen parties.

BUDDING ARTIST PARTY (Ages 10-12)

Invitations: Paint Palette

Decorations: Easels, if desired, large jars of paint colors, brushes and paper.

This party is great for those older children who are in between early elementary and the sophistication of the early teens. Works nicely in park setting with play equipment nearby.

Food:

Lunch, if desired

Cake - palette shape with color splotches

Ice Cream

Multicolored punch

Entertainment:

Provide mural paper for a group creation. Or if you've longed for a colorful concrete area, provide masking tape to mark off a large area and then mark off small geometric areas within. Paint one solid color in one area, a different solid color in next and so on. (Use washable tempera). Finally give out sheets of paper to each guest and ask for an individual creation. Hang and have an art show (with ribbons if desired).

Favors:

Magic markers

Water colors

HOBO PARTY (Teen or Adult)
(Three House Progressive)

Invitations: Written on paper grocery sacks - guests asked to come dressed as hobos.

I Hors d'oeuvres

Drinks in tin cans (leave labels on) can fit plastic glass down in can if you choose.

Assorted cheeses

Crackers

II Main Course

More-More**

French Bread**

Tossed Salad

III Dessert

Purchase doughnuts and split in half. Butter lightly, sprinkle with cinnamon/sugar and toast in broiler until hot.

Coffee or Hot Chocolate

SPECIAL TOUCHES

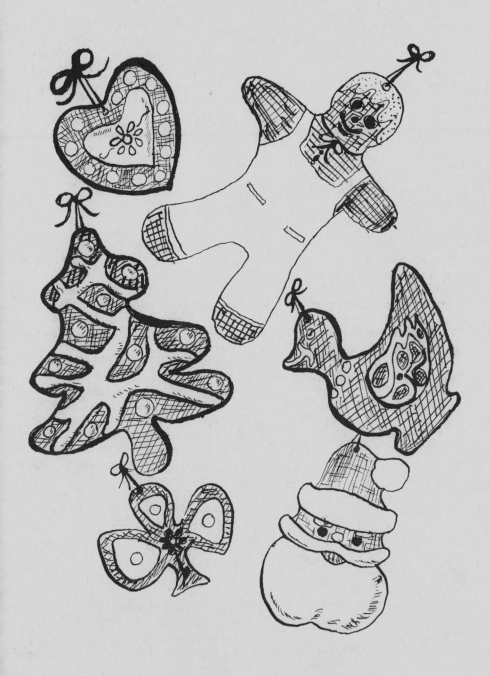

COOKING WITH FLOWERS

NASTURTIUM CAPERS

Do Ahead   Yield: 1 pint

2 c. fresh nasturtium seeds
   (picked green not packaged)
1 c. water
¼ c. salt
1 c. sugar
1 c. cider vinegar

Wash and drain seeds. Mix water and salt, pour over seeds in glass jar or crock. Cover and let stand 2 days. Drain and pour into sterile glass jar. Heat sugar and vinegar to boiling, pour over seeds, seal. Makes 1 pint.

Mrs. W. Evans Bruner
Atlanta, Georgia

CHEESE STUFFED BLOSSOM APPETIZERS

Do Ahead   Yield: 15-20

15-20 squash blossoms
   (3" from base to tip)
1 (3 oz.) pkg. cream cheese
1 T. milk
$^1/_3$ c. grated Parmesan cheese
dash pepper
1½ T. chopped canned
   California green chilies
flour
2 eggs
1 T. water
salad oil

Use male blossoms (those on which no immature fruit shows at the base of the flower) from squash or pumpkins. It is best to pick blossoms in the morning when vines are shaded. Cut blossoms with stems and put in water as a bouquet of flowers. Loosely cover with a plastic bag and refrigerate. Blossoms will keep this way until early evening. For longer storage, package blossoms (unwashed and untrimmed) in plastic bags and refrigerate up to three days. To prepare, rinse with gentle spray of cool water, shake off excess. Trim stems close to blossoms. Remove stamens. Blend cream cheese, milk, Parmesan cheese, pepper and chilies. Spoon about 1" filling into each blossom; twist tips to close. Roll blossoms in flour to lightly coat; set aside. Beat eggs with water. Heat ¼" salad oil in pan over medium-high heat. With a fork, dip one blossom at a time in beaten egg and put in pan. Fry, turning as needed, until golden brown. Drain on paper towels in a warm oven. *Found this several years ago in Sunset Magazine and it has become a summer tradition!*

Mrs. H. Alfred Bolton III

CRYSTALLIZING FLOWERS

1 or 2 egg whites (depends
   on amount of flowers)
sugar (granulated)
flowers (rose petals, violets)
   <u>Do not use flowers that
   have been sprayed.</u>

Brush flowers with well-beaten egg whites and dip into sugar so that flowers are well coated. Place close together on thick paper on a cake rack. Bake in a very slow oven (200°-225°) to dry out. Repeat process of dipping, coating and drying two or three times until thoroughly coated. When cool and dry, store in air tight container. Using a small amount of fondant colored the same as the rose petals, and tweezers, you can stand each petal in fondant and reconstruct a small rose.

Mrs. W. Evans Bruner
Atlanta, Georgia

CANDIED MINT LEAVES
(Quick Method)

mint leaves (also rose petals
   and violets)
   <u>Do not use flowers that
   have been sprayed</u>
1 c. sugar
½ c. water

Thoroughly wash and dry young tender mint leaves. Boil sugar and water to hard ball stage (250°). Remove from heat and cool to luke-warm. Dip leaves in syrup with tweezers or a silver fork. Drop onto a well sugared plate and cool. Place on waxed paper in a cool dry place until thoroughly dry. Store in air tight container.

Mrs. W. Evans Bruner
Atlanta, Georgia

DAY LILY CASSEROLE

300°
5-10 min.

day lily blossoms
whole milk
salt
butter

Preheat oven. Pick blossoms just as they open. <u>Be sure blossoms have not been sprayed</u>. Remove niche where each joins stem. Fill casserole with blossoms; cover scantily with milk, salt to taste and dot generously with butter. Place casserole in oven for 5-10 minutes or until blossoms are tender. Serve at once.
Delicious flavor!

Mabel C. Phillips
Baton Rouge, Louisiana

VIOLET SALAD

Serves 4

1 qt. mixed greens
(Boston lettuce, curly endive, romaine, etc.)
1 c. fresh violets
½ c. small tender violet leaves

Dressing:
⅓ c. vinegar
1 T. lemon juice
⅔ c. olive oil
1 tsp. cognac

Wash and shake greens and violets in a towel. Place in plastic bag in refrigerator to crisp. Make dressing of vinegar, lemon juice, olive oil and cognac. Toss greens in bowl with dressing and sprinkle violets and leaves on top. Serve immediately.

Mrs. W. Evans Bruner
Atlanta, Georgia

GINGERBREAD HOUSE

Dough:
- 1¾ c. heavy cream
- 9½ c. flour
- 2¾ c. brown sugar
- 1½ c. molasses
- 1 T. ginger
- 1 T. grated lemon rind
- 2 T. baking soda

This entire recipe can be eaten, but since they rarely are, a copy can be made of scraps of plywood and decorated using the icing recipe and all edible candies. The advantage of using wood is that it can be washed, stored and reused year after year.

Make dough recipe in 2 batches; one is used for the house and the second will make several dozen cookies or ornaments for decorating the house. Whip cream. Add all ingredients except flour. Stir 12 minutes. Add flour and knead until smooth. Cover and place in a cool area overnight. Work on floured board and roll dough out ⅛" thick. Using a cardboard pattern, cut pieces for the roof, sides and base as shown in illustration. Brush pieces with water and place on greased cookie sheet. Bake at 300° for 10 minutes. Let cool.

Icing:
- 3 egg whites, room temperature
- 1 lb. box powdered sugar
- ½ tsp. cream of tartar

For making icing: Place all ingredients in electric mixer and mix for 10 minutes. Keep bowl covered with damp cloth while using icing, as it dries hard. Depending on how heavy you use the icing, you may need to make 2 or 3 batches. It is best to make 1 and work one area at a time. You may prefer to decorate house parts partially before assembling-piping windows and doors using small tip on pastry bag. When icing is completely dry, assemble house using icing as cement to hold pieces together. Tooth picks and bamboo

(Continued)

GINGERBREAD HOUSE (Continued)

skewers may also be used in assembling the pieces. As you assemble each piece, hold it until frosting is set. Lay roof pieces on top; they should meet, but not overlap. Cement gaps between them with icing. To decorate have fun and use your imagination! Large and small gumdrops are easily pulled off to nibble. Orange slices make cute shutters for windows. Hershey squares make an attractive walkway. Cookies may be stacked for the chimney. Icing may be used for snow on the base and the house may be sprinkled with a snowdrift of sugar.

Mrs. James F. Lewis
Savannah, Georgia

FLOWER POT DESSERT

Serves 18

18 (2-3") new clay pots
  (wash in dishwasher)
cake
½ gal. vanilla ice cream
Creme de Menthe, optional
chocolate sauce, optional
8 egg whites
½ c. sugar
1½ tsp. cream of tartar

Put small round of cake in bottom of clay pot. (Can line with aluminum foil if desired.) Beat egg whites until stiff, gradually add sugar for meringues. Fill pots with ice cream. layer with chocolate and/or Creme de Menthe for additional flavor. Push paper straw into ice cream. Pile meringue on top carefully sealing edges of pot, leaving straw opening exposed. Bake at 400° until meringue is brown and puffy. Serve immediately, or freeze until needed. Use fresh flower in straw to match color scheme.

Mrs. Warren K. Scoville

BAKER'S DOUGH

4 c. flour (all-purpose)
1 c. salt
1½ c. water

Mix flour and salt. Slowly add water mixing to dough consistency. Form ball with hands. Knead dough for a full 20 minutes on well-floured board. Add more flour as needed to prevent sticking. Roll out and make cookie shaped ornaments (be sure to make hole) or candle holders and bread baskets.

For Bread Baskets:
  Generously grease the <u>outside</u> of an oven-proof container or flower pot, coffee can, etc. Roll out dough to ¼-⅜" thickness and cut even parallel 1" strips. Lay these diagonally on outside of container, lattice style. Trim with "rope" effect. To make "ropes" roll lengths of rope to even thickness and twist 2 or 3 together. Bake baskets on shape container.

To Bake:
  Cook in a 325° - 350° oven for 1 to 3 hours, depending on thickness (ropes especially). Do not over-brown. (Do not bake baskets upright - keep open side down.) When cool spray or brush with several coats of clear polyurethane.

Tips:
  A potato ricer makes wonderful "hair", "grass", etc.
  "Puffy" cookie ornaments look better than thin, flat ones.
  Use cookie cutters for shapes, then decorate.
  For an extra-rich brown color, brush on margarine or egg whites and
    cook 15-20 minutes extra.
  A child's "Playdough Fun Factory" has excellent small rope shapes.
  Use a little water to seal braids or ends together.
  If baked dough gets spongy, rebake.

BIRD PUDDING

2 parts corn meal
2 parts ground suet
2 parts sugar
1 part flour

You may substitute peanut butter for suet. Mix, add water and cook. If you're a Georgia Cracker, cook like grits; a Yankee, cook like mush. Pour into pan, allow to cool and harden, then cut chunks to use as needed.

R. D. Dixon, Jr.

CORN SHUCK CREATIONS

To Prepare:
Pull back shucks, cut out corn and let shucks dry naturally. Do not wrap or bag them. A dry, warm attic is better than a damp basement for drying.

To Color:
When thoroughly dry, use a commercial or natural dye. Dip to desired color and dry thoroughly.

To Create:
Mist well the natural or colored shucks. Use the inside leaves, the most pliable and the prettiest natural color. Trim ends evenly with scissors, pinch ends together and wrap with pick and wire. Tape the ends securely with florist tape. Each shuck will make a "loop". Three "loops" wired together will make a corn shuck flower. Use a pompom or artificial stamen for center. For wreaths push picks in a wrapped floral form. Spray well with clear plastic spray when finished.

Mrs. Henry H. Moxley

NUT BASKETS

leftover nuts - same size
   assorted or 1 variety
   (peanuts and pecans work
   well) unshelled
white all-purpose glue
bowl for form

Bake nuts in slow (200°) oven for 1 hour to kill any insects. Line bowl with plastic wrap or grease. Begin in center of bowl and glue nuts together for base. On sides, glue 1 layer at a time and let dry. When completely dry, turn out, peel off plastic wrap and spray well with several coats of polyurethane spray. If larger form is desired use outside of inverted bowl. Build up from rim to base. Be sure to glue only the nuts together - do not use so much glue that it runs down bowl.

Edith D. Phillips
Baton Rouge, Louisiana

APPETIZERS

MELON MINT COCKTAIL

Easy
Do Ahead

½ c. sugar
½ c. water
3 T. chopped mint leaves
juice of 1 lemon
juice of 1 orange

Boil sugar and water for 5 minutes. Pour syrup over 3 T. chopped mint leaves. Cool. Strain. To cooled syrup add lemon juice, orange juice; chill.

cantaloupe balls
watermelon balls
sprigs of mint

Immediately before serving the cocktail, place the balls in cocktail glasses and pour the syrup over them. Garnish with sprigs of mint.
Syrup can be refrigerated for several days. Fruit should be done day of use. Good as first course or light dessert.

Mrs. W. Everett Beal

AVOCADO AND SHRIMP COCKTAIL

Easy   Serves 6

1½ dozen shrimp, cooked
   and deveined
1 lge. avocado, diced
½ c. Russian dressing, well
   chilled
chopped lettuce

Cut each shrimp in several pieces. Place shrimp and avocado on chopped lettuce in cocktail glasses. Pour dressing over them.

Mrs. W. Newton Crouch

CLAM APPETIZER

Easy   Serves 4   350°
                                                              25 min.

2 T. olive oil
2 T. minced onion
2 cloves garlic, minced
1 (7½ oz.) can minced clams
   (and half of juice)
¼ c. Italian seasoned bread
   crumbs (Arnold's)
2 T. Parmesan cheese
2 T. bread crumbs

Saute onion and garlic in oil. Add can of drained clams and ½ of liquid. Mix in bread crumbs. Put in four clam shells. Sprinkle with 2 T. Parmesan cheese and 2 T. bread crumbs. Bake at 350° for 25 minutes.

Mrs. James H. Cobb III

SARDINE PATE IN LEMON SHELLS

2 T. lemon juice
1 thin slice onion
4 sprigs parsley
1 (8 oz.) pkg. cream cheese
2 (4 oz.) cans sardines, drained
Tabasco sauce
lemon shells
parsley sprigs
melba toast

Place first 6 ingredients in food processor and puree until smooth. Fill lemon shells (scooped of pulp) with the pate and decorate with sprigs of parsley. Serve with hot toast.
May also be used as a spread with toast.

Mrs. Nathaniel Hendricks
Atlanta, Georgia

MELON AND SHRIMP CREME FRAICHE

Serves 6

3 melon - cantaloupes
  halved or similar melon
  in serving size
small shrimp, peeled, deveined
  and cooked until just firm

Creme Fraiche
  1½ tsp. buttermilk (or
  ⅓ c. sour cream)
  1 c. heavy cream
  catsup
  Tabasco
  grated lemon rind

Use enough shrimp to pile attractively in melon halves. Top with creme fraiche to which catsup and Tabasco have been added to taste. Garnish with grated lemon rind and serve well chilled.

Creme Fraiche, found widely in France, is cream that has matured and fermented to the point where it has thickened slightly and has a faintly acid taste, very pleasant with many cold dishes. To approximate Creme Fraiche, shake buttermilk or sour cream with heavy cream in a jar. Keep in a warm place until cream has thickened (5 to 8 hours on a hot day, 24 hours on a cool day). Shake jar again and refrigerate. The cream will keep, refrigerated, for up to 10 days.

For a crowd make melon balls and skewer with shrimp on toothpick with bowl of Creme Fraiche dusted with grated lemon rind and seasoned with catsup and Tabasco as above.

Mrs. Nathaniel Hendricks
Atlanta, Georgia

SHRIMP REMOULADE

Easy
Do Ahead

Serves 6-8

3 (4½ oz.) cans shrimp
3 garlic cloves, cut fine
⅓ c. horseradish mustard
2 T. catsup
2 T. paprika
½ tsp. cayenne pepper
⅓ c. tarragon vinegar
½ c. olive oil
½ c. finely chopped green
    onions, top included

Drain shrimp. Crush garlic in a bowl and stir in all ingredients except shrimp. When thoroughly blended add the shrimp. Marinate in the refrigerator 2 hours or longer stirring occasionally. Serve on small portions of shredded lettuce for appetizer or provide party picks and serve with crackers for cocktail party.

Mrs. James R. Fortune, Jr.

BACON WRAPPED DATES

Easy

Yield: 3 dozen

350°
15 min.

1 lb. hotel-sliced bacon
1 box pitted dates
regular toothpicks
frilled toothpicks

Cut bacon slices into three sections. Wrap dates in 1 section; fix with regular toothpick. Bake for 10 minutes; then turn on broiler until bacon is crisp. Be sure to watch closely while under broiler as they crisp very quickly. Replace regular pick with frilled pick and arrange on tray.
This may also be done with water chestnuts or watermelon rind pickle instead of dates.

Mrs. James E. Scharnhorst

RUMAKI

Do Ahead   Serves 8   Broiler
                                                       15 min.

1 (8 oz.) can water chestnuts
1 lb. chicken livers, halved
12 - 14 bacon slices (cut in
    thirds)
4 T. brown sugar
4 T. soy sauce

Dip liver halves in soy sauce and brown sugar. Slice water chestnuts in half. Hold each piece of liver and water chestnut and wrap around with bacon slice. Secure both ends with toothpick. Refrigerate up to 1 day if you are not ready to use them. When ready to cook, place on broiler pan and broil each side until bacon is crisp. Can prepare 1 day in advance, but cook at last minute.

Mrs. Mark C. Kapiloff

BOYOS

Do Ahead†   Yield: 90 to 100   400°
                                                       20 min.

Basic Dough:
    1 c. vegetable oil
    2½ c. water
    1 tsp. salt
    8-10 c. White Lily only
       (plain flour)

Filling:
    2 pkgs. frozen spinach,
       drained well
    2 c. grated cheese
    2 beaten eggs
    1 T. salt - to taste

    1 egg, beaten
    grated cheese

Bring water, oil and salt to a boil. Remove from heat and stir in flour. Work until consistency of pie dough. Knead until smooth. Shape into walnut size balls. Place in bowl and cover with waxed paper to prevent dryness. Roll each into flat oval shape. Mix all filling ingredients together. Fill each oval dough with ½ tsp. to 1 tsp. filling. Roll up and fold edges into finger shaped pieces. Brush lightly with beaten egg, sprinkle with grated cheese. Bake on well greased sheet at 400° for 20 minutes or until golden brown.

Mrs. Ken Levin
Atlanta, Georgia

DRUMSTICK APPETIZERS

Do Ahead   Serves 8

3 lb. chicken wings - cut in
    ½ and use meatier
    "drumstick" for frying
¾ c. buttermilk
½ c. flour
½ c. Parmesan cheese
1 tsp. Accent
1 tsp. salt
1 tsp. paprika
⅛ tsp. pepper
½ tsp. oregano

Blend dry ingredients together. Dip chicken pieces in buttermilk and roll in dry ingredients. Fry in oil in electric fry pan at 365° for 5 minutes.

Mrs. J. Thomas Grayson

COCKTAIL MEATBALLS

Do Ahead†   Yield: 5 dozen

1 lb. lean ground beef
½ c. dry bread crumbs
⅓ c. minced onion
½ c. milk
1 egg
1 T. parsley flakes
1 tsp. salt
⅛ tsp. black pepper
½ tsp. Worcestershire sauce
½ c. shortening
1 (12 oz.) bottle chili sauce
1 (10 oz.) jar grape jelly

Mix ground beef, bread crumbs, onion, milk, egg, parsley flakes, salt, pepper and Worcestershire sauce together. Shape into 1" balls. Melt shortening in large skillet and brown meatballs. Remove meatballs from skillet and pour off fat. Heat chili sauce and jelly in skillet, stirring constantly until jelly is melted. Add meatballs and stir until thoroughly coated. Simmer uncovered 30 minutes. Makes 5 dozen appetizers. Serve hot.

Mrs. Richard M. Shapard

CURRIED BEEF BALLS

Easy†   Yield: 7 dozen   300°
Do Ahead   20-25 min.

1 lb. ground beef
1 pkg. stuffing mix
¾ c. hot water
¼ c. melted butter or
    margarine
1 well beaten egg
2 tsp. curry powder

Combine all ingredients, shape into 1¼" balls and bake on cookie sheet, covered (aluminum foil) at 300° for 20-25 minutes.

Mrs. James D. Goodwin
Baton Rouge, Louisiana

DUCHESS (PUFF PASTRIES)

Do Ahead   Yield: 4 dozen   450 & 350°
                                                        15-20 min.

½ c. butter
⅛ tsp. salt
1 c. boiling water
1 c. sifted flour
3 eggs, unbeaten

Add butter and salt to boiling water and stir over medium heat until mixture boils. Reduce heat, add flour all at once and beat vigorously, until mixture leaves sides of pan. Remove from heat and add 1 egg at a time, beating thoroughly after each addition. Shape puffs very small using about 1 tsp. paste for each one. Bake on a greased cookie sheet at 450° for about 8 minutes or until points begin to brown, then reduce heat to 350° and continue baking 10-12 minutes longer. Remove to wire cooling rack. When cold cut open and fill with shrimp or anchovy butter. I prefer anchovy.

Anchovy Butter:
  1 c. butter
  4 T. anchovy paste
  2 tsp. lemon juice
  4 drops onion juice

Cream butter thoroughly, add anchovy paste, lemon juice and onion juice until well mixed. Put small amount in each "puff". May be heated or served cold. (Better heated.)

Mrs. Enrique Montero

Alternate Filling:
  3½ c. ground cooked
    ham
  ⅔ c. chopped gherkins
  4 T. horseradish
  2 T. lemon juice
  4 hard cooked eggs,
    chopped
  salad dressing
  salt and pepper

Mix all ingredients. Put small amount in each puff.

Mrs. Franklin P. Lindsey, Jr.

MARINATED MUSHROOMS

Easy
Do Ahead

⅔ c. dry white wine
⅔ c. white wine vinegar
½ c. salad oil
½ c. finely chopped onion
4 T. fresh chopped parsley
1 clove garlic, crushed
2 bay leaves
2 tsp. salt
½ tsp. dried fresh thyme
dash ground pepper
1 lb. fresh mushrooms,
    washed and drained

In a saucepan combine all ingredients except mushrooms and bring to a boil. Add mushrooms. Simmer 10-12 minutes, uncovered. Ladle into a warm jar. Cool and store in refrigerator. Let stand in refrigerator at least 12 hours before serving. These will keep a long time in the refrigerator (3 weeks).

Mrs. William L. Wages

STUFFED MUSHROOMS

Easy   Yield: 2 dozen   Broil
Do Ahead

1 (3 oz.) pkg. cream cheese
1 small can Underwood deviled
    ham
approximately 24 small
    mushrooms

Soften cream cheese and mix with deviled ham. Clean mushrooms and remove stems. Fill mushroom caps with cream cheese mixture. Broil or bake until hot.
This can be made ahead and heated at the last minute.

Mrs. James R. Fortune, Jr.

OLIVE CHEESE BALLS

Easy   Yield: 48 balls   400°
Do Ahead   20 min.

1 stick butter (melted)
1 c. shredded Cracker Barrel
    Brand Sharp Natural
    Cheddar cheese
1¼ c. plain flour
¼ tsp. salt
48 olives, drained and
    dried (overnight)

Mix butter and cheese with flour. Add salt. Form into small balls, forming around olives and seal well. Let stand in refrigerator overnight. Bake at 400° for 20 minutes or until brown. Yields 48 balls.

Mrs. Louis Arnett

PORK STRIPS

Easy   Serves 6   300°
                                                    2 hrs.

2 lbs. fresh pork tenderloin
1½ T. soy sauce
2½ T. Hoi Sin Sauce
    (oriental grocery item)
1 T. dry sherry
⅛ tsp. Chinese 5 Spice Powder
    or garlic
¼ tsp. red food coloring
    (if desired)
½ T. sugar

Trim fat and gristle from meat. Mix soy sauce, Hoi Sin Sauce, sherry, 5-Spice Powder, food coloring and sugar. Rub above on meat and let stand 1 hour. Put meat on rack in roasting pan containing 1½ - 2 c. water and roast slowly at 300° for 2 hours or until done. Do not let meat touch water. Add water if necessary during cooking. When halfway through, brush meat with mixture and turn. Serve hot, cut in thin slices.

Mrs. William S. Colvin

SAUSAGE BALLS

Easy†   Yield: 6 dozen   350°
Do Ahead   15 min.

1 lb. ground pork sausage
1 lb. very sharp New York
    Cheddar cheese, grated
2 c. Bisquick

Combine sausage and cheese. Gradually add Bisquick, working it in with hands. Shape into balls the size of a walnut and bake on ungreased cookie sheet. These do not spread much, so many may be placed on sheet at one time.

Mrs. James E. Scharnhorst

SAUSAGE TWISTS

Easy   Yield: 16   375°
                                                                 13 min.

1 lb. pork sausage
   (bulk) hot
Pillsbury Crescent Dinner
   rolls
parsley flakes

Preheat oven to 375°. Unroll dough, separate into 8 triangles; cut each in half. Shape sausage into small balls (16) and put on each triangle. Roll up, start at shortest side of triangle and twist.   Place on ungreased cookie sheet. Sprinkle with parsley flakes and bake for about 13 minutes at 375°, or until brown. You will have enough sausage to double the recipe easily.

Mrs. James D. Goodwin
Baton Rouge, Louisiana

PICKLED SHRIMP I

Do Ahead   Serves 25

5 lbs. shrimp, raw
3 med. onions, thinly
   sliced
1 med. size can dry
   mustard
2 tsp. curry powder
3 tsp. celery seed
1 tsp. salt (taste dressing
   and add more if needed)
3 c. white vinegar
½ bottle catsup
2 T. soy sauce
2 T. Worcestershire sauce
3 tsp. capers and juice
3 or 4 whole cloves
5 bay leaves
dash of Tabasco
3 c. oil

Three days before serving, cook shrimp in boiling, salted water. After water returns to boil, cook shrimp for 3 minutes, and pour off water and let shrimp cool. Make layers of shrimp and onions in glass or crockery container. Mix dry mustard, curry powder, celery seed and salt together in mixing bowl. Add vinegar, catsup, soy sauce, Worcestershire sauce, capers, cloves, bay leaves, and Tabasco. Stir and mix well and gradually add 3 c. oil. Pour all over shrimp and onions. Cover tightly with foil and refrigerate for three days, stirring each day. Drain well and serve on large platter on bed of lettuce. Serve with cocktail picks. The success of this depends on only cooking shrimp for 3 minutes after coming to a boil, then stirring well each day for three days.

Mrs. C. Whitten Walter
Birmingham, Alabama

PICKLED SHRIMP II

Do Ahead

shrimp
Italian Wishbone salad
    dressing
onions
capers
green pepper
button mushrooms
salt
lemon pepper

Clean and boil shrimp - any amount. (Just under-cook the shrimp.) Drain and cool. Pour Italian Wishbone salad dressing over shrimp (cover with dressing). Add thin sliced onions, capers, salt and lemon pepper. May add slivered green pepper and button mushrooms. Let marinate 24 hours. Keep refrigerated.

Mrs. Thomas V. Pollard

PEPPERED PECANS

Easy
Do Ahead

250°

¼ lb. of butter or margarine
½ c. Worcestershire sauce
1½ lb. shelled pecan halves
salt and cayenne pepper
    (to taste)

Melt butter or margarine in baking pan and add Worcestershire sauce. Mix well. Add pecan halves and stir well. Place in 250° oven and bake slowly, stirring every few minutes until the pecan halves have absorbed all the liquid. Remove from oven and sprinkle with salt and cayenne pepper. Stir again. Serve as you would any other salted nuts.

Mrs. James D. Goodwin
Baton Rouge, Louisiana

SPICED PECANS

Easy
Do Ahead

1 c. sugar
¼ c. water
1 T. butter
1 tsp. cinnamon
3 c. whole pecans

Mix sugar, water, butter, cinnamon in a saucepan. Place over medium heat; bring to a boil. When mixture starts to boil, cook exactly 2 minutes, stirring constantly. Pour in pecans; stir quickly until pecans are coated and all syrup is absorbed. Pour out on sheet of waxed paper. Separate. Cool and serve.

Mrs. Carl H. Cartledge, Jr.

HOT SAUSAGE IN SOUR CREAM

Easy

2 lbs. lean highly seasoned
   sausage
1 (8 oz.) jar Major Grey's
   Chutney, chopped fine
8 oz. sherry
1 c. sour cream

Roll sausage into bite-size balls and cook in a skillet until done. Pour off grease and transfer sausage to a chafing dish. Into the skillet put chutney, enough sherry to fill chutney jar and sour cream. Cook gently for a few minutes and pour over sausage.

Mrs. Robert Smalley

CHAFING DISH OYSTERS AND MUSHROOMS

1 lb. fresh mushrooms,
   sliced
6 T. butter
6 T. flour
2 c. cream
salt and freshly ground
   pepper
dash Tabasco
1 qt. oysters
toasted bread triangles

Saute mushrooms in butter. After they have cooked a few minutes, sift flour over the mixture and stir gently. As it thickens, add cream and seasonings. Pick over the oysters and simmer in their own liquid in another pan until the edges curl. Add oysters to mushroom sauce. Serve from chafing dish onto toasted bread triangles.

Mrs. Nathaniel Hendricks
Atlanta, Georgia

CHEESE STRAWS I

Do Ahead†   Yield: 3 dozen   350°
                                           18-20 min.

½ c. butter
1 lb. sharp cheese (grated
   fine)
1 egg
1 T. cold water
1¾ c. plain flour
½ tsp. salt
¼ tsp. cayenne
½ tsp. paprika

Cream butter, cheese. Add egg and water. Beat. Sift flour, salt, cayenne, and paprika. Add dry ingredients to mixture; beat well after each. Chill dough 10 minutes. Pack into pastry press, squeeze shapes onto baking sheet. Bake 18-20 minutes at 350°.

Mrs. David Clements

CHEESE STRAWS II

Do Ahead†   Yield: 12 dozen   350°
                                                         10-15 min.

1 lb. extra sharp cheese   Grate cheese. Add butter or margarine.
2 c. butter or margarine   Let these reach room temperature.
4 c. flour (plain)   Cream in electric mixer until they are
1 tsp. salt   consistency of shortening for cake.
½ tsp. red pepper   Gradually add flour and salt and
                                pepper. Use star plate of cookie press
                                to shape. Bake.

                                Mrs. Charles L. Smith

CHEESE WAFERS

Easy   Yield: 100   350°
Do Ahead   10 min.

2 c. grated sharp cheese   Mix all together; form into small
  (½ lb.)   balls. Place balls on ungreased cookie
2 c. plain flour   sheet and press down with a fork.
2 sticks soft butter   Bake.
2 c. Rice Krispies
¼ tsp. red pepper   Mrs. Harvey Y. Andress
½ tsp. paprika   Galax, Virginia
½ tsp. salt

CHEESE CRACKERS

                              Yield: 12 dozen   325°
                                                         17 min.

1 lb. grated New York very   Leave cheese and butter out the night
  sharp cheese   before to really soften. Mix all
1 c. butter (2 sticks)   ingredients, working with your hands.
3 c. plain flour, sifted   Shape into four rolls and roll in
1 tsp. salt   waxed paper. Store in refrigerator
½ tsp. red pepper   until firm. Slice thin. Cook at 325°
½ c. finely chopped   for 17 minutes. Watch closely as
  pecans   they burn easily!

                                Mrs. Wm. R. Hancock
                                Mrs. Thomas V. Pollard

CHEESE BALL

Do Ahead

8 oz. English Kraft cheese
1 (8 oz.) pkg. cream cheese
1 (4 oz.) square bleu cheese
2 T. Worcestershire sauce
4 drops Tabasco sauce
¼ c. minced onion
dash of garlic salt
½ c. mayonnaise
pecans, finely chopped
parsley, finely chopped
paprika

Grate English Kraft cheese. Let cheeses stand at room temperature until soft. Add seasonings and blend with mixer on low speed. Beat on medium speed until fluffy, scraping side and bottom of bowl. Cover; chill. Make into one large ball and roll in pecans or shape mixture into 30-40 1" balls and roll in nuts, paprika, or parsley. At Christmas it is pretty to mold into 2 logs, rolling one in parsley and one in paprika.

Mrs. Herbert A. Bolton, Jr.
Mrs. Joseph T. Johnson

HAM CHEESE LOGS

Easy   Serves 8
Do Ahead

4 oz. sharp Cheddar cheese,
  shredded (1 c.)
1 (8 oz.) pkg. cream cheese,
  softened
1 (4½ oz.) can of deviled
  ham
½ c. pitted, chopped ripe
  olives
½ c. finely chopped pecans

Have Cheddar cheese at room temperature. In small mixer bowl, beat together Cheddar cheese and cream cheese until blended. Beat in deviled ham; stir in olives and chill. Shape into two 8" logs. Roll in pecans. Serve with crackers.

Mrs. John M. Cogburn, Jr.

DIPS

BROCCOLI DIP
†

1 roll garlic cheese
½ can cream of mushroom
  soup, undiluted
1 onion, chopped finely
½ c. celery, chopped finely
1 (8 oz.) can chopped
  mushrooms, drained
1 pkg. frozen chopped
  broccoli
crackers

Saute onion and celery. Melt together cheese and soup. Add sauteed onion and celery. Add mushrooms. Cook broccoli as directed and drain well on paper towel. Add to cheese mix and serve hot with crackers or corn chips.

Mrs. John Umstead
Chapel Hill, North Carolina

CHILI CON QUESO CON CARNE

Yield: 1 quart

1 lb. ground beef
¼ c. chopped green onion
1 (8 oz.) can tomato sauce
1 (4 oz.) can green chili
  peppers, drained, seeded and
  chopped
1 tsp. Worcestershire sauce
16 oz. process American cheese,
  cut into small pieces or Kraft
  Old English cheese
dash garlic powder

In large skillet brown meat. Add green onion. Cook over low heat until tender but not brown. Add tomato sauce, chili peppers, Worcestershire and cheese. Cook stirring until all cheese melts. Stir in garlic powder. Serve in chafing dish over a low heat source with tortilla or corn chips. Good hot dip in the winter. This can be prepared ahead up to the point of adding the cheese. This part should be done just before serving.

Mrs. Lutie C. Johnston

Editor's note: Omit ground beef for Chili Con Queso.

CLAM DIP

Easy
Do Ahead

Serves 75

½ c. margarine, melted
9 (8 oz.) pkg. cream cheese
6 cans minced clams, drained
(save juice)
2 tsp. each:
chopped chives
salt
Worcestershire sauce
sage
minced onion
rosemary
dash Tabasco sauce
Ruffles or other "sturdy"
chips

Mix first three ingredients together; cook slowly over medium heat. Add other ingredients and thin with clam juice. Serve warm in a chafing dish with Ruffles.
A tradition at the annual Atlanta Sigma Chi Alumni Christmas Party.

Mrs. H. Alfred Bolton III

HOT CRAB APPETIZER *

Easy
Do Ahead

375°
15 min.

1 (8 oz.) pkg. cream cheese
1 (6 oz.) can flaked crabmeat
2 T. finely chopped onions
1 T. milk
½ tsp. cream style
horseradish
¼ tsp. salt
dash pepper
⅓ c. sliced almonds, toasted

Combine first seven ingredients. Mix well. Spoon mixture into ovenproof dish. Sprinkle with almonds. Bake at 375° for 15 minutes. Use as a dip for Fritos or a spread for crackers or cocktail rye bread.

SHRIMP DIP

2 cans small shrimp
1 lime
⅔ c. mayonnaise (approx.)
1 tsp. French's mustard
1 sm. grated onion
(really to taste)

Mash shrimp and other ingredients and mix together. Let stand for a few hours or overnight.

Mrs. James R. Fortune, Jr.

VEGETABLES FOR DIPPING

Artichokes
Broccoli
Carrot sticks
Cauliflowerettes
Celery sticks
Cherry tomatoes
Cucumber slices
Green pepper strips
Kohlrabi cubes
Mushrooms
Radishes
Spring onions
Yellow squash
Zucchini slices

Prepare vegetables. Serve with one or more dips.

BAGNA CAUDA

Easy

Serves 8-10

¾ c. butter
¼ c. olive oil
2-3 cloves garlic, minced
  (or more to taste)
8 anchovy fillets, finely
  chopped
assorted fresh vegetables

Melt butter with oil and garlic in a fondue pot. Add anchovies and let mixture bubble slowly about 5 minutes. Wash raw vegetables and cut into bite-size pieces; arrange on a tray alongside fondue pot. Dip vegetables briefly into the pot - just to coat not to cook.

Mrs. H. Alfred Bolton III

CURRY DIP

Easy
Do Ahead

1 c. mayonnaise
3 tsp. curry powder
3 T. catsup
1 T. Worcestershire sauce
1 tsp. grated onion
¼ tsp. salt and pepper
dash of horseradish

Combine all ingredients. Chill until serving time. Serve with crisp, raw vegetables.
Also good as a sauce for cooked asparagus.

Mrs. Dan Baker

RAW VEGETABLE DIP

Easy
Do Ahead

8 oz. cream cheese, softened
½ pkg. Good Seasons Italian
  Salad Dressing mix
6 oz. tomato juice

Blend all ingredients until smooth. Chill and serve.

Mrs. John Umstead
Chapel Hill, North Carolina

QUICK VEGETABLE DIP

Easy
Do Ahead

½ c. mayonnaise
½ c. sour cream
1 T. dill weed

Mix and chill. Serve with raw vegetables.

SHRIMP DIP FOR VEGETABLES

Easy
Do Ahead

Serves 16

1 (8 oz.) pkg. cream cheese,
  softened
¼ c. mayonnaise
¼ c. French dressing
2 tsp. prepared mustard
dash Tabasco sauce
1 (8 oz.) can shrimp, drained
  and crumbled

Mix all ingredients except shrimp. Add shrimp. Chill. Serve with raw vegetables. Makes 2½ cups.

Mrs. C. E. Williams, Jr.

SPREADS

CAVIAR LOG

Easy
Do Ahead

1 (4¾ oz.) can liver pate
1 (2 oz.) jar black caviar
4 (3 oz.) pkgs. cream cheese
melba toast rounds

Have pate, caviar, and cheese at room temperature. Place cream cheese on waxed paper. Use the paper to roll and shape cheese into a log. Spread evenly with liver pate, then carefully cover with caviar. Lightly cover with clear plastic wrap; chill at least 1 hour. Serve with melba toast. Makes 1 log.

Mrs. William Hewitt

CHUTNEY CHEESE SPREAD

Easy
Do Ahead

1 (8 oz.) pkg. cream cheese
1 T. chutney
sm. pkg. toasted almonds
½ tsp. curry powder

Add chopped chutney to cream cheese. Mix well with curry powder and chopped toasted almonds. This spread keeps well and ingredients may vary according to taste.

Mrs. J. Denny Hall

CHOPPED CHICKEN LIVERS

Do Ahead

½ lb. chicken livers
¼ c. butter
3 eggs, hard boiled
2 med. onions, chopped
¼ c. butter
2-3 T. mayonnaise
salt and pepper to taste

Saute chicken livers in butter until done. Drain. Hard boil 3 eggs. Simmer onions in butter until tender and soft, about 20 minutes. Do not brown. Drain. Mix all together and chop fine or grind (blend). Add mayonnaise and salt and pepper. Serve with crackers.

Mrs. Carole Goldstein

CHICKEN LIVER PATE

Easy†
Do Ahead

Serves Many

½ lb. chicken livers
1 tsp. salt
pinch cayenne
½ c. softened butter
¼ tsp. nutmeg
1 tsp. dry mustard
⅛ tsp. ground cloves
2 T. finely minced onion

Simmer chicken livers 15-20 minutes in water barely to cover. Drain. Put in blender or Cuisinart using French knife with remaining ingredients. Blend well. Pack in crock and refrigerate.

Mrs. John H. Cheatham

HALIBUT PARTY SPREAD

Easy
Do Ahead

Serves Many

¾ lb. halibut - poached*
 (use 12 oz. pkg. frozen
 halibut)
1 (8 oz.) pkg. cream cheese,
 softened
1 T. frozen freeze-dried
 chives
1½ T. lemon juice
1½ T. chopped green
 chilies
¼ tsp. salt
¼ tsp. garlic salt
¼ tsp. Tabasco sauce

Flake halibut with fork, discarding skin and bones. Combine fish with cheese, chives and chilies and seasonings. Blend thoroughly. Press mixture into waxed paper lined mold or bowl. Refrigerate several hours (a day or two is fine). Unmold on serving platter. May garnish with stuffed olives. Serve with crackers. I double recipe and use 5½ c. fish mold. This serves a large crowd.

Mrs. Taylor B. Manley, Jr.

*To poach: place fish in simmering, salted water with 2 lemon slices and 1 slice onion. Cover and simmer 10 minutes. Drain.

PECAN SPREAD *

Easy
Do Ahead

Serves 8 - 12

350°
20 min.

½ c. chopped pecans
2 T. butter
½ tsp. salt
1 (8 oz.) pkg. cream cheese,
  softened
2 T. milk
1 (2½ oz.) jar dried beef
¼ c. finely chopped green
  pepper
2 T. dried onion flakes
½ tsp. garlic salt
¼ tsp. pepper
½ c. sour cream
pimiento for color

Heat and crisp pecans in buttered salt. Mix all other ingredients except sour cream. Blend with electric mixer. Fold in sour cream. Put in baking dish. Sprinkle crisp pecans on top. Bake in 350° oven for 20 minutes. Serve hot on crackers.

STEAK TARTARE

1 whole egg
1 T. red wine vinegar
3 T. good olive oil
1 scant tsp. Dijon mustard
1 tsp. salt, or more to
  taste
1 tsp. or to taste, freshly
  ground pepper
1 lb. top round steak,
  ground
3 T. minced onion
1 T. capers (optional)
parsley or caviar

Mix all ingredients but beef and onion in food processor or blend well by hand to consistency of dressing, then add chopped steak, onions and mix well. Rinse, drain and add capers if desired. Form mixture into ball and roll in finely chopped parsley or spread outside with caviar. Serve cold with basket of melba toast triangles or wheat thins.

Mrs. Nathaniel Hendricks
Atlanta, Georgia

SHRIMP SPREADS

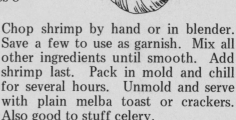

SHRIMP BUTTER

Easy†   Serves 8

1 lb. cleaned and cooked
   shrimp
8 oz. cream cheese
¾ c. soft butter (no
   substitute)
juice of 1 lemon
4 T. mayonnaise
1 T. minced onion

Chop shrimp by hand or in blender. Save a few to use as garnish. Mix all other ingredients until smooth. Add shrimp last. Pack in mold and chill for several hours. Unmold and serve with plain melba toast or crackers. Also good to stuff celery.

Mrs. William J. Kendrick

SHRIMP CANAPE

1½ lbs. shrimp
½ c. light rum
½ c. butter
½ tsp. onion juice
½ tsp. dry mustard
lemon juice to taste
salt and pepper to taste

Marinate boiled, peeled shrimp in rum for 1 hour or more. Run twice through a fine meat grinder. Cream butter. Combine with shrimp, onion juice, mustard, lemon juice, salt and pepper. Mix thoroughly. Chill. Serve on crackers.

Mrs. James R. Fortune, Jr.

SHRIMP AND CURRY MOLD

Do Ahead†

4 lbs. shrimp
3 slices lemon
2 bay leaves
1 tsp. salt
1 onion, chopped
water
2 tsp. curry powder
1½ c. homemade mayonnaise
2 onions grated
juice of 2 lemons
salt and pepper to taste

Cook shrimp, lemon, bay leaves, salt, and onion together in water until shrimp are done. Drain. Put shrimp through meat grinder. Mix remaining ingredients well with ground shrimp. Line mold with wet cheese-cloth. Fill with shrimp mixture and chill. Unmold and serve with thin toast.

Mrs. John H. Cheatham

BEVERAGES

AMBROSIA

Easy   Serves 1

$\frac{1}{3}$ oz. lemon juice   Shake and strain lemon juice, cointreau
$\frac{1}{2}$ oz. cointreau   and brandy into a chilled champagne
1 oz. brandy   glass.   Add champagne to fill glass.
champagne
                                        H. Alfred Bolton III

BANANA DAIQUIRI

Easy   Serves 3

1 ripe banana   Put all ingredients into blender plus
1 tsp. sugar *   9 to 11 cracked ice cubes.   Blend
$\frac{2}{3}$ lemon or $\frac{1}{2}$ lime   until lumps of ice disappear.   Serve
3 oz. light rum   in cocktail glass and garnish, if desired,
1$\frac{1}{2}$ oz. banana brandy   with mint or lemon twist.
9-11 ice cubes
*More sugar may be added if   Mrs. Franklin P. Lindsey, Jr.
a sweeter taste is preferred

CHABLIS COOLER

Easy   Serves 1

superfine sugar   Sugar-frost a tall 14 oz. glass.   Pour
$\frac{1}{2}$ oz. grenadine   grenadine, lemon juice, vanilla and
$\frac{1}{2}$ oz. lemon juice   vodka into glass.   Stir well.   Add
$\frac{1}{4}$ tsp. vanilla   3 large ice cubes.   Fill glass to
1 oz. vodka   rim with Chablis.   Stir.
iced pink Chablis
                                        H. Alfred Bolton III

FROZEN PEACH DAIQUIRI

Easy†   Serves 6
Do Ahead

1 (10 oz.) pkg. frozen peaches   Place ingredients in blender.   Mix
juice of 1 fresh lime   well.   Store in freezer.   Garnish each
4$\frac{1}{2}$ oz. light rum   serving with mint sprig.
4$\frac{1}{2}$ tsp. bar sugar
2 c. crushed ice   Mrs. J. Gordon Dixon
mint sprigs

HOT BUTTERED RUM

Easy   Serves 1

2 whole cloves
2 whole allspice
1 stick cinnamon
1 tsp. sugar
boiling water or hot
    apple cider
2 oz. rum
dab butter

Place spices and sugar in a thick mug with a little boiling water. Let stand for about 5 minutes. Then add rum, butter and boiling water or apple cider to taste. Add more sugar if desired.

William S. Colvin

MILK PUNCH

Easy   Serves 12
Do Ahead

½ gal. milk
1½ c. bourbon
5 T. sugar

Mix well to dissolve sugar. Pour over ice in 8 oz. glasses.

Mrs. Taylor B. Manley, Jr.
Mrs. Warren Wells

OLD RED EYE

Easy   Serves 4
Do Ahead

12 oz. tomato juice
6 oz. vodka
juice 1 lime
pinch salt, pepper, celery salt
1 tsp. Worcestershire sauce
dash Tabasco sauce

Stir ingredients in large pitcher and pour over ice cubes in cocktail glass. Garnish with slice of lime and celery stick.

Lutie C. Johnston

YANKEE SOUR

Easy   Serves 4

6 oz. whiskey
1 (6 oz.) can lemonade,
    undiluted
½ (3 oz.) can orange juice,
    undiluted
1 T. grenadine
½ doz. cherries and juice
1 tray of ice

Blend all ingredients in blender. Serve in frosted glasses if desired. This is a pretty pink drink which can be garnished with fruit.

Mrs. Alyn R. Jones, Jr.
Zebulon, Georgia

TOMATO JUICE APPETIZER

Easy
Do Ahead

Serves 8-12

1 c. sour cream
3 c. tomato juice
¼ c. sugar
1 tsp. salt
⅛ tsp. pepper
1½ tsp. onion juice
¾ tsp. Worcestershire sauce

Beat together using a rotary beater - not a blender.   Chill several hours before serving.

Mrs. William L. Joiner
First President of The Utility Club

SANGRIA

Do Ahead

Serves 8

1 whole orange
1 bottle (fifth) light, dry
   red wine
1 ripe Elberta peach, peeled
   and sliced
6 slices lemon
1½ oz. cognac
1 oz. triple sec
1 oz. maraschino liqueur
1 T. or more sugar to taste
6 oz. club soda, chilled

Cut entire peel of orange in a single strip, beginning at stem and continuing until spiral reaches bottom of fruit. White part should be cut along with outer peel so that orange fruit is exposed.   Leave peel attached to orange bottom so that fruit may be suspended in pitcher. Pour wine into glass pitcher. Add peach slices, lemon slices, cognac, triple sec, maraschino liquer and sugar.   Stir to dissolve sugar.   Carefully place orange in pitcher, fastening top end of peel over rim.   Let mixture marinate at room temperature at least 1 hour. Add soda and a tray of ice cubes to pitcher. Stir and serve.

Mrs. William C. Hewitt

KAHLUA

Easy
Do Ahead

Yield: ½ gallon

1 qt. water
3 c. sugar
4 T. freeze dried instant
   coffee
1 T. vanilla
1 fifth vodka

Bring water, sugar and coffee to boil. Turn heat down and simmer slowly for 1 hour. Cool. Add vanilla and vodka. Drink!

Mrs. Taylor B. Manley, Jr.

BRANDY BRICKLE

Easy   Serves 2

1 oz. brandy
½ oz. Creme de Cacao
1 heaping T. Butter Brickle
   ice cream
½ c. cracked ice

Place ingredients in blender and blend for 15 seconds. Or, place ingredients in shaker and shake well for 30 seconds and strain into cocktail glasses.

Lutie C. Johnston

IRISH COFFEE

Easy   Serves 1

1 tsp. sugar
1½ oz. Irish whiskey
5 oz. hot coffee
1 T. whipped cream

Rinse out a large wine glass or Irish coffee glass with hot water. Shake and, if you like, dip into additional sugar to coat the rim. Put sugar, whiskey and coffee into glass and stir well. Top with whipped cream.

Mrs. Eugene F. Robbins, Jr.

EGG NOG I

For 24:
   24 eggs, separated
   3 c. sugar
   1 qt. brandy or bourbon
   1 qt. heavy cream

For 6-8 people:
   6 eggs, separated
   ¾ c. sugar
   ¾ c. bourbon
   1 c. whipping cream

In a large bowl, beat yolks thoroughly; then add sugar to yolks and cream until smooth. Add bourbon very slowly so as not to cook the eggs too quickly. Whip cream and fold into above mixture. Lastly, fold in stiffly beaten whites.

Mrs. Charles Moore

Editor's note: Makes a very thick, divine egg nog which must be eaten with a spoon.

EGG NOG II

Do Ahead   Serves 30

15 egg yolks
2½ c. sugar
½ tsp. salt
1 qt. heavy cream
1 qt. milk
1 c. bourbon
¼ c. sherry
¼ c. rum
15 egg whites, beaten stiff

Separate eggs and place whites in refrigerator. Blend sugar and yolks and salt until frothy. Let stand. Whip cream. Add milk to sugar and eggs, blending well. Combine liquor and cream. Whip egg whites. Fold all together with wooden spoon. Refrigerate for 3-4 hours before serving.
A Christmas favorite - never any left!

Mrs. William S. Colvin

WONDERFUL WASSAIL

Do Ahead   Serves 40

3 oranges
whole cloves
5 c. pineapple juice
  (2 No. 2 cans)
3 qt. apple cider
2 sticks cinnamon
½ tsp. nutmeg
½ c. honey
¹/₃ c. lemon juice
2 tsp. lemon rind
2 c. rum or brandy
  (optional)

Stud 3 oranges with whole cloves, about ½ inch apart. Place in baking pan with a cup or so of water. Bake at 325° for 30 minutes. In the meantime, heat cider and cinnamon sticks and honey in large saucepan. Bring to boil over medium heat; simmer covered for 5 minutes. Add remaining ingredients. Pour over spiced oranges that have been transferred from oven to punch bowl.

Mrs. James E. Scharnhorst

COFFEE PUNCH

Easy   Serves 15-18
Do Ahead

2 qt. strong coffee
1 pt. cold milk
2 tsp. vanilla extract
½ c. sugar
2 qt. vanilla ice cream
½ pt. whipping cream
ground nutmeg

Combine coffee, milk, vanilla and sugar; chill. Break ice cream into chunks in punch bowl just before serving; pour chilled coffee mixture over ice cream. Whip cream; spoon into mounds on top of punch. Sprinkle with nutmeg. (This mixture may be made 1 day ahead.)

Mrs. Don R. Rainwater

CHEROKEE SHERRY APPETIZER

Easy†   Serves 12
Do Ahead

1 (12 oz.) can frozen orange juice
1 (12 oz.) can frozen lemonade
1 (12 oz.) can frozen limeade
1 qt. ginger ale
sherry

Mix together all but sherry and freeze. Do not use any other liquid. To serve put a scoop of ice into glasses and pour sherry over it. Stick short straws into ice.

Mrs. R. O. Crouch, Jr.

WINE PUNCH

Easy   Serves 12

1 bottle red wine
1 c. orange juice
1 c. pineapple juice
2 lemons sliced
3 oranges sliced

Combine all of the ingredients and pour over a block of ice.

Mrs. John H. Goddard

RASPBERRY-CHAMPAGNE PUNCH

Easy
Do Ahead

1 qt. ripe or frozen raspberries
3 T. lemon juice
¾ bottle Chablis, chilled
1¾ bottles champagne, chilled
crushed ice

Put berries in a bowl, reserving enough to garnish glasses. Cover with lemon juice and ½ Chablis. Chill. Before serving, add ice, champagne and remaining wine. Serve in chilled punch glasses with a berry in each glass.

Mrs. William C. Hewitt

PINEAPPLE CRUSH

Easy   Yield: 22 cups
Do Ahead

3 c. water
2 c. sugar
1 (46 oz.) can pineapple juice
1½ c. orange juice
½ c. lemon juice
3 mashed ripe bananas
3 qts. ginger ale or
2 qts. ginger ale and 1 bottle
   of champagne

Mix sugar and water in large pan. Boil, remove and stir in juices and mashed bananas. Pour into freezer trays or cake pans and freeze until firm. Cut into small cubes. Pour ginger ale or ginger ale and champagne over iced punch cubes.

Mrs. Ralph W. Mitchell

RED-PINK FRUIT PUNCH

Easy
Do Ahead

Serves 50

2 (46 oz.) cans pineapple juice
2 (46 oz.) cans grapefruit-
pineapple juice
2 (46 oz.) cans red Hawaiian
Punch
1 lge. bottle ginger ale

Mix juices together in advance and chill. Add ginger ale just before serving or chill all ingredients in advance and mix together just before serving.

Mrs. T. J. Berry

Editor's Note: Hundreds of Griffin kindergarteners and their families have enjoyed this at First Methodist Kindergarten's annual Christmas program. Easy to make, easy to transport, and very tasty.

FRUIT PUNCH

Easy
Do Ahead

Serves 75

2 gal. tea (¼ lb. box)
3 (46 oz.) cans pineapple juice
3 (46 oz.) cans orange juice
1 (5 oz.) can frozen lemon juice
2½ lbs. sugar
3 qts. ginger ale, chilled
ice or sherbet

Dissolve sugar in hot tea. Add juices and cool. Add ginger ale just before serving. Pour over ice or any kind of sherbet.

Mrs. Malcolm M. Hemphill

CHATHAM ARTILLERY PUNCH

Easy
Do Ahead

Serves 200

1½ gal. Catawba wine
½ gal. St. Croix wine
1 qt. Gordon gin
1 qt. Hennessy brandy
1 pt. Benedictine
1½ qts. rye whiskey
1½ gal. strong tea
2½ lbs. brown sugar
juice of 1½ doz. oranges
juice of 1½ doz. lemons
1 bottle maraschino cherries
1 case champagne

Mix all ingredients but champagne 36-48 hours before using. Add champagne when ready to serve.
Served in Savannah in 1819 to President James Monroe on the occasion of the sailing of the first steamship to cross the Atlantic. Great for wedding receptions.

Mrs. John H. Goddard

ICE RING

Boil water and cool for clear ice ring. Pour in small amount; freeze. Add layer of fruit, freeze. Add water bit by bit, freezing well until fruit is stationary.

RUSSIAN TEA

Do Ahead   Yield: 12-14 cups

2 T. whole cloves
¼ c. hot water
2½ T. black tea
3 qts. water
1¼ c. sugar
juice of 3 oranges
juice of 3 lemons
2 c. pineapple juice
sugar

Soak whole cloves in ¼ c. hot water 10-15 minutes. Bring 3 quarts water to boil, add tea and sugar and steep for a few minutes (to taste). Strain leaves. Strain cloves; add juices and tea. Sweeten to taste. Heat just before serving.

Mrs. John Lerner

INSTANT HOT CHOCOLATE

Do Ahead

1 (2 lb.) box Nestles Quik
1 (1 lb.) box powdered sugar
1 (11 oz.) jar Coffeemate
1 (8 qt.) box powdered milk

Mix well together and sift. Store in air-tight container. To serve: Put 2 heaping tablespoons in cup and add hot water.

Mrs. Ralph W. Mitchell

Editor's Note: This makes nice teachers' gifts when put in small decorative containers.

INSTANT RUSSIAN TEA

Easy   Yield: 75 cups
Do Ahead

1 lge. jar Tang (2½ c.)
1 c. instant tea with lemon
   and sugar mix
1 c. sugar
2 tsp. cinnamon
1 tsp. ground allspice
1 tsp. ground cloves

Mix all ingredients together. Use 1 T. of mix per cup.

Mrs. Eugene F. Robbins, Jr.

Editor's Note: A nice change from instant coffee - and just as easy to prepare.

Notes

SOUPS

CREAM OF BROCCOLI SOUP

Serves 6

4 T. margarine
1 onion, chopped
4 T. flour
4 c. milk
¼ tsp. pepper
1 T. Worcestershire sauce
1½ tsp. salt
1-4 drops Tabasco sauce
1-2 c. cut broccoli stalks
½ c. powdered milk
chives (optional)

In 1½ qt.-2 qt. saucepan, saute onion in margarine. Stir in flour and cook until bubbly. Add 3 c. milk, pepper, Worcestershire, salt and Tabasco. Cover saucepan and heat to simmering. In blender, liquefy the remaining cup of milk, broccoli and powdered milk. Add to soup and simmer covered 6-10 minutes. Do not boil. Serve immediately. Garnish with chives if desired.

Mrs. John M. Cogburn, Jr.

CREAM OF CHICKEN CURRY

Easy
Do Ahead

Serves 3

1 can cream of chicken soup
1½ c. half and half
½ tsp. curry powder

Mix well and chill. Serve cold.

Mrs. Seaton G. Bailey

CREAM OF CRAB SOUP

Serves 4-6

¼ c. grated onions
¼ c. butter
1 chicken bouillon cube
1 c. boiling water
3 T. flour
1 qt. milk
1 lb. crabmeat
1 tsp. celery salt
1 T. Worcestershire sauce
pepper to taste
Accent
sherry to taste

Saute the onions in butter. Dissolve the bouillon cube in boiling water. Mix the flour with a little milk, making a smooth paste. Add more milk gradually as mixture cooks, stirring to keep smooth, but do not let it boil. Add all ingredients and keep hot.

Mrs. Jim L. Gillis, Jr.
Soperton, Georgia

SHE-CRAB SOUP

Serves 4-6

½ c. butter
1 T. flour
1 qt. milk
2 c. white crab meat and
   crab roe
mace
few drops onion juice
salt and pepper
½ tsp. Worcestershire sauce
4 T. dry sherry
¼ pt. cream (whipped)

Melt butter and blend in flour. Add milk, crab meat, roe and all seasonings except sherry. Cook slowly over hot water for 20 minutes. Add ½ T. warmed sherry to individual soup bowls. Add soup and top each with whipped cream. Serve hot!

Mrs. James K. Duffes

CREME VICHYSSOISSE

Serves 6-8

6 leeks (white part only)
2 med. onions
½ lb. butter
¾ lb. white potatoes (peeled and
   cut in small pieces)
2 qts. chicken stock
1 c. cream
salt and pepper to taste
chopped chives

Chop onions and leeks finely. Cook them very slowly in ¼ lb. butter - do not brown, just cook until soft. Add stock and potatoes. Add salt and pepper to taste and cook until potatoes are done. Put through a very fine strainer. Add remaining butter, allow it to melt, then add cream. Chill thoroughly, When serving sprinkle finely chopped chives on top.

Mrs. Robert Smalley

CHEDDAR CHOWDER

Do Ahead   Yield: 2 qts. or 6 large servings

2 c. salted water
2 lge. potatoes, peeled and cut
    in small pieces
4 carrots, diced thin
½ c. diced celery
1 sm. onion, chopped
¼ c. margarine
¼ c. flour
2 c. milk
¾ lb. sharp Cheddar cheese,
    shredded
1 (8 oz.) can cream-style corn
2 (4½ oz.) cans small shrimp,
    drained
salt
chives

Put water in saucepan and add next four ingredients. Bring to a boil, cover and simmer for 10 minutes. In small kettle, melt margarine and blend in flour. Gradually stir in milk and cook, stirring until smooth and thickened. Add cheese and stir until it melts. Add the vegetables and liquids, shrimp and corn. Add salt to taste and serve. Garnish with chives if desired.

Mrs. William S. Conner

COLD RASPBERRY SOUP

Do Ahead   Serves 4-5

2 c. fresh or frozen raspberries
½ c. sugar
½ c. sour cream
2 c. water
½ c. red wine

Push raspberries through a fine-mesh strainer. Combine the puree with sugar and sour cream. Add cold water, wine and chill thoroughly.

Mrs. W. Evans Bruner
Atlanta, Georgia

BAKED BEEF MINESTRONE

Do Ahead   Serves 8   350-400°
                                                          3 hrs. 10 min.

2 lbs. lean beef stew meat
1 lge. onion, chopped
2 T. olive or salad oil
1 c. water
2 cloves garlic, minced
1 c. each sliced carrots, zucchini
   and celery
1 sm. green pepper, sliced (seeded)
3 c. shredded cabbage
2 (16 oz.) cans stewed tomatoes
½ tsp. each salt, sugar, rosemary,
   basil and thyme
¼ tsp. pepper
3 (14 oz.) cans beef broth
3 c. cooked shell macaroni
grated Parmesan cheese

Cube beef. Place in large casserole with tight fitting lid (4 qt.) with onion and oil. Bake, uncovered, at 400° for 40 minutes. Add water, cover and reduce heat to 350°. Cook 1 hour. Add vegetables, seasoning and broth. Cover and bake 1½ hours at 350°. To serve spoon some macaroni into soup bowl, ladle soup over macaroni. Sprinkle Parmesan cheese on top.
Best soup ever - a hearty meal! Oven does it all!

Mrs. William S. Colvin

PENNSYLVANIA DUTCH RIVEL SOUP

Easy   Serves 8

2 c. flour (sifted)
½ tsp. salt
2 eggs, well beaten
6 c. chicken broth (seasoned)

Combine flour, salt and beaten eggs and blend until mixture is crumbly. Pour into boiling broth and cook 10 minutes. The rivels will look like rice when cooked. Serves 8

Mrs. R. Lee Pfrogner

GAZPACHO

Do Ahead   Serves 6

1 lge. tomato, peeled and sliced
½ lge. cucumber, peeled and sliced
½ med. onion, sliced
¼ med. green pepper, seeded and
   sliced
1 pimiento, drained
2 (12 oz.) cans tomato juice
⅓ c. olive or salad oil
⅓ c. red wine vinegar
¼ tsp. Tabasco
1½ tsp. salt
⅛ tsp. coarsely ground black
   pepper
1 clove garlic, minced
1 tsp. oregano

Puree in blender the vegetables in ½ - 1 c. tomato juice. Add to remaining juice, stir in seasonings well. Chill several hours. Serve with any of the following condiments: chopped tomatoes, chopped cucumber, chopped onion, chopped chives, chopped stuffed olives, chopped green pepper, crumbled crisp bacon, chopped avocado, chopped hard-boiled egg.

Mrs. William S. Colvin

FRENCH ONION SOUP

Do Ahead   Serves 6-8

1½ lb. or 5 c. thinly sliced onions
3 T. butter or margarine
1 T. oil
1 tsp. salt
¼ tsp. sugar
3 T. flour
2 qts. boiling brown stock,
    canned bouillon or 1 qt.
    boiling water, 1 qt. stock
½ c. dry white wine or dry
    white vermouth
salt and pepper to taste
3 T. cognac if desired
olive oil
garlic
croutes (hard toasted French
    bread)
grated Swiss or Parmesan cheese

Cook onions slowly in butter and oil in covered saucepan for 15 minutes. Uncover, raise heat to medium and stir in salt and sugar. Cook for 30-40 minutes, stirring frequently, until onions are an even deep golden brown. Sprinkle in flour and stir about 3 minutes. Remove from heat, blend in boiling stock, add wine and season to taste. Simmer partially covered 30-40 minutes, skimming if necessary. Just before serving, stir in the cognac. Pour into soup tureen or individual bowls. Place bread or croutes in bowls and pass cheese separately, or if bowls are ovenproof, sprinkle cheese on croutes and bake 10 minutes at 325°, then broil until tops are brown. Serve immediately.

To Make Croutes:
Place French bread slices cut ¾-1" thick on a cookie sheet in a preheated 325° oven for 30 minutes or until thoroughly dry and lightly browned. Halfway through baking, baste each side of bread with a tsp. olive oil and after baking, rub each piece with cut garlic.

The soup is delicious. It does take time, and it is worthwhile to double the recipe.

Mrs. John P. Gross
Birmingham, Alabama

SOUP IN A PUMPKIN SHELL

Serves 10-12

1 attractive pumpkin
oil
2-3 chicken breasts
3 qts. water
1 onion, chopped
butter
1 c. bread crumbs
1½ qts. chicken bouillon (canned
   or made with cubes)
salt and pepper
fresh mushrooms, optional
seasoned croutons

Cut top at slant and scoop out pumpkin. Rub outside of pumpkin with oil and set in shallow pan of water. Boil chicken breasts in approximately 3 qts. water. Saute chopped onion in butter and add bread crumbs. Put mixture in pumpkin. Dice chicken and add to the mixture in the pumpkin. Add chicken broth from cooked chicken (about 1½ qts.) and add another 1½ qts. of chicken bouillon made from cubes or bought. Add salt and pepper to taste and sliced fresh mushrooms. Bake at 350° for 1-1½ hours or if prepared ahead and refrigerated, bake 2-2½ hours. Add seasoned croutons when serving. Place pumpkin on tray and serve soup from the table. For creamed soup, add ½ c. cream for each 2 qts. liquid.

Mrs. William S. Conner

VEGETABLE SOUP

Easy†   Serves 6

1 lb. hamburger
1 (1 lb.) can tomatoes
1 (1 lb.) can mixed vegetables or
   1 (10 oz.) pkg. frozen mixed
   vegetables
1 can consomme
1 c. water
1 med. onion, chopped
bay leaf
salt and pepper to taste

Brown hamburger and drain. Add all other ingredients. Bring to boil; boil for 5 minutes. Cover, reduce heat and simmer for 1 hour.

Mrs. Joseph T. Johnson

CREOLE GUMBO

Serves 6-8

2 T. fat
2 T. flour
1 green pepper, chopped
3 onions, chopped
1 c. celery and parsley, mixed
⅛ tsp. nutmeg
3 cloves
salt to taste
dash of red pepper
1 lge. chicken (boiled
  and cut in pieces,
  save stock)
1 pt. oysters
meat from 5 or 6 crabs
2 c. peeled shrimp
1 qt. okra

Make roux of fat and flour, add seasonings, celery, pepper and onions and saute. Skim fat from chicken stock. Put all ingredients in large container and pour stock over, adding enough water to cover well. Cover and cook on low heat for 2-2½ hours. Serve with rice (cooked dry).

Mrs. J. Ralph Phillips
Baton Rouge, Louisiana

BRUNSWICK STEW

Do Ahead†

3 lbs. pork
3 lbs. beef
6 lbs. chicken
2 (17 oz.) cans sm. English
  peas
2 (17 oz.) cans cream style corn
2 (17 oz.) cans whole tomatoes
6 med. onions, chopped
5 lbs. potatoes, mashed
2 lbs. okra cut for frying
3 T. Worcestershire sauce
1 whole sm. bottle catsup
1 tsp. Tabasco sauce
⅔ c. fresh lemon juice (save
  peelings to add later)
1 tsp. nutmeg
1 tsp. red pepper
2 tsp. black pepper

Cover meat with water and boil for 1½ hours until tender. Season with salt. Save all liquid. Debone chicken, pork and beef. In a large, thick aluminum pot add chunks of meat, all canned ingredients drained, onions, mashed potatoes, okra, spices and lemon juice. Simmer on top of the stove for 8 hours, stirring at least every hour. To add an extra zip, last hour add lemon peels. Remove them when ready to serve or freeze. Meat will shred.

A southern barbecue tradition!

Mrs. Sid Esary

OYSTER STEW

Serves 3-4

1½ T. flour
1½ tsp. salt
dash Tabasco sauce
2 T. cold water
1 pt. oysters
¼ c. butter
3 c. milk
1 c. light cream

Combine first 4 ingredients and blend to a smooth paste. Stir in 1 pt. oysters and their liquor. Add ¼ c. butter. Simmer oyster mixture over very low heat, about 5 minutes, or just until edges curl, stirring gently. Meanwhile scald 3 c. milk and 1 c. light cream. Pour in oyster mixture. Remove from heat; cover. Let stew stand 15 minutes to blend flavors. Have tureen and soup dishes hot. Reheat stew briefly to serving temperature. Dash with paprika.

Mrs. William T. Scott, III

Notes

BREADS

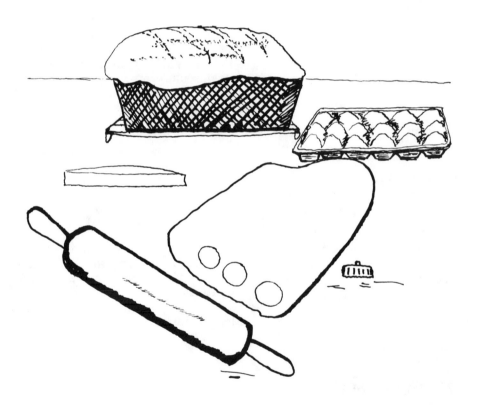

ANGEL BISCUITS *

400°
20 min.

2 pkgs. yeast
2 T. lukewarm water
1 c. Crisco
5 c. self-rising flour
¾ tsp. baking powder
¼ c. sugar
1 tsp. salt
2 c. buttermilk
1 tsp. soda

Dissolve yeast in water. Sift dry ingredients and cut in Crisco. Add yeast mixture and buttermilk to dry ingredients. Knead for 30 seconds. Refrigerate until needed. When ready to roll out, flour rolling surface and hands. Place dough on surface and turn over two or three times before rolling. Can be cut with large cutter or glass and folded over as Parkerhouse rolls, or cut two and stack together for biscuit effect. May cut with biscuit cutter and fold placing sideways close together to fill the baking pan so all sides are touching. This makes a soft biscuit everywhere but the tops and bottoms. When cut, place on greased pan and bake at 400° for 20 minutes.

BEER BISCUITS

Easy

375° 425°
10-20 min.

1 (20 oz.) pkg. Bisquick Mix
1 can beer (room temperature)
2 T. sugar

Mix and let stand 30 minutes. Spoon in greased muffin tins and bake. (375° for 20 minutes or 425° for 10 minutes.)

Mrs. Arthur K. Weathers

BUTTERMILK BISCUITS

Easy†

Yield: 1 dozen

450°
12 min.

1 c. flour
¼ tsp. salt
2 tsp. baking powder
¼ tsp. soda
2½ T. shortening
½ c. buttermilk

Sift dry ingredients into bowl, cut in shortening. Add buttermilk all at once and stir into ball. Roll out, cut and bake.

Mrs. Thomas W. Fetzer

CHEESE BISCUITS

Easy†   375°
                                                         10-15 min.

1 glass Old English Cheese   Mix well. Roll out on floured board.
   (or ½ lb. sharp grated cheese)   Cut in small rounds. Bake at 375°
½ c. butter   until lightly browned (about 10-15
1 c. flour   minutes).
⅛ tsp. red pepper

                                    Mrs. Robert Smalley

JALAPENO CORN BREAD

†   Yield: 12 large servings   450°
                                                      20-25 min.

1½ c. corn meal   Sift dry ingredients. Add remaining
3 tsp. baking powder   ingredients and mix well. Fill greased
½ tsp. salt   muffin pans half full and bake 20 or
3 eggs   25 minutes at 450°.
1 c. sour cream
1 c. grated cheese   Mrs. Billy Peeples
1 sm. can cream style corn   Waynesboro, Virginia
½ c. chopped Jalapeno peppers
½ c. shortening

ONION CORN BREAD

Easy   Serves 6-8

2 med. onions   Brown onions in shortening. Prepare
2 T. shortening   muffin mix according to package di-
1 pkg. corn muffin mix or   rections; pour into greased pie plate.
   your favorite recipe   Spread with onions. Beat sour cream,
¾ c. sour cream   egg, salt and pepper together; pour
1 egg   over top. Bake according to muffin
½ tsp. salt   mix directions.
dash of pepper

                                    Mrs. Don R. Rainwater

SOUR CREAM CORN BREAD

Yield: 18 muffins   400°
                            30 min.

½ c. cooking oil
1 (8½ oz.) can cream
   style corn
1 c. sour cream
1 c. self-rising corn meal
2 eggs
1 tsp. salt
1 level T. sugar

Mix all together. Bake in greased 9"
pie pan, or skillet or muffin tins.
Bake at 400° for 25 to 30 minutes.
Serve hot.
So moist it tastes like cake!

Mrs. David Clements
Mary Beth Nichols

EGG BREAD

Serves 4-6   400°-375°
                         Approx. 45 min.

3 eggs
2 c. buttermilk
1 c. meal
1 c. cold rice (cooked)
1 T. butter and 1 T.
   lard melted
1 tsp. salt
½ tsp. soda dissolved in as
   little water as possible

Beat eggs well, stir in rice, meal and
milk. Add salt and melted shortening
and lastly soda. Heat buttered baking
dish before filling. Bake in pre-
heated 400° oven for 15 minutes.
Reduce temperature to 375° and bake
another 30 minutes or so - until
puffed and brown.

Mrs. John H. Cheatham

SPOON BREAD

Serves 6   375°
                         25-30 min.

2 c. milk
½ c. corn meal*
1 tsp. salt
½ tsp. baking powder
½ tsp. sugar
2 T. melted butter
3 eggs, separated

*If self-rising corn meal is used,
omit the salt and baking powder.

Scald milk. Add corn meal and cook
over low heat until thick. Add salt,
baking powder, sugar and butter. Beat
egg yolks until lemon colored. Add
to corn meal mixture and mix well.
Beat egg whites until soft peaks form.
Fold into corn meal mixture. Put into
greased 1½ qt. casserole. Bake uncovered at 375° for 25-30 minutes.

Mrs. Franklin P. Lindsey, Jr.

MUFFINS

BLUEBERRY MUFFINS

Easy

400°
20-25 min.

2 c. cake flour, sifted
¾ tsp. salt
⅓ c. sugar
2 tsp. baking powder
¼ c. melted margarine
2 eggs, beaten
¾ c. milk
1 c. fresh blueberries
(optional: 1 tsp. grated
lemon or orange rind)

Sift flour, salt, sugar, and baking powder. In a separate bowl, blend melted margarine, beaten eggs, and milk. Mix dry ingredients with wet ingredients. Fold blueberries into batter before the dry ingredients are completely moist. (Do not overmix). Fill well-greased tins ⅔ full. Bake at once in preheated 400° oven 20-25 minutes. Best eaten at once. But if you must reheat them, wrap in foil and heat 5 minutes in a 450° oven.

Mrs. John R. Carlisle

BRAN MUFFINS

Do Ahead

Yield: 3 dozen

375°
20-25 min.

1 c. water
2 c. Bran Buds
1½ c. sugar
½ c. Crisco
2 eggs beaten
1 pt. buttermilk
1 c. All Bran
2½ tsp. soda, dissolved
   in buttermilk
½ tsp. salt
2½ c. flour
raisins, dates, nuts,
   optional

Pour water over Bran Buds. Let stand 1 hour. Cream sugar and Crisco. Add eggs. Add Bran Buds, buttermilk, and All Bran. Mix dry ingredients and add to above. Add raisins, dates or nuts as desired. Bake as many as you need at 375° for 20 to 25 minutes. Keep mixture tightly covered in refrigerator for up to 6 weeks.
Great for gift-giving in refrigerator containers.

Mrs. John P. Gross
Birmingham, Alabama

CHERRY-NUT MUFFINS

†

375°
20-25 min.

½ c. Crisco
½ c. brown sugar
½ c. white sugar
3 eggs, beaten separately
3 T. cherry juice
¼ tsp. baking powder
dash salt
1 c. flour
1 c. pecans, chopped
1 c. maraschino cherries,
   chopped

Cream Crisco and sugars. Add eggs and cherry juice. Beat well. Add flour, baking powder and salt; beat. Fold in pecans and cherries. Pour in greased cupcake tins and bake at 375° for 20-25 minutes.

Mrs. David Rumph
Mineral Wells, Texas

MOTHER'S DATE MUFFINS

Do Ahead†

Yield: 6 doz.
tiny muffins

400°
15 min.

1 (1 lb.) box pitted dates
   (or raisins)
1 tsp. soda
2½ c. all-purpose flour
1 tsp. cloves
1 tsp. cinnamon
1 tsp. nutmeg
½ c. butter
1 c. sugar
2 eggs
1 c. chopped nuts

Cover dates (or raisins) barely with water in a saucepan. Boil until tender (about 15 minutes). Strain and save liquid. Let liquid cool. Dissolve soda in liquid and set aside. Sift together flour, cloves, cinnamon and nutmeg and set aside. Cream together butter and sugar. Add eggs, mixing well. Add liquid saved from the dates. Gradually add flour mixture, blending thoroughly. Fold in dates and nuts. Using a muffin pan for tiny muffins, fill each greased muffin hole with muffin mixture (about half full). Bake at 400° for 15 minutes. Cool and frost with Coffee Icing.
Coffee Icing: Blend ¼ c. butter and enough confectioners sugar to make a stiff mixture. Add enough strong, cooled coffee to butter mixture to make it a spreadable consistency.

Mrs. F. Ted Wilder, Jr.

APRICOT BREAD

Do Ahead†   Yield: 1 large cake   325°
                                                       1 hr. - 15 min.

1 c. margarine
2 c. sugar
4 eggs
1 c. apricot preserves
1 c. buttermilk
3 c. all-purpose flour
1 tsp. cinnamon
¼ tsp. ground cloves
1 tsp. soda (dissolved in
  buttermilk)
1 tsp. vanilla
1 c. chopped pecans
½ c. chopped dried
  apricots

Cream margarine and sugar. Add eggs one at a time, beating after each one. Add preserves. Sift dry ingredients together several times. Then alternately add dry mixture and buttermilk to creamed mixture. Add vanilla and stir well. Fold in nuts and dried apricots. Pour into greased tube or Bundt pan. After baking one hour, cover loosely with foil. Bake 15 minutes more. Then test with toothpick.

This keeps well. It is delicious when sliced, dotted with butter and toasted.

Mrs. Lester L. Luttrell

BANANA BREAD

Do Ahead†   Serves 12   350°
                                                       Loaf-45 min.
                                                       Tins-25 min.

⅔ c. margarine
1½ c. sugar
2 eggs
1½ c. flour
2 tsp. baking powder
¼ tsp. salt
4 T. milk
1 c. mashed bananas
½ c. chopped pecans
1 tsp. vanilla

Cream margarine and sugar; add eggs. Sift flour, baking powder and salt together. Add flour mixture and milk to creamed ingredients. Then add mashed bananas, nuts and vanilla. Pour into a greased 8 x 13" pan or bake as cupcakes. We prefer cupcakes, and this will make 2 dozen.

Mrs. Hugh Dempsey
Mrs. J. Henry Walker

CRANBERRY BREAD

Do Ahead†   Yield: 1 loaf   350°
                                                     1 hr.

2 c. all-purpose flour
   (sifted)
1 c. sugar
1½ tsp. baking powder
½ tsp. soda
1 tsp. salt
¼ c. shortening (I use solid
   Crisco)
¾ c. orange juice
1 T. grated orange rind
1 egg, well beaten
½ c. chopped nuts
1 or 2 c. fresh or frozen
   cranberries

Sift together flour, sugar, baking powder, soda and salt. Cut in shortening until mixture resembles coarse corn meal. Combine orange juice and grated rind with egg. Pour all at once into dry ingredients, mixing just enough to dampen. Fold in chopped nuts and berries. (If berries are frozen, do not thaw - chop frozen.) Spoon into greased 9 x 5 x 3" loaf pan and bake at 350° about 1 hour or until golden brown.
Great in mini-loaves as teacher's gifts. One of my favorite Christmas breads.

Mrs. William S. Colvin

PUMPKIN BREAD

Do Ahead†
                         Yield: 3 loaves   350°
                                                     1 hr.

3⅓ c. plain flour
2 tsp. soda
1½ tsp. salt
1 tsp. cinnamon
1 tsp. nutmeg
3 c. sugar
1 c. oil
4 eggs
⅔ c. water
2 c. (No. 2 can) pumpkin
1 c. nuts, chopped

Sift twice in bowl, flour, soda, salt, cinnamon, nutmeg and sugar. Make well in dry mixture and add oil, eggs, water, pumpkin and nuts. Mix well. Divide into three greased loaf pans. Bake for 1 hour at 350°.

Mrs. Thomas F. Jones

Variation: Add ½ tsp. ginger and increase cinnamon and nutmeg to 3 tsp.

BUTTERSCOTCH STICKY BUNS

Easy   Serves 5-6   400°
                                                        9-11 min.

½ c. chopped nuts
1 (10 oz.) pkg. refrigerator
    biscuits
¼ c. butter or margarine,
    melted
½ c. sugar
1 tsp. cinnamon
½ (6 oz.) pkg. butterscotch-
    flavored morsels
⅓ c. evaporated milk

Sprinkle nuts into a greased 9" cake pan. Separate biscuits, dip on both sides in melted butter. Dip into mixture of sugar and cinnamon. Place over nuts in pan. Bake at 400° for 9-11 minutes. Combine butterscotch morsels and evaporated milk in small saucepan. Cook, stirring constantly, over medium heat until smooth and melted. Pour over hot biscuit buns. Let stand 5 minutes. Turn out of pan onto plate.

Mrs. H. Alfred Bolton III

MARSHMALLOW PUFFS

Easy†   Serves 8   375°
Do Ahead   10-15 min.

¼ c. sugar
1 tsp. cinnamon
2 cans Pillsbury Crescent rolls
16 lge. marshmallows
¼ c. melted butter
¼ c. chopped nuts

Glaze:
    ½ c. powdered sugar
    ½ tsp. vanilla
    2-3 tsp. milk

Mix sugar and cinnamon. Dip marshmallows in butter and roll in sugar mix. Wrap in dough triangle covering completely and squeeze edges to seal. Dip in butter, flatten one end and place upright, twist top to a peak and bend. Place buttered side down in a deep cup pan. Bake, drizzle glaze on tops and sprinkle with nuts. Can refrigerate for 2-3 hours before baking.

Mrs. Fred L. Omundson

PECAN ROLLS

Do Ahead†   Yield: 8 pans   350°
                                            30 min.

1½ c. milk (scalded)
1½ c. sugar
4 tsp. salt
¾ c. shortening (solid)
5 pkgs. active dry yeast
2 c. warm water
6 eggs, beaten
4 c. wheat germ
12-13 c. flour

Syrup:
  2 c. butter
  6 c. brown sugar
  1 c. light corn syrup
  6 c. chopped (coarse)
    pecans

Scald milk, stir in sugar, salt and shortening. Cool to lukewarm. Dissolve yeast in the warm water, stir in lukewarm mixture, beaten eggs and ½ flour and all wheat germ. Work in remaining flour. (Don't dump all in - you use only enough to keep mixture from being sticky.) Knead 8 minutes. Divide dough and place in 2 greased bowls. Cover and let rise in warm place until doubled in bulk (1½-2 hours). Mix syrup ingredients in heavy pan. Heat until butter melts - stir well. Grease eight 9" round cake pans. Spread ⅔ c. syrup in bottom of each pan. Punch down dough. Form into small round rolls - 12 in each pan. Cover with clean cloth and let rise until double in bulk (1 hour). Bake at 350° for 30 minutes or until brown. While still hot, turn out of pan into another pan. Cool and cover with plastic wrap and aluminum foil. Freeze.

Mrs. William S. Colvin

SAVANNAH COFFEE CAKE

†   350°
                                    30 min.

½ c. butter
1 c. sugar
2 eggs
1 c. sour cream
1 tsp. soda
1½ c. flour
1½ tsp. baking powder
½ c. sugar
2 tsp. cinnamon
1 c. nuts (chopped)

Cream butter and 1 c. sugar. Add eggs and sour cream. Sift together soda, flour, and baking powder. Add to creamed mixture. Spoon one-half of batter into 8 x 12" baking pan which has been greased and floured. Mix together ½ c. sugar, cinnamon and nuts. Sprinkle one-half sugar mixture on batter then pour in rest of batter. Sprinkle rest of sugar mixture on top. Bake 30 minutes at 350°.

Malvina M. Beal

ANADAMA BREAD

†

375°
40-45 min.

1½ c. water
1 tsp. salt
⅓ c. yellow corn meal
⅓ c. molasses
1½ T. shortening
1 pkg. dry yeast
¼ c. lukewarm water
4 to 4½ c. flour

Bring salted water to boil in saucepan. Add the corn meal, stirring constantly. Remove from heat and stir in molasses and shortening. Cool to lukewarm. Mix yeast with ¼ c. water and let stand 5 minutes. Blend yeast into corn meal mixture then mix in flour, first with spoon then by hand. The dough will be sticky. Knead and let rise until double (1½ hours). Punch down and turn into greased loaf pan. Let rise until double. Brush top with melted butter and sprinkle with corn meal and salt. Bake 375° about 40-45 minutes until dark brown.

The name Anadama comes from a New England fisherman whose lazy wife always served him corn meal mush and molasses for dinner. One day tired of it, he mixed it with flour and yeast and baked it as bread saying, "Anna, damn her".

Mrs. James S. Murray
Durham, New Hampshire

"TIP"

To measure molasses; grease measuring cup.

CHEDDAR SWIRL BREAD

Do Ahead†   Yield: 2 loaves   350°
                                            35-40 min.

1 c. milk
¼ c. shortening
½ c. sugar
2 tsp. salt
2 pkg. dry yeast
½ c. warm water
2 eggs
6 c. (approximately)
   plain flour
melted butter
Cheddar cheese (grated)
dried onion flakes

Scald milk; stir in shortening, sugar, salt and cool to lukewarm. Sprinkle yeast on warm water in large bowl; stir until dissolved. Stir in milk mixture, eggs and 3 c. flour; beat 2 minutes with mixer (medium speed). Mix in remaining flour a little at a time to make a soft dough. Knead until smooth. Place dough in a greased bowl and cover; let rise in warm place until doubled (about 1½ hours). Turn onto bread board and knead until smooth; divide in half and roll each half with rolling pin into flat 12 x 7" rectangle. Brush each with melted butter, sprinkle with grated sharp Cheddar cheese to cover well and sprinkle on a few dried onion flakes. Roll each rectangle up like a jelly roll (roll up short 7" end). Place seam down in greased loaf pan. Cover and let rise until double, about 1 hour. Bake at 350° for 35 to 40 minutes until brown. Remove from pan and cool on wire racks.

A great basic bread dough - for coffee cake sprinkle rectangle with nuts, butter, cinnamon and sugar. For herb bread substitute your favorite herbs for the cheese and onions, or create your own special bread.

Mrs. Cedric Kuhn
Athens, Georgia

CRUSTY WHITE BRAIDS

Do Ahead†   Yield: 2 loaves   375°
                       30 min.

4 - 4½ c. <u>unbleached</u> flour
2 pkg. active dry yeast
2 c. warm water
½ c. cooking oil
2 T. sugar
1 T. salt

In large mixing bowl combine 2 c. of the flour and the 2 pkg. yeast. Add water, cooking oil, sugar and salt to the dry mixture. Beat at low speed of electric mixer for ½ minute, scraping sides of bowl constantly. Beat 3 minutes at high speed. By hand, stir in enough of the remaining flour to make a moderately stiff dough. Turn out on lightly floured surface; knead until smooth and elastic, 8-10 minutes. Shape into a ball. Place dough in greased bowl, turning once to grease surface. Cover, let rise until double, about 1½ hours. Punch dough down. Divide in half. Divide each half in thirds; shape into 6 balls. Cover; let rest 10 minutes. Roll each ball to a 16" rope. Line up 3 ropes, 1" apart, on greased baking sheet. Braid very loosely, beginning in the middle. Pinch ends together and tuck under. Repeat with remaining ropes. Cover, let rise in warm place until almost double, about 40 minutes. Bake in 375° oven for 30 minutes or until bread is done. Cool slightly before attempting to slice.

Mrs. H. Ray Simonton

DILLY BREAD

Do Ahead†   Serves 8   350°
                                                         30 min.

2 to 2¼ c. unsifted flour
  (plain)
2 T. sugar
1 tsp. salt
1 T. instant minced onion
2 tsp. dill seed
¼ tsp. baking soda
1 pkg. dry yeast
1 T. butter
¼ c. very hot tap water
  (125-135 degrees)
1 c. creamed cottage cheese
  (room temperature)
1 egg
  (room temperature)

In a large bowl thoroughly mix ¼ c. flour, sugar, salt, instant minced onion, dill seed, baking soda and undissolved dry yeast.   Add softened butter. Gradually add very hot tap water to dry ingredients and beat 2 minutes at medium   speed   of electric mixer, scraping   bowl   occasionally.   Add cottage cheese, egg, and ½ c. flour or enough flour to make a thick batter. Beat at high speed 2 minutes, scraping bowl occasionally.   Stir in enough additional   flour   to make a stiff batter. Cover; let rise in a warm place, free from draft; until doubled in bulk, about 1 hour and 15 minutes. Stir batter down. Turn into a greased loaf pan.   Cover; let rise in a warm place, free from draft, until doubled in bulk, about 50 minutes. Bake in moderate   oven   (350°) about 30 minutes, or until done. Remove from pan and cool on wire rack.   Brush with melted butter and sprinkle with coarse salt.

Mrs. William F. Early

SYRIAN BREAD ENVELOPES

Do Ahead†   Serves 12   400°
                                                    9-10 min.

1 pkg. dry yeast
3½ - 4 c. sifted all-purpose
   flour
1¼ c. warm water
2 T. cooking oil
1 tsp. salt
¼ tsp. sugar

In large bowl, combine yeast and 1½ c. flour. Combine warm water, oil, salt and sugar. Add to dry mixture in bowl and beat on low speed of electric mixer for ½ minute - scraping sides of bowl constantly. Beat 3 minutes at high speed. Stir in by hand enough of remaining flour to make stiff dough. Turn out on floured surface and knead until smooth and elastic, about 5 minutes. Cover with bowl and let rise 45 minutes. Punch down and divide into 12 equal parts. Shape in balls and let rise 10 minutes. Roll on floured surface to 5" circles. Place 2" apart on ungreased baking sheet. Cover and let rise 20 to 30 minutes. Remove from sheet after cooking 9-10 minutes at 400° and immediately wrap in foil to cool.

Mrs. James S. Murray
Durham, New Hampshire

FRENCH BREAD

Do Ahead†   Yield: 2 loaves   400°
                                                      35 min.

1 pkg. yeast
1½ c. hot water
1 T. sugar
melted butter
1½ tsp. salt
1 T. shortening
4 c. flour (plain)

Dissolve yeast in ½ c. water, set aside. In another bowl, dissolve salt and sugar in remaining water. Add shortening and yeast mix. Add a little flour at a time, mix well. Work through dough with spoon at 10 minute intervals for 5 consecutive times. Turn onto lightly floured surface and divide in half. Shape into two balls. Let rest 10 minutes. Roll each ball into 12 x 9" rectangle. Roll as for jelly roll and seal edges. Place on baking sheet. Cover with towel and let stand 1½ hours. Bake 30-35 minutes at 400°

Mrs. Donald L. Hutcheson
Mrs. Bates Bowers, Jr.

OATMEAL BREAD

Do Ahead†   Yield: 2 loaves   325°
                                                          50 min.

1 c. rolled oats
2 c. boiling water
2 pkgs. active dry yeast
⅓ c. warm water
2½ tsp. salt
½ c. honey (molasses may
   be used)
2 T. soft butter
about 6 c. unbleached flour
unbeaten egg white

Put rolled oats in large bowl. Pour boiling water over. Let stand about ½ hour (must still be warm). Dissolve yeast in the warm water. Let stand about 5 minutes. Add the salt, honey and butter to the soaked oats. Add the yeast mixture. Add and stir in the first 2 c. of flour, then 2 more c. Knead the last 2 c. of flour into the dough. (If the dough is still very sticky, add a little more flour.) Wash out bowl, grease lightly, put bread dough back in, turn over once, cover with a towel and let rise until double in a warm place (about 2-3 hours). Punch dough down, divide, and place in two 9 x 5 x 3" loaf pans. Shape the dough out to the ends covering the bottoms of the pans. Cover and let rise again (about 1 hour or a little more). Bake at 325° on a rack about 4" from the bottom for about 50 minutes. When done, take out of pans immediately. Brush tops with unbeaten egg white and cool on racks right side up.

I like to start this right after breakfast on a day I plan to be home most of the day. Don't try to hurry bread-making. Enjoy!

Mrs. H. Ray Simonton

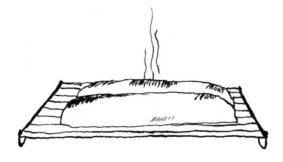

WHOLE WHEAT BREAD

Do Ahead†   Yield: 4 loaves   350°
                                                                45 min.

2 c. unseasoned mashed
   potatoes
1 c. whole bran cereal
½ c. molasses
¼ c. butter or margarine
2 T. salt
3 c. boiling water
2 pkg. yeast
½ c. lukewarm water
9 c. sifted flour (white)
3 c. whole wheat flour
¾ c. corn meal

Put all flour in oven at 200° and heat until warm. Combine, in large bowl, mashed potatoes, bran cereal, molasses, butter and salt. Stir in boiling water. Cool to lukewarm. Sprinkle yeast on ½ c. lukewarm water; stir to dissolve. Add yeast and 4 c. flour to bran mixture. Beat with electric mixer at medium speed until smooth, about 2 minutes. Gradually add flour, making soft dough that leaves sides of the bowl. Turn on floured surface and knead until smooth and satiny, about 8 to 10 minutes. Place in lightly greased bowl, turning once to grease top. Cover and let rise until doubled, 1 - 1½ hours. Divide dough in fourths. Shape into loaves and place in 4 greased 9 x 5 x 3" loaf pans. Let rise until doubled. Bake at 350° for 45 minutes or until bread tests done. Remove from pan and cool on racks.

Mrs. John P. Gross
Birmingham, Alabama

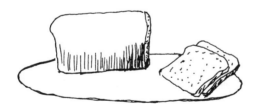

HOMEMADE BREAD IDEA

Make your favorite white bread recipe and after the last time you punch dough down and shape into loaves, slice the loaf into desired sized slices and dip each slice in melted butter then into a mixture of cinnamon and sugar. Place into loaf pan like regular loaf of bread, let rise and bake according to your recipe directions. Can be wrapped in foil and reheated.

ALL-BRAN REFRIGERATOR ROLLS

†   Yield: 3 dozen   425°
                                                      10-15 min.

1 pkg. dry yeast
½ c. lukewarm water
½ c. Crisco
6 T. sugar
1 tsp. salt
½ c. All-Bran (cereal)
½ c. boiling water
3 c. plain all-purpose
    flour
1 egg

Soften the yeast in the warm water. Place the shortening, sugar, salt and All-Bran in a large mixing bowl. Add the boiling water and let cool to lukewarm. Stir. Add the dissolved yeast, 1 egg slightly beaten, and the sifted flour. Stir well. It will be a very soft dough. Cover tightly and place in the refrigerator at least overnight. When ready to use, make out in any desired shape, place on greased baking sheet. Let rise until double in bulk (about 1½ hours) at room temperature. Bake at 425° until light brown. Rolling, cutting round, creasing with the back of a knife, and folding over is the quickest way to make out and makes an attractive "pocketbook" type roll. Any unused portion will keep well in the refrigerator several days.

Mrs. T. B. Manley, Sr.

CRESCENT ROLLS

Do Ahead†   Yield: 4-5 dozen   350°
                                                      10 min.

1 c. warm water
1 pkg. yeast
½ c. sugar
3 eggs
½ c. melted shortening
    or oil
1 tsp. salt
5 c. flour

Mix first three ingredients. Add rest in order. Mix well by hand in bowl until dough does not cling to bowl sides or fingers. Oil top of dough, cover with Saran and let double in size. Divide into four equal parts. Roll as for pie crust, spread with soft butter and cut into wedges. Roll from widest part to point, stretching and curving as you roll. Let rise again on greased baking sheet. Bake.

Mrs. Fred L. Omundson

YEAST ROLLS

Do Ahead†   Yield: 6 dozen   400°
                                                                15 min.

¾ c. shortening
⅓ c. sugar
1 c. hot water
2 eggs, well beaten
2 pkg. yeast
1 c. cold water
6 c. flour
2 tsp. salt
margarine

Cream sugar and shortening together. Add cup of boiling water. Cool. When lukewarm add well-beaten eggs and yeast dissolved in cup of cold water. Add flour, then salt. Mix well. Put into greased bowl in refrigerator to rise. Let dough chill thoroughly (best overnight). Make out rolls in desired shape and put on greased cookie sheet. Brush with margarine. Let rise at least 2 hours until double in bulk. Bake at 400° for 15 minutes.

Mrs. Ivey L. Burson

FEATHER LIGHT DUMPLINGS

2 c. plain flour
1 tsp. salt
3 tsp. baking powder
⅔ c. whole milk
corn oil

Sift flour. Add salt and baking powder. Stir in milk and knead dough on floured surface until firm. Roll out into ⅛" thickness and cut into strips 1 x 3". Drop a few at a time into boiling corn oil. Cover for a few seconds; continue adding dumplings, being certain that the liquid is kept at a rolling boil. When all dumplings have been added, cover tightly and continue cooking 12 minutes. Drain in basket or on paper towels.

Mrs. John H. Goddard

GRANOLA

Easy
Do Ahead

6 c. rolled oats (uncooked)
1 c. shredded coconut
1 c. wheat germ
½ c. shelled (salted) sunflower
  seeds
¾ c. halved cashew nuts
½ c. cooking oil
½ c. honey
⅓ c. water
1½ tsp. salt
1½ tsp. vanilla
1 c. raisins

In large bowl combine oats, coconut, wheat germ, sunflower seeds and cashews. Mix together oil, honey, water, salt and vanilla. Pour over oatmeal mixture. Stir well to coat. Spread oat mixture on 2 greased baking sheets (with sides). Bake at 350° for 30 minutes, stirring frequently. Cool thoroughly. Add raisins. Store in airtight container until ready to serve. Will easily store 3-4 weeks.

Mrs. E. F. Carlisle III

CORN PANCAKES

For a heavier "supper" pancake, add 1 can drained white corn to pancake batter. Cook according to package directions.

MY PANCAKES

Yield: 16-18

2 c. sifted flour (plain)
4 tsp. baking powder
2 T. sugar
1 tsp. salt
2 egg yolks, beaten until
  thick
1 c. milk
¼ c. melted butter
2 egg whites, beaten until
  stiff but not dry

Sift flour, measure 2 cups; add baking powder, salt and sugar. Then mix and sift. Beat egg yolks until light, then stir in milk; add to flour mixture and beat or stir until smooth. Stir in fat. Fold in beaten egg whites. Bake on hot griddle until bubbles appear on top - turn only once.

Mrs. Gerald L. Bilbro

PANCAKE "TIP"

Any pancake recipe or mix can be improved by separating the eggs and folding in the beaten whites at the end.

BUTTERMILK PANCAKES

Yield: 18

2 c. all-purpose flour
1 tsp. baking soda
1 tsp. salt
2 T. sugar
2 eggs, separated
2 1/3 c. buttermilk
2 T. butter, melted

Sift together dry ingredients. Add buttermilk, beaten egg yolks, and melted butter. Stir until moistened. Beat egg whites until stiff. Fold into batter. (For thinner batter, add more buttermilk.) Bake on hot (375°) lightly greased griddle or skillet.

Mrs. H. Ray Simonton

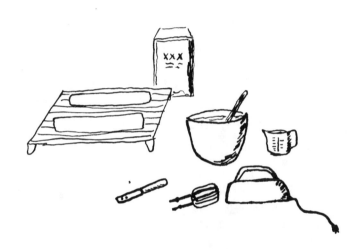

PINEAPPLE FRITTERS

Leftover pancake batter makes good Pineapple Fritters. Dip pineapple slices in flour and then in pancake batter. Fry in small amount of hot fat. Drain. Good with ham, pork chops, etc.

POPOVERS

Easy   Yield: 8   425°
                                                30 min.

1 c. milk
1 c. flour
2 eggs
2 T. melted butter, cooled
½ tsp. salt

Blend in blender or Cuisinart until just combined. Do not over blend. Half fill 8 buttered ½ c. metal molds and set on preheated baking sheet in 425° oven. Bake 30 minutes or until well puffed and crisp.

Mrs. Robert Smalley

SANDWICHES

TEA SANDWICH TIP

Trim and spread bread while frozen - much easier to work with. Spread all tea sandwiches with a very thin layer of butter. The butter will not alter the taste and will keep the sandwiches from being soggy.

To store: Cover sandwiches with waxed paper, then cover with a damp tea towel and refrigerate until needed.

CARROT SANDWICHES

Mix India Relish, mayonnaise, ground peanuts and grated carrots to taste. Spoon onto small buttered bread rounds.

CREAM CHEESE RELISH SANDWICHES

Mix softened cream cheese with prepared sweet pickle relish. Spread on thinly buttered bread.

CUCUMBER SANDWICHES (Open Faced)

1 (3 oz.) pkg. cream cheese
1 T. mayonnaise
1 T. sour cream
1 T. minced onion
dash of Worcestershire sauce
sprinkle of garlic powder
   (optional)
salt and pepper to taste
cucumber
parsley

Cut out rounds (small) of bread with cookie cutter or biscuit cutter. Mix all ingredients except cucumber and parsley. Spread on bread. Top with thin slice of cucumber and sprig of fresh parsley.

Mrs. William C. Hewitt

ROLLED-UP DEVILED HAM SANDWICHES

Mix 1 can deviled ham with small amount of mustard and grated onion to taste. Trim wheat bread. Roll with rolling pin, butter thinly, spread with ham. Roll up and chill. Cut in thirds, stand on end and decorate with a tiny sprig of fresh parsley.

Mrs. W. Barron Cumming

VEGETABLE SANDWICH FILLING

2 carrots
2 tomatoes
1 or 2 onions
2 sm. cucumbers
1 bell pepper
1 envelope unflavored
    gelatin
1 c. Miracle Whip Salad
    dressing
2 tsp. Tabasco sauce
salt to taste

Prepare vegetables by washing and coring. Do not peel anything except onion. Grind 5 vegetables in blender. Drain. Save juice. Mix one envelope plain gelatin with vegetable juice. Place this in hot water until dissolved. Add to salad dressing. Add Tabasco, a little salt and mix with vegetables. Chill; if too thick, add more salad dressing. Use white and wheat bread.

Mrs. Charles L. Smith

STUFFINGS

CHESTNUT STUFFING

Yield: Stuffs 10 lb. goose or
           12 lb. turkey

2 lbs. mild sausage
6-8 c. bread crumbs
2 lbs. chestnuts, peeled
2 eggs, beaten with fork
2 med. cloves of garlic
2 oz. cognac
salt and pepper to taste
¼ tsp. thyme
1 bay leaf

Mix ingredients and place in refrigerator, allowing flavors to blend overnight. Fill cavity of goose or turkey. To prepare chestnuts, peel thin strips of shell from side of each chestnut. Drop in saucepan of cold water to cover by one inch. Bring to a boil. Remove from heat. Peel off shell and brown inner skin.

Mrs. John H. Goddard

SAUSAGE-APPLE STUFFING

Do Ahead   Serves 5-6

giblets and neck
1 c. stock
1 tsp. salt
¼ tsp. pepper
½ tsp. sage
4 c. red apples, unpeeled
   and sliced very thin
4 c. dry bread crumbs
1 c. celery, cut fine
3 T. butter
¼ lb. pork sausage

To make stock, simmer giblets and neck of fowl until tender in a pint of water in saucepan. Drain off 1 c. liquid and cool. Add seasonings and apples to bread crumbs. Cook celery in butter for 3 minutes. Add sausage and stir until meat is browned. Combine broth and chopped giblets with bread mixture. Fill cavities of birds. Stuffing for 5-7 cornish hens or 6-8 lb. turkey.

Apples and sausage always make a fantastic combination!

Mrs. William T. Scott III

SOUTHERN STUFFING

Serves 12-20   350°
                      45 min-1 hr.

2 c. chopped celery
1 c. chopped onion
2 c. milk
6 c. coarsely crumbled
   corn bread
4 c. cracker meal
6 c. turkey or chicken
   broth
3 tsp. seasoning salt
2 tsp. celery salt
6 eggs
1 tsp. black pepper

Heat a little fat in skillet. Saute celery and onion until barely tender. In large bowl combine all ingredients; mix well and pour into 4 qt. casserole. Bake in moderate oven (350°) for 45 minutes or until done. Makes enough stuffing for a 12 lb. turkey.

Mrs. William L. Wages

EGGS and CHEESE

EGGS

EGGS BOURGUIGNONNE

Do Ahead   Serves 3

⅓ c. onion, finely chopped
⅓ c. shallots, finely chopped
2 T. garlic, minced
2 T. butter
¼ c. flour
1 c. whole canned tomatoes
¼ c. liquid from snails
1 (4½ oz.) can snails
¼ c. carrots, diced and cooked
salt and pepper
6 eggs

Saute onion, shallots and garlic in butter over medium heat. Stir in flour and brown thoroughly over a low heat. Blend in tomatoes and liquid from snails. Add snails, carrots, salt and pepper. Cook slowly, 10 to 15 minutes, stirring constantly.

Make three 2 egg omlets and fold ¼ cup sauce into each omelet.

Mrs. H. Alfred Bolton III

EGGS RACHEL

Serves 6

1 (10 oz.) pkg. frozen puff - pastry shells

Sauce:
1 c. sliced fresh mushrooms
  or 4 oz. canned
2 T. butter
1 T. flour
1 c. milk
2 T. white wine
½ tsp. salt

Eggs:
8 eggs
½ c. sour cream
2 T. dried chives
½ tsp. salt
¼ tsp. black pepper
¼ c. butter

Bake the pastry shells according to package directions. Keep warm. Make mushroom sauce by sauteing 1 cup mushrooms in 2 T. butter. Sprinkle 1 T. flour over mushrooms. Stir. Blend in 1 cup milk. Bring to boil stirring and add 2 T. white wine and ½ tsp. salt. Keep warm. Make eggs by beating together eggs, sour cream, chives, salt and pepper. Melt butter in large skillet. Soft scramble eggs. Use to fill warm shells. Spoon mushroom sauce over eggs. Serves 6 people. May be multiplied to serve any number.

Mrs. Taylor B. Manley, Jr.
Mrs. Warren K. Wells

EGG SAUSAGE CASSEROLE

Do Ahead   ·   Serves 6-8   350°
30-45 min.

6 slices white bread, trimmed
and cubed
6 eggs, slightly beaten
1 c. sharp Cheddar cheese,
grated
1 lb. pre-cooked small sausage
links
1 tsp. dry mustard
salt and pepper
2 c. whole milk

Butter casserole or Pyrex dish heavily.
Line with bread cubes. Mix all other
ingredients; pour over cubes, cover
tightly and let stand overnight in
refrigerator. Bake 350° for 45
minutes.

Mrs. Robert S. Ogletree, Jr.

CHEESE EGGS

Do Ahead   Serves 12   350°
15-20 min.

2 doz. eggs
2 tsp. lemon juice
1 tsp. dry mustard
2 tsp. Worcestershire sauce
capers
salt and pepper
1½ lbs. Velveeta cheese
¼ c. butter
½ c. flour
½ c. dry cocktail sherry
1½ c. milk
buttered cracker crumbs

Hardboil and split two dozen eggs.
Mash yolks. Add lemon, mustard,
Worcestershire, capers, and salt and
pepper as in making deviled eggs.
Melt cheese. Stuff yolk mixture into
egg halves. Place in shallow casserole.
Melt butter. Stir in flour. Add sherry,
cheese and milk. Cook over medium
heat until blended. Pour mixture
on top of eggs. Sprinkle with
buttered cracker crumbs. Bake at
350° for 15-20 minutes.

Mrs. J. Gordon Dixon

Variation: Add 4 young green chopped
onions and ½ lb. ground cooked ham
(can use canned Deviled Ham) to
yolk mixture.

Mrs. Herbert A. Bolton, Jr.

SAUSAGE CUPS AND CHIVE EGGS

Do Ahead   Serves 6-8   375°
                                                          30 min.

1½ lbs. sausage
½ tsp. onion powder
1 c. uncooked oats
1 egg
¼ c. milk

Blend ingredients together and shape into cups in muffin tins. Bake at 375° for 30 minutes. Dip grease off during cooking. Makes 12-18 medium cups.

12 eggs
¾ c. milk
¾ tsp. salt
½ tsp. pepper
2 (3 oz.) pkgs. cream cheese
  with chives
butter

Fill cups with scrambled eggs cooked as follows:
In bowl combine eggs, milk, salt, and pepper. Beat just until combined. Heat butter in a large skillet, pour in egg mixture, cook over low heat. As eggs start to set on bottom, gently lift cooked portion to let uncooked portion flow under. Add cheese cubes and cook until eggs are moist and shiny.

Mrs. H. Alfred Bolton III

SAUSAGE PUFF

                            Serves 6   350°
                                                         45 min.

4 slices white bread
1 lb. sausage
1 tsp. mustard
¼ c. green onions
1 c. shredded Swiss cheese
4 eggs beaten
1 pt. half and half
¼ to ½ tsp. salt
⅛ tsp. pepper
dash nutmeg

Put bread slices in 8 inch square baking dish. Brown and drain sausage. Stir in mustard - spoon evenly over bread. Sprinkle sausage with finely chopped onions and then with cheese. Mix remaining ingredients and pour over mixture. Bake in 350° oven for 45 minutes or until golden brown or knife comes out clean.

Mrs. James R. Fortune, Jr.

QUICHE

Serves 4-6   400°
                          15 min.

½ pt. cream
3 eggs
¼ tsp. nutmeg
salt and pepper
½ lb. sharp Cheddar cheese or
  1 lb. Swiss cheese, grated
8 slices bacon, fried and
  crumbled (optional)
1 sm. onion, chopped and
  sauteed
1 regular size pie shell
  (baked)

Assemble ingredients. Mix together in medium size bowl. Pour mixture into prepared pie shell and bake 15 minutes at 400°.

Mrs. Donald L. Hutcheson

QUICK QUICHE

Serves 8-10   350°
                          50-60 min.

2 (9") shallow pie shells
8 strips crisp bacon
1 sm. onion, finely chopped
1 c. Swiss cheese, grated
¼ c. Parmesan cheese
½ tsp. salt
¼ tsp. pepper
½ c. diced ham
1½ c. light cream
4 eggs
sm. can mushrooms (optional)

Sprinkle bacon, cheese and mushrooms on bottom of crust. Put remaining ingredients in blender for 10 seconds. Pour in pie shells. Bake 50-60 minutes at 350°.

Mrs. James F. Lewis
Savannah, Georgia

SPINACH QUICHE

Serves 6-8   350°
                          About 40 min.

2 c. finely chopped onions
¼ c. butter
1 (10 oz.) pkg. frozen chopped
  spinach
¾ c. grated Swiss cheese
3 eggs
1 c. milk
1 tsp. salt
⅛ tsp. pepper
dash nutmeg
1 unbaked 9" pie shell
  or
2 frozen smaller pie shells

Peel and chop onions. Saute slowly in butter. Cook spinach according to package directions and drain thoroughly. Combine onions, spinach, Swiss cheese, beaten eggs. Add milk and seasonings. Pour into pastry shell and bake at 350° about 40 minutes, for large pie, shorter time for small one. Test by inserting knife into center. If it comes out clean, it is done.

Mrs. John J. Flynt, Jr.

CHEESE

CHEESY FONDUE

Do Ahead   Serves 8-10

½ c. finely chopped onion
1 T. butter or margarine
1 (8 oz.) pkg. cream cheese,
  softened
1 (10¾ oz.) can condensed
  Cheddar cheese soup
¼ c. drained, chopped, canned
  tomatoes
½ tsp. Worcestershire sauce
Italian bread cubes

In saucepan, cook onion in butter until tender. Add cream cheese. Gradually blend in soup, tomatoes, and Worcestershire. Heat until cheese melts. Stir occasionally. When ready to serve, transfer to fondue pot. Spear bread with fondue fork or toothpick and dip into hot cheese. Makes 2¼ c. dip.

Mrs. Newton Crouch

SWISS CHEESE FONDUE

Serves 6-8

1 (1 lb.) loaf French or
  Italian bread cut into bite
  size pieces with at least
  one crusty side
½ lb. natural Swiss cheese,
  shredded
½ lb. Gruyere, shredded*
5 tsp. corn starch
2 T. Kirsch
1 clove garlic
¼ tsp. salt
¼ tsp. monosodium glutamate
⅓ tsp. pepper
2 c. Sauterne
*If Gruyere is not available,
use 1 lb. Swiss cheese

Rub earthenware chafing dish or 2 qt. top of range casserole with cut garlic. Put cheese, salt, monosodium glutamate, and pepper into the dish. Pour sauterne over the cheese. Stir constantly over medium heat until cheese is melted. Blend in mixture of corn starch and Kirsch. Continue stirring while cooking 2 or 3 minutes or until fondue begins to bubble. Keep the fondue gently bubbling throughout serving time. Serve at table. Spear bread cubes with a fork, dunk and twirl in the fondue. Be sure to spear your bread securely for the lady who loses her bread must kiss everyone at the table or a man supply the next bottle of wine.

Rolf Duerr
Newport News, Virginia

GARLIC CHEESE GRITS

Easy Serves 8 to 10 350°
Do Ahead 15-20 min.

1 c. grits, uncooked
4 c. water
1 T. salt
1 stick butter or margarine
1 roll garlic cheese
½ lb. sharp cheese
2 T. Worcestershire sauce

Cook grits in the salted water. When cooked, add the butter, garlic cheese, sharp cheese and Worcestershire sauce. Stir until the butter and cheese have melted. Put in greased casserole and sprinkle with paprika. Bake in pre-heated 350° oven for 15 to 20 minutes. Use as main supper dish or starch.

Mrs. W. Everett Beal

JALAPENO CHEESE GRITS

Easy Serves 4-6 250°
Do Ahead 1 hr.

3 c. boiling water
1 tsp. salt
¾ c. quick cooking grits
2 beaten eggs
¾ stick margarine
8 oz. sharp Cheddar cheese
1 roll Jalapeno cheese
1 (4 oz.) can green chilies, chopped
3 or 4 shakes of Tabasco sauce

Add grits gradually to water and salt, stirring until thick - about 5 minutes. Add eggs and let come to a good boil. Add margarine and cheese. Stir until melted. Add Tabasco sauce. Put in a greased 9 inch square dish and sprinkle with paprika. Bake for 1 hour at 250°.

Mrs. Richard M. Barnes
Plattsburg, Missouri

CRISPY MACARONI AND CHEESE

Easy Serves 6 350°
Do Ahead 30 min.

1 can cream of celery soup
½ c. milk
½ tsp. prepared mustard
generous dash of pepper
3 c. cooked macaroni
2 c. shredded Cheddar cheese
1 c. French fried onions

Blend soup, milk, mustard, pepper with mixer until smooth. Stir in macaroni and 1½ cups of cheese. Bake for 20 minutes. Top with French fried onions, remaining cheese and bake 10 minutes more.

Mrs. Allen W. Marshall III

MACARONI AND CHEESE DELUXE

Do Ahead   Serves 6-8   350°
               45 min.

1 (8 oz.) pkg. elbow macaroni
2 c. small curd cream style
 cottage cheese
1 c. sour cream
1 egg, slightly beaten
¾ tsp. salt
dash pepper
8 oz. sharp cheese, shredded
 (2 c.)
paprika

Cook macaroni according to package directions. Drain well. Combine cottage cheese, sour cream, egg, salt and pepper. Add shredded cheese, mixing well. Add macaroni. Turn into a greased 9 x9 x2" baking dish. Sprinkle with paprika. Bake at 350° for 45 minutes.

Mrs. Billy Peeples
Waynesboro, Virginia

BLENDER SOUFFLE

Do Ahead   Serves 6-8   350°
               1 hr.

8 oz. sharp cheese, grated
10 slices bread, buttered
 and trimmed
4 eggs
2 c. milk
1 tsp. salt
½ tsp. Worcestershire sauce
½ tsp. dry mustard

Mix ½ of all ingredients in blender, then the other ½ (all won't fit in food processor). Put together in 1½ qt. casserole. Cook 1 hour at 350°. Never fails. Can be made a day ahead.

Mrs. Robert Smalley

CHEESE SOUFFLE

     Serves 4   325°
               1 hr.

2 T. butter
2 T. flour
¾ c. hot milk
½ tsp. salt and pepper
½ lb. cheese (sharp), grated
4 eggs, separated

Make sauce with butter, flour, milk, and salt and pepper. Add cheese. Stir in egg yolks. Cool. Fold in stiffly beaten egg whites and pour in greased casserole. Bake at 325° for about an hour.

Mrs. Lewis T. Murphy

CHEESE-HAM-SPINACH STRATA

Do Ahead   Serves 12   325°
                                                         1 hr.

18 slices of day old bread,
   remove crusts
12 slices sharp American cheese
2 c. diced/cubed ham
2 (10 oz.) pkgs. chopped,
   frozen spinach
1 tsp. butter
2 T. chopped onion
½ tsp. black pepper
6 eggs, slightly beaten
3½ c. milk
½ c. grated or shredded
   Cheddar cheese

Cook and drain spinach and season with butter, onion and black pepper. Cover bottom of greased 13 x 9" dish with 6 slices bread and top with 6 slices cheese. Next add ½ spinach mixture and sprinkle 1 cup diced ham. Repeat layers of bread, cheese slices, spinach, and ham. Gently push down entire strata with hand or wide spatula. Take 6 remaining bread slices and cut diagonally into halves and arrange 12 triangles in 2 overlapping rows on top of strata. Combine eggs and milk. Pour combined egg and milk mixture on top of entire dish. Cover and let stand refrigerated several hours or overnight. Bake at 325° for 45 minutes. Remove from oven to sprinkle entire dish with grated Cheddar cheese, return to oven and bake an additional 15 minutes.

Mrs. Arthur C. Krepps II

Editor's note: Broccoli may be substituted for spinach.

Notes

SALADS and DRESSINGS

FRUIT SALADS

APPLESAUCE SALAD

Easy
Do Ahead

Serves 4-6

1 c. sweetened applesauce
1 (3 oz.) pkg. raspberry gelatin
1 orange
1 (6½ oz.) bottle of 7-Up

Heat applesauce. Add powdered gelatin to hot sauce and set aside to cool. Add juice and grated rind of one orange. Gradually add 7-Up and refrigerate until set.
Tart taste perks up meal and you can vary color with choice of gelatin to fit any meal.

Mrs. Fred Omundson

APRICOT SUPREME SALAD

Do Ahead

Serves 10

1 (3 oz.) pkg. orange gelatin
½ c. water
1 (16 oz.) can apricots
1 (5¼ oz.) can crushed
    pineapple
1 c. miniature marshmallows
1 c. pecan pieces
1 c. juice from apricots and
    pineapple

Oil pan before pouring in mixture. Dissolve gelatin in ½ c. boiling water. Add 1 c. of fruit juices, drained from apricots and pineapple. Reserve rest. Chop apricots fine. Allow gelatin to thicken; then add apricots and pineapple; also add marshmallows and pecans. Set until firm.

Topping:
    1 T. flour
    ¼ c. sugar
    1 T. butter
    ½ c. mixed fruit juices
    ½ beaten egg
    ½ c. whipped cream
    ¾ c. grated Cheddar
        cheese

Topping: Mix 1 T. flour, ¼ c. sugar, 1 T. butter, ½ c. mixed fruit juices. Cook over medium heat, gradually adding ½ beaten egg, until thickened or egg appears cooked. Allow mixture to cool and fold in ½ c. whipped cream. Pour over congealed mixture and top with grated cheese.

Mrs. William C. Hewitt

BLUEBERRY SALAD

Easy
Do Ahead

Serves 10-12

1 (16 oz.) can blueberries
1 (6½ oz.) can crushed pineapple
2 (3 oz.) pkgs. blackberry gelatin
2 c. water

Topping:
1 (8 oz.) pkg. cream
cheese
1 c. sour cream
½ c. sugar
½ tsp. vanilla
½ c. chopped nuts

Dissolve gelatin in 2 c. boiling water and 1 c. juice drained from pineapple and blueberries. Add drained fruit. Let congeal. Blend together Topping ingredients and spread on top of salad. Sprinkle ½ c. chopped nuts on top. Use 2 qt. oblong dish.

Mrs. Ronald S. Cain
Mrs. David Rumph
Mineral Wells, Texas

SOUR CHERRY SALAD

Do Ahead

Serves 16

1 (16 oz.) can red, sour, pitted
cherries
1 (16 oz.) can crushed pineapple
reserved juice of fruit
1 orange (juice and grated rind)
1 lemon (juice and grated rind)
2 (3 oz.) pkgs. cherry gelatin
1 envelope unflavored gelatin
¾ c. sugar
1 c. chopped nuts (pecan)

Drain and save juices from cherries and pineapple. Add orange and lemon juices to above liquid. Measure and add water to make 3¾ c. liquid. Heat the liquid and the sugar to a boil. Pour over the cherry gelatin and dissolve. Soak the gelatin in ¼ c. cold water and add to hot cherry mixture. Cool. Add cherries, cut in half, pineapple, nuts, grated rinds, and a few drops of red food color. Pour into mold and chill.

Mrs. T. B. Manley, Sr.

FROZEN CRANBERRY SALAD

Do Ahead†

Serves 4-6

1 lb. cranberries
1 c. water
¼ c. orange juice
1½ c. sugar
1 c. water

2 egg whites
2 T. sugar

Simmer the cranberries in the first cup of water until they all "pop". Press through a sieve. Then add orange juice and syrup, which is the second cup of water and 1½ c. of sugar boiled for 5 minutes. Chill. Then add 2 egg whites beaten with 2 T. sugar. Fold into chilled mixture and freeze. After about 2 hours it should be stirred again and frozen.

Mrs. Dale H. Carley

CRANBERRY-PINEAPPLE SALAD

Easy   Serves 8-10
Do Ahead

1 sm. can cranberry sauce
1 (8¼ oz.) can crushed pineapple,
  drained
1 c. boiling water
1 envelope plain gelatin
1 (3 oz.) pkg. raspberry gelatin
½ c. cold water
½ c. pecans, chopped
orange juice

Dissolve raspberry gelatin in hot water. Add 1 c. cold fruit juice - pineapple juice plus enough orange juice to make 1 c.   Soften gelatin in cold water. Mash the cranberry sauce slightly. Add plain gelatin to raspberry gelatin, then add cranberry sauce, pineapple and pecans. Pour into mold. Chill until set.

Mrs. Lin Thompson, Jr.

FROZEN FRUIT SALAD

Easy   Serves 16-20
Do Ahead

2 (3 oz.) pkgs. cream cheese
1 c. whipping cream
¼ c. sugar
½ c. mayonnaise
¼ c. lemon juice
1 (16 oz.) can sliced peaches
1 (16 oz.) can pineapple
  chunks
1 (16 oz.) can dark sweet
  pitted cherries
1 c. chopped pecans
12-14 maraschino cherries
3 ripe bananas (sliced
  crosswise)

Soften cream cheese with ¼ c. juice from peaches.   Add mayonnaise, cream whipped with sugar and lemon juice.   Add drained fruit, stir, add bananas and place in bowl in freezer until it begins to freeze. Stir again and put in cans or quart milk carton to freeze. (Can freeze all in one container.) Slice when ready to serve.

Mrs. R. O. Crouch, Jr.
Mrs. Olin Hunter

Editor's note: Can freeze in muffin tins for individual salads.

ORANGE SALAD

Easy   Serves 8
Do Ahead

1 sm. can mandarin oranges,
  drained - discard liquid
1 sm. can crushed pineapple,
  drained, save liquid
1 c. strong tea, boiling
1 c. liquid (pineapple plus any
  other fruit liquid)
1 (3 oz.) pkg. orange gelatin,
  dissolved in tea
1 sm. can water chestnuts,
  chopped

Combine all ingredients. Pour into 1 qt. mold. Chill.

Mrs. Paul McCubbin
Campbellsville, Kentucky

PINEAPPLE SALAD

Easy　　　　　　　　　　Serves 10-12
Do Ahead

1 (3 oz.) pkg. lime or lemon
　gelatin
2 c. hot water
25-30 marshmallows
1 sm. can crushed pineapple
½ c. mayonnaise
1 (8 oz.) pkg. cream cheese
1 c. whipping cream

Dissolve gelatin in hot water, and cut marshmallows in small pieces and stir in gelatin. Cool slightly and mix in cream cheese. Set aside to stiffen. Just before mixture is congealed, whip with rotary egg beater. Add pineapple, mayonnaise and fold in whipped cream. Chill until set.

Mrs. Ken Fletcher

PEACH SURPRISE

Do Ahead　　　　　　　　Serves 16

1 envelope plain gelatin
2 (3 oz.) pkgs. peach gelatin
2 c. cold water
2 c. hot water
2 (8½ oz.) cans crushed
　pineapple
1 c. miniature marshmallows
2 lge. bananas, cubed
½ c. pineapple juice
½ c. sugar
2 T. flour
1 egg, beaten
1 (3 oz.) pkg. cream cheese
1 pkg. Dream Whip
shredded coconut

Drain pineapple and reserve juice. Combine gelatins. Dissolve in hot water, add cold water and cool until starts to thicken. Add pineapple, marshmallows and bananas. Pour into 9 x 13" pan. Let set until firm. Combine pineapple juice, sugar, flour and egg and cook over low heat until thick. While still hot add cream cheese and stir until well mixed. Cool completely. Prepare Dream Whip according to package directions. Fold in cooled cooked mixture. Pour on top of congealed gelatin mixture. Sprinkle top with shredded coconut. Refrigerate several hours before serving.

Mrs. Douglas J. Brown

STRAWBERRY NUT SALAD *

Easy   Serves 8
Do Ahead

1 (6 oz.) pkg. strawberry gelatin
1 c. boiling water
2 (10 oz.) pkgs. frozen
   strawberries, thawed with
   juice
1 (1 lb. 4 oz.) can crushed
   pineapple, drained
3 med. bananas, diced
1 c. chopped nuts
1 (16 oz.) carton sour cream

Combine gelatin and water. Fold in remaining ingredients except sour cream. Put ½ of mixture in large mold and refrigerate until firm. Top with sour cream and put on remainder of mixture. Refrigerate.

Editor's note: As variation, add 2 peeled and diced apples.

VEGETABLE SALADS

ASPARAGUS CONGEALED SALAD

Easy   Serves 6
Do Ahead

¾ c. sugar
½ c. vinegar
1 c. liquid from asparagus
   (add water to make 1 c.)
1 tsp. salt
½ c. cold water
2 envelopes unflavored gelatin
1 (No. 2) can asparagus,
   drained
1 (5 oz.) can water chestnuts,
   drained and sliced thin
1 c. chopped celery
2 T. lemon juice
1 T. minced onion
1 (4 oz.) jar pimiento cut
   in strips

Combine sugar, salt, vinegar, cup of liquid; bring to boil. Dissolve gelatin in cold water; add to hot mixture along with onion; cool. Combine remaining ingredients, add liquid and chill until set.

Mrs. Allen W. Marshall, III

Editor's note: Pecans may be substituted for the water chestnuts.

CONGEALED AVOCADO SALAD

Easy
Do Ahead

Serves 8

1 (3 oz.) pkg. lime gelatin
1 c. boiling water
1 (3 oz.) pkg. cream cheese
1 avocado, chopped
1 sm. onion, chopped fine
2 stalks celery, chopped
½ c. mayonnaise

Dissolve gelatin in boiling water. Cool to syrupy stage. Combine softened cream cheese with other ingredients and add to gelatin mixture. Spoon into mold and chill until set.

Mrs. Thomas W. Gary

THREE BEAN SALAD

Easy
Do Ahead

Serves 6

1 (15 oz.) can kidney beans
1 (1 lb.) can all-green lima beans
1 (1 lb.) can cut green beans
½ c. chopped green pepper
½ c. chopped onion
¾ c. sugar
½ c. oil
½ c. vinegar
1 tsp. salt
½ tsp. black pepper
½ tsp. dill weed or
    celery seed

Rinse beans in cold water, drain. Add green pepper and onion. Stir together remaining ingredients until sugar is dissolved. Pour over beans. Mix lightly. Place in shallow glass dish so that beans are in the liquid. Cover; chill overnight. To serve, drain excess dressing.

Mrs. Newton Crouch

COMBINATION VEGETABLE BEAN SALAD

Easy
Do Ahead

Serves 20

1 (1 lb.) can cut green beans
1 (1 lb.) can wax beans
1 (1 lb.) can kidney beans
1 (1 lb.) can black-eyed peas
1 (1 lb.) can English peas
1 (1 lb.) can whole kernel white
    corn
2 (4 oz.) jars sliced mushrooms
1 lge. onion, chopped
1 lge. bell pepper, chopped

Dressing:
    ½ c. sugar
    1 c. wine vinegar
    ½ c. salad oil
    ½ tsp. dry mustard
    salt to taste

Drain and combine vegetables in a large bowl. Prepare dressing and pour over beans. Chill. Stir several times. *Great for a picnic. Keeps for weeks; improves with age.*

Mrs. William Valdon Smith

CONGEALED BROCCOLI MOLD

Easy   Serves 8
Do Ahead

1 (10 oz.) can beef consomme
1 envelope gelatin, dissolved in
   ¼ c. cold water
2 tsp. lemon juice
1 c. mayonnaise
1 (10 oz.) pkg. chopped cooked
   broccoli
1 - 2 grated hard-boiled eggs
1 T. grated onion
slivered almonds

Heat consomme, add soaked gelatin, cool. Add other ingredients. Pour into 1½ qt. mold and refrigerate until set.

Mrs. Eugene F. Robbins, Jr.

SEA FOAM CUCUMBER SALAD

Easy   Serves 8-10
Do Ahead

1 (3 oz.) pkg. lime gelatin
1 c. boiling water
1 T. vinegar
1 T. grated onion
1 (3 oz.) pkg. cream cheese
1 c. mayonnaise
1 c. grated cucumber

Add water to gelatin and stir until dissolved. Add mayonnaise and vinegar to the softened cream cheese. Mix these together well, then whip this mixture into the gelatin. When the above is a nice even color, add onion and cucumber. Chill.
Very tasty and different way to use cucumber.

Mrs. Lin H. Thompson, Jr.

BAVARIAN STYLE KRAUT SALAD

Easy   Serves 6-8
Do Ahead

1 (No. 303) can Bavarian Style
   Sauerkraut, drained
1 c. chopped onion
1 c. chopped celery
1 med. green pepper, chopped
1 sm. jar pimientos, chopped
1½ c. sugar
⅓ c. vinegar

Mix all ingredients and chill thoroughly.
This will keep for several weeks if stored in an air-tight container.

Mrs. William Early

MAKE AHEAD LETTUCE SALAD

Easy   Serves 16
Do Ahead 24-48 hrs.

1 head lettuce, shredded
½ c. celery, chopped
¼ c. green pepper, chopped
½ c. onion, chopped
2 c. fresh chopped spinach
1 (10 oz.) pkg. frozen peas
  (cooked slightly and
  cooled)
1 pt. Hellmann's mayonnaise
2 T. sugar
1 c. Parmesan cheese
½ c. crumbled bacon

Grease 9x13" pan. Arrange first 6 ingredients in order given. Do not stir. Spread mayonnaise over all evenly. Add next 3 ingredients in order. Cover tightly and refrigerate 24 hours. Cut in squares.

Mrs. William T. Early
Mrs. James R. Fortune, Jr.

WILTED LETTUCE SALAD

Easy   Serves 4-6

1 lge. bunch leaf lettuce
4 spring onions and tops,
  chopped or ½ a Vidalia onion,
  chopped
lemon pepper or coarsely ground
  black pepper
4 - 6 slices bacon
1 tsp. sugar
2 T. vinegar
½ - 1 tsp. salt

Select very fresh spring lettuce leaves. Wash carefully, pat dry on paper towels, and tear into pieces. Put in salad bowl. Add chopped onions and sprinkle with lemon pepper. Fry bacon until crisp, drain. Add sugar, vinegar, and salt to sizzling bacon drippings. Stir, heat, and pour immediately over lettuce. Toss lightly to coat all leaves. Crumble bacon over top and toss.

Mrs. Lutie C. Johnston

COLD MACARONI AND CHEESE SALAD

Easy   Serves 6
Do Ahead

6 oz. shell macaroni
  (about 1½ c.)
1 c. sliced celery
1 c. shredded carrot
¼ c. chopped onion
1 can condensed Cheddar
  cheese soup
¼ c. cooking oil
2 T. vinegar
1 tsp. sugar
1 tsp. prepared mustard
1 tsp. Worcestershire sauce
½ tsp. salt
dash pepper

Cook macaroni according to package directions; drain and cool. Combine macaroni, celery, carrot, and onions. In small mixer bowl combine soup, oil, vinegar, sugar, mustard, Worcestershire sauce, salt and pepper, beat until well-blended; spoon atop macaroni mixture. Mix well. Chill several hours.

Mrs. Allen W. Marshall, III

POTATO SALAD SUPREME

Do Ahead   Serves 12

6 c. cold sliced cooked potatoes
  (about 2½ lbs.)
1 c. minced onions
½ c. finely snipped parsley
½ c. finely chopped celery
1½ tsp. salt
¼ tsp. pepper
2 envelopes unflavored gelatin
½ c. water
16 packaged cooked thin ham
  slices, 7"x4½"
1½ c. mayonnaise or salad
  dressing
watercress or lettuce

Day before:
Combine in large bowl, sliced potatoes, onions, celery, parsley, salt and pepper. In a measuring cup sprinkle gelatin on water; stir over hot water until dissolved. Coarsely snip 8 ham slices; add to potato mixture along with mayonnaise and gelatin mixture; toss all together. Line a 10x5x3" loaf pan completely with foil, letting it extend about 3 inches above each edge. Now along 10 inch side of loaf pan lay three overlapping ham slices, which extend across bottom of pan and up opposite long side. Repeat on other long side of pan, making a double thickness of ham on bottom of pan. Cover each end of pan with ham slice. Have tops of all ham slices even with edge of pan. Pack potato salad mixture into ham-lined pan, cover top of salad with overhanging foil, refrigerate. For serving, unmold on a chilled plate, peel off foil, slice, surround with watercress and cherry tomatoes.

Mrs. R. Lee Pfrogner

GERMAN SLAW *

Easy   Serves 8
Do Ahead

1 head cabbage, chopped
1 lge. onion, sliced thin
1 green pepper, chopped
½ c. sugar
½ c. vinegar
½ c. salad oil
1 T. salt
1 tsp. dry mustard
1 tsp. celery seed
1 T. sugar

Layer cabbage, onion and pepper in bowl. Pour ½ c. sugar on top. Boil together vinegar, salad oil, salt, dry mustard, celery seed and sugar. Pour hot mixture over top. Cover tightly and refrigerate. Will keep for several weeks.

FRESH SPINACH SALAD

Easy   Serves 8
Do Ahead

2 lbs. fresh spinach
2 heads red leaf lettuce or
   1 head iceberg lettuce
½ lb. bacon
¼ c. sugar
1 tsp. salt
1 tsp. dry mustard
1 T. onion juice
¼ c. cider vinegar
¾ c. salad oil
1 T. poppy seed
1½ c. large curd cottage
   cheese

Thoroughly wash and drain the spinach; break off stems and tear apart large leaves. Combine with the lettuce, broken in bite-size pieces. Fry bacon until crisp; cool and crumble it and add to the greens. For the dressing, combine sugar, salt, mustard, onion juice, vinegar and salad oil. Shake or beat well. Add poppy seed, shake again. Use about half of this dressing to mix in the greens. Add cottage cheese to remaining dressing; mix with the salad greens.

H. Alfred Bolton III

SPINACH SALAD WITH BACON AND APPLE

Easy   Serves 8
Do Ahead

1 lb. fresh spinach
5 slices bacon
1 T. bacon drippings
⅓ c. sliced almonds
¼ c. salad oil or olive oil
3 T. tarragon wine vinegar
⅛ tsp. salt
dash pepper
1 tsp. sugar
½ tsp. dry mustard
1 red apple, pared and diced
3 green onions with some
   of the green tops thinly
   sliced

Wash spinach thoroughly, discarding stems; drain well. Chill at least 2 hours. Pan fry bacon until crisp; drain on paper towels. Discard all except 1 T. of bacon drippings. Put almonds in pan with bacon drippings and stir over medium heat until toasted. Remove and drain on paper towel. If you wish, you can prepare dressing ahead. Combine the salad oil, vinegar, salt, pepper, sugar and mustard; set aside. Before serving, break the spinach into bowl. Add green onion, apple and almonds; crumble in the bacon. Mix dressing and drizzle over salad.

Mrs. Ralph W. Mitchell

AT'S SALAD

Easy
Do Ahead

Holland Rusk
Roquefort cheese
slice of tomato
homemade mayonnaise with
    catsup (See Salad Dressing)
chopped bacon
hard-boiled egg
top with anchovy

Stack ingredients in order given for each serving.   (Make as many as needed) and serve.

Mrs. Robert Smalley

TOMATO SALAD

Easy
Do Ahead

Serves 6

2 (16 oz.) cans Delmonte Stewed
    Tomatoes, drained
2 (3 oz.) pkgs. lemon gelatin
3 T. vinegar
2 T. onion, finely chopped
dash of salt
¼ c. water and juice from
    tomatoes

Bring liquids to a boil.   Add jello and stir   until   dissolved.   Add   other ingredients   to   gelatin   mixture   and pour   into a 6x8" Pyrex dish or any type mold.
This   is   a   tart   salad   and   a   good substitute   for   tossed   salad.   It   can   be made   in   advance - plus   it   is   so   easy   to prepare!

Mrs. Hugh Dempsey

ASHEVILLE SALAD *

Easy
Do Ahead

2 (3 oz.) pkgs. cream cheese
2 (13 oz.) cans tomato soup
3 T. unflavored gelatin dissolved
    in ⅓ c. cold water
⅓ c. minced onion
⅓ c. celery
⅓ c. green pepper
½ c. chopped pecans
1 c. mayonnaise

Heat   tomato   soup   and   melt   cream cheese   in   the   soup.   Dissolve   gelatin in   cold   water   and   pour   into   hot mixture.   Mix   well   and   add   the   other ingredients.   Pour   into   greased   mold and   refrigerate   until   set.

TOMATO ASPIC

Do Ahead   Serves 10

1 qt. canned V-8 tomato
   juice
2 pkgs. unflavored gelatin
1 pkg. lemon gelatin
3 hard-boiled eggs,
   chopped
1 med. onion, minced
3 lge. stalks celery
1 med. green pepper
stuffed olives to taste
lemon juice, vinegar, salt and
   red pepper to taste

Dissolve plain gelatin in ½ c. cold tomato juice, then add heated tomato juice to this, as well as to the lemon gelatin. Mix and add the rest of the ingredients and season to taste. Pour into mold or ring and congeal in refrigerator.

Mrs. Sam Stacy

MY GRANDMOTHER'S ASPIC

Do Ahead   Serves 8

2 envelopes plain gelatin
¼ c. cold water
2 c. tomato juice
1½ tsp. grated onion
1 T. plus ¾ tsp. vinegar
dash red pepper
1½ c. finely chopped celery
1 sm. bottle olives, finely
   chopped (smallest bottle
   available)

Put gelatin in water and let stand 10 minutes. Then heat over boiling water until dissolved. Add gelatin to tomato juice. To this mixture add onion, vinegar and red pepper. (Salt to taste is optional.) Refrigerate the mixture until it begins to gel then add olives and celery.

Mrs. F. Ted Wilder, Jr.

MEAT SALADS

AVOCADO SALAD WITH SHRIMP SAUCE

Do Ahead   Serves 8-10

3 avocados, mashed
4 T. lemon juice
3 T. gelatin
2 tsp. salt
3 T. onion juice
1 tsp. sugar
⅛ tsp. cayenne pepper
¾ c. mayonnaise

Sauce:
  1 pt. sour cream
  ½ c. catsup
  2 T. Worcestershire sauce
  ¼ tsp. dry mustard
  ½ lb. shrimp, cut fine
  1½ T. grated onion
  2 T. horseradish
  1 tsp. salt
  1 tsp. paprika
  1 T. lemon juice
  crisp garnishes, carrot
    sticks, etc.

Separate avocado from shells with spoon. Sprinkle with lemon juice. Put through ricer and sieve. Soak 3 T. gelatin in ½ c. cold water for 10 minutes. Then add 1¼ c. boiling water. Chill until mixture starts to set. Blend avocado and gelatin mixtures and add salt, onion juice, sugar and cayenne. Set in refrigerator until partly congealed, then beat 3 minutes with rotary beater and add ¾ c. mayonnaise. Taste for seasoning. Add drop or two of green food coloring. Put in greased ring mold or individual molds. Chill. Mix remaining ingredients to make sauce. Save a few whole shrimp for garnish. Serve salad with sauce.

Mrs. Franklin P. Lindsey, Jr.

MEXICAN CHEF SALAD

Do Ahead   Serves 6-8

1 lb. ground beef
1 (15 oz.) can kidney beans,
  drained
1 head of lettuce, salad size
  pieces
¼ tsp. salt
3 - 4 tomatoes in wedges
1 onion, chopped
1 c. shredded Cheddar cheese
1 (8 or 10 oz.) pkg. Doritos, Taco
  Flavor, crushed
1 chopped green pepper
2 sm. avocados, peeled and sliced
1 c. Thousand Island dressing
hot sauce to taste (mix with
  dressing)
1 (3 oz.) bottle stuffed olives
  (if desired)

Brown beef and drain. Add salt and kidney beans. Simmer 10 minutes. In large bowl combine lettuce, tomato, cheese, green pepper, onion and salad dressing. Mix lightly. Just prior to serving, add meat and beans and chips. Toss again. Garnish with alternate slices of avocado, tomato wedges and olives (if desired), making a sunburst pattern.

Mrs. John Umstead
Chapel Hill, North Carolina

Variation: Instead of above dressing, use 1 package Good Seasons Italian Dressing (prepared).

Mrs. John R. Carlisle

CHICKEN-HAM SALAD

Easy   Serves 4-6

2 c. diced cooked chicken
1 c. diced cooked ham
1 T. diced onion
½ c. mayonnaise
1 T. French Dressing
½ c. chopped celery
tomatoes
lettuce

Mix together all ingredients except tomatoes and lettuce. Salad may be served in hollowed tomatoes or on sliced tomatoes on a lettuce leaf.

Mrs. Lewis T. Murphy

CORNED BEEF MOLD

Do Ahead   Serves 6-8

1 pkg. plain gelatin
½ c. cold water
¼ c. chopped onion
3 tsp. lemon juice
1 tsp. salt
1 c. mayonnaise
1½ c. shredded cabbage
1 can corned beef
    (separated with fork)
1 c. chopped celery
½ c. pickle relish

Soften gelatin in water in saucepan. Dissolve over low heat, stir. Remove from heat. Stir in onion, lemon juice and salt; stir in mayonnaise. Blend rest ingredients. Put in 1 qt. mold. Chill 2 hours. Serve with mustard sauce.

Mrs. Thomas W. Fetzer

KING CRAB SALAD

Easy
Do Ahead

Serves 2

2 hot dog buns
mayonnaise
1 (6 oz.) pkg. Wakefield's King
  Crab
1 sm. can asparagus
1 T. lemon juice
French dressing
lettuce leaf (2)

Place asparagus in small low dish, pour French dressing over it and marinate for at least 1 hour. If crabmeat is frozen, thaw. Spread mayonnaise on hot dog buns (open face), put lettuce leaf on top. Add asparagus, using some French dressing spooned over it; add crabmeat that has been tossed in lemon juice.
Good as salad luncheon. Hard boiled eggs add to the looks as well as taste.

Mrs. William Valdon Smith

GREEK SALAD

Do Ahead

Serves 6

6 boiling potatoes
½ c. thinly sliced green onions
¼ c. finely chopped parsley
½ c. salad dressing
1 lge. head of lettuce
2 tomatoes cut into 6 wedges each
1 peeled cucumber cut lengthwise,
  8 fingers
1 avocado peeled and cut into
  wedges
4 slices of Greek Feta cheese
1 bell pepper cut into 4 rings
4 slices canned cooked beets
1 lb. peeled and cooked shrimp
1 sm. can anchovy filets
1 sm. can black olives
medium hot Salonika peppers
  (bought in bottles)
4 fancy cut radishes
4 whole green onions
½ c. distilled white vinegar
¼ c. each olive and salad oil
  blended
oregano
capers (bought in bottles)

Cube and boil potatoes until tender but not soft when tested. Drain and cool potatoes and place in bowl. Add sliced green onions and chopped parsley to potatoes and sprinkle lightly with salt. Fold in salad dressing. Line a large platter with lettuce leaves and place the potato salad in a mound in the center of the platter. Cover with remaining lettuce which has been shredded. Place tomato wedges, cucumber wedges, avocado slices, and whole green onions around the outer edge making a solid base of the salad. Slices of Feta cheese should be arranged on the top of the salad, with the bell pepper slices over the cheese. On the very top, place the sliced beets with a shrimp on each beet slice and an anchovy filet on each shrimp. All remaining and leftover ingredients may be arranged over the salad as desired. Sprinkle capers liberally over salad. The entire salad is then sprinkled with the vinegar and then with the blended oil. Sprinkle oregano liberally over all.

Mrs. Bates Bowers, Jr.

MAYONNAISE CHICKEN

Do Ahead   Serves 6-8

3 T. gelatin
3 c. chicken stock
2 c. mayonnaise
1 hen, cooked and diced or
    5 lb. chicken breasts, well
    seasoned
½ c. sweet pickles, diced
2 pimientos, chopped
2 c. celery, diced
1 tsp. Tabasco sauce
1 c. almonds, chopped
1 (8½ oz.) can small sugar
    peas, drained
pimiento
parsley
olives

Dissolve gelatin in ½ c. chicken stock. Heat the rest of stock and pour over this. Add the 2 c. mayonnaise, chicken, pickles, pimientos, celery, Tabasco, almonds, and peas. Stir well and put in greased mold. Refrigerate until set. Unmold and garnish with pimiento, parsley and olives.

Edith D. Phillips
Baton Rouge, Louisiana

CREAMY TUNA MOLD

Easy   Serves 4
Do Ahead

1 envelope unflavored gelatin
1 can Cream of Celery soup
1 (3 oz.) pkg. cream cheese,
    softened
1 (6½ oz.) can tuna, drained
    and flaked
½ c. shredded carrot
⅓ c. chopped celery
2 T. chopped parsley
1 T. lemon juice
1 - 2 T. Kraft Green Onion
    Salad Dressing, optional

Sprinkle gelatin on ½ c. cold water to soften; place over boiling water; stir until gelatin is dissolved. Blend soup and cream cheese; add gelatin, tuna, carrot, celery, parsley, lemon juice and Green Onion Salad Dressing, if desired. Pour into a 1 qt. mold. Chill until firm. Unmold; serve on crisp salad greens.

Mrs. Bob Scroggins

TUNA AVOCADO SALAD

Do Ahead   Serves 6

3 med. sized avocados
1 (14 oz.) can pineapple chunks,
  drained
2 oranges, peeled and cut up
¼ tsp. crumbled dried mint leaves
French dressing
1 (7 oz.) can solid-pack tuna,
  drained

Cut avocados in half and remove seed. Scoop out pulp with melon ball cutter; reserve avocado shells. Combine avocado balls, pineapple chunks, oranges and mint leaves. Marinate in French dressing 30 minutes. Break tuna into pieces with fork. Add to avocado mixture and toss lightly. Fill avocado shells with tuna-fruit mixture and serve on crisp salad greens.

Mrs. Will Hill Newton II

SALAD DRESSINGS

BLENDER MAYONNAISE

Easy   Yield: About 1¼ cups
Do Ahead

1 egg
5 tsp. lemon juice or Real Lemon
½ tsp. dry mustard
½ tsp. salt
½ tsp. red pepper
1 c. Crisco oil

In blender combine egg, lemon juice, mustard, salt, and red pepper. Blend. On stir position of blender, add the cup of oil in a small steady stream. Stop blender immediately. Repeat entire recipe for a double amount. Do not try to double ingredients in blender.

Mrs. Thomas V. Pollard

Variation: May substitute ½ tsp. paprika for red pepper.

Mrs. E. Herben Turner

ARGYLE SALAD DRESSING

Do Ahead   Serves 8-12

4 egg yolks
2½ T. vinegar
1 T. sugar
1 tsp. salt
1 T. margarine or butter
¼ tsp. dry mustard
dash cayenne pepper
12 marshmallows, cut finely
1 c. cream, whipped
½ c. pecans, chopped

Cook first seven ingredients in double boiler until it begins to thicken. While hot, add marshmallows. Stir until smooth. When cool add whipped cream and nuts.
This unusual blend of ingredients yields a delicious dressing similar to a spicy, homemade mayonnaise.

Mrs. Champ S. Vance

AVOCADO AND ARTICHOKE DRESSING

Easy
Do Ahead

Serves 4-6

½ c. olive oil
1 T. tarragon vinegar
1 T. fresh lemon juice
2 T. Dijon mustard
2 T. dry vermouth
salt and white pepper to
    taste

Combine all ingredients in jar and shake well. Chill thoroughly before serving.

Mrs. Warren K. Wells

FRENCH DRESSING

Easy
Do Ahead

Yield: 1½ pints

1 c. sugar
½ c. vinegar
1 c. salad oil
1½ tsp. salt
1 tsp. Worcestershire sauce
1 tsp. ground onion (or more)
1 clove garlic (optional)
catsup (to color)
paprika

Blend sugar with vinegar. Add oil and blend. Add remaining ingredients and beat well. Bottle and refrigerate. Keeps well. Shake well before using.

Mrs. Barbara J. Searcy
St. Simons Island, Georgia

FRUIT SALAD DRESSING

Easy
Do Ahead

Serves 10-12

1 c. mayonnaise (any good
    brand)
¼ c. honey or Dark Karo
4 tsp. lemon juice
1 tsp. celery seed

Mix all ingredients and serve over fresh or canned fruit salads.

Mrs. Herbert A. Bolton, Jr.

ITALIAN SALAD DRESSING

Easy
Do Ahead

Yield: Approximately 1 quart

1 tsp. dry mustard
2 tsp. sugar
4 tsp. salt
2 tsp. Accent
2⅔ c. salad oil
1 c. cider vinegar
8 garlic cloves, halved

Mix all ingredients in quart bottle.
Shake well before using on tossed
salad.   Not necessary to refrigerate.

Mrs. John R. Carlisle

ROQUEFORT DRESSING

Easy
Do Ahead

Yield: ½ gallon

1½ qts. mayonnaise
1¼ c. sweet milk
1 tsp. lemon juice
1½ tsp. salt
½ tsp. pepper (white or
    black)
½ tsp. garlic powder or
    4 cloves grated garlic
8 oz. Bleu cheese, crumbled

Mix all ingredients and refrigerate.
Can be refrigerated for a month or
two.

Mrs. David Clements

ROQUEFORT-SOUR CREAM DRESSING

Easy
Do Ahead

Yield: 1 quart, plus

⅓ c. shallots and tops,
    chopped coarsely
2 c. mayonnaise
2 cloves garlic on toothpicks
½ c. chopped parsley
1 c. sour cream
juice of 1 lemon
½ lb. Roquefort or Bleu
    cheese, crumbled
¼ c. vinegar (wine)
¼ c. water

Chop shallots in Cuisinart by placing
pieces 1½" long in container with
chopper blade and turning on and
off rapidly several times. Remove and
follow same procedure with parsley.
Mix all ingredients together. Place in
refrigerator in tightly closed jar overnight. Before serving, remove garlic
clove. This is easily made by hand.

Mrs. Paul J. Mitchell, Jr.

RUSSIAN SALAD DRESSING

Easy
Do Ahead

Yield: 1⅔ cup

1 c. Hellman's Real Mayonnaise
⅔ c. chili sauce
2 T. milk
1 T. sweet pickle relish

Combine ingredients. Chill. Serve
on tossed greens.

Mrs. George W. Kirby

SALSA FRIA

Easy
Do Ahead

Yield: ½ gallon

2 (1 lb.) cans of stewed
   tomatoes, mashed
2 onions, chopped
1 (4 oz.) can green chilies,
   chopped
2 carrots, sliced thinly
2 stalks celery, chopped
1 tsp. oregano
1 T. salt
1 tsp. ground coriander
2 T. salad oil
2 T. Tequila

Mix all ingredients and keep chilled
*Great to serve over cottage cheese,
in omelet, over pork chops or chicken.*

Mrs. Richard M. Barnes
Plattsburg, Missouri

THOUSAND ISLAND DRESSING

Easy
Do Ahead

Yield: 1 pint

1 c. Kraft mayonnaise
½ c. Heinz tomato catsup
½ c. sweet pickles, chopped
1 T. minced onion
1 tsp. chili powder
¼ tsp. garlic salt
¼ tsp. Tabasco sauce
⅛ tsp. pepper

Mix all ingredients and refrigerate.

Mrs. Carter Y. Greenway

Notes

FRUITS

BAKED APPLES

Easy   Serves 8   300°
                                                         2 hrs.

10 apples, sliced but not   Put sliced apples in 9 x 13" Pyrex
  peeled   dish.   Fill dish to 1" with water.
water   Sprinkle with salt.   Pour lime juice
¼ tsp. salt   over apples.   Pour sugar over entire
juice of 2 limes   dish of apples.   Put cinnamon hearts on
½ c. (or more) sugar   top and place pats of butter on top
¼ c. cinnamon hearts   of this.   Bake at 300° for 2 hours or
5 pats of butter   until done.

                               Mrs. James R. Fortune, Jr.

APPLE AND BANANA DELIGHT

Easy   Serves 4   325°
Do Ahead   1¼-1½ hrs.

3 apples, peeled and sliced   Layer the first four ingredients using
3 bananas, sliced   as many layers as possible because of
¼ c. brown sugar   shrinkage in a buttered casserole. Make
1 stick butter or margarine   a crumble mix of next three ingredients
2 T. brown sugar   and spread over top.
2 T. flour
2 T. butter or margarine   Mrs. Joe G. Hunter, Jr.
                               Opelika, Alabama

CRUSTY APPLESAUCE

Easy   Serves 6   350°
                                                         20 min.

5 c. (2 No. 2 cans) applesauce   Dot bottom of baking dish with 1
2 c. Post Toasties   T. butter.   Add 2½ c. (1 can) apple-
1 c. brown sugar   sauce.   Add layer (1 c.) Post Toasties.
2 T. butter   Sprinkle with ½ c. brown sugar.
                               Repeat.   Dot top with 1 T. butter
                               and bake.

                               Mrs. Charles Smith

BAKED APRICOTS

Serves 8   300°
                                        1 hr.

2 (1 lb.) cans apricot halves
1 c. (packed) brown sugar
1 box Ritz crackers (crushed)
butter (use generously)

Place a layer of well drained apricots in a buttered baking dish. Cover with one-half brown sugar, then a layer of crushed Ritz crackers. Dot with lumps of butter. Repeat. Top should be thick and crusty. Bake at 300° for 1 hour.
Excellent accompaniment for meat.

Mrs. W. Evans Bruner
Atlanta, Georgia

BAKED FRUIT CASSEROLE

Do Ahead   Serves 8   375°
                                                        25 min.

½ c. margarine
⅔ c. sugar
⅓ c. flour
¼ tsp. salt
⅓ c. sherry
1 (1 lb. 4 oz.) can sliced
   pineapple
1 (1 lb.) can pear halves
1 (1 lb.) can sliced peaches
1 (6 oz.) jar maraschino
   cherries

Melt margarine and make a paste with the sugar, flour and salt. Cook until thickened - then add sherry. Butter a large casserole dish and arrange fruit as follows: pear halves on pineapple slices, peaches on side of pears with a cherry on top of pear halves.* Pour sauce over fruits and marinate overnight. Take out of refrigerator 1 hour before baking. *Any fruit combination can be used.

Mrs. Hugh Dempsey

HOT CURRIED FRUIT

Easy   Serves 8   350°
Do Ahead   1 hr.

½ c. butter
1 c. brown sugar
2 T. curry powder
1 lge. can pears
1 lge. can peaches
1 (1 lb. 4 oz.) can pineapple
  chunks
1 jar mixed fruit for salad
1 jar maraschino cherries
(exact amount of fruit is not
important - use combination
you enjoy)

Melt butter in small saucepan. Dissolve sugar in butter and add curry powder. Drain fruits well and cut in bite-sized pieces. Put fruit into large oven-proof bowl, pour sauce over, bake 350° for 1 hour uncovered.

Mrs. William M. Woodward

GRILLED GRAPEFRUIT

Easy   Serves 2   Broil
                                       2-3 min.

1 lge. grapefruit, halved
4 T. granulated sugar
  (approx.)
2 oz. Kirsch
maraschino cherries
mint sprigs

Remove grapefruit core and loosen meat from skin. Sprinkle generously with sugar and then Kirsch. Broil 2-3 minutes or until top starts to brown. Garnish with cherries and mint.

Mrs. Allen J. Brock
Atlanta, Georgia

SPICED BAKED ORANGES

Easy   Serves 6-8
Do Ahead

4 whole navel oranges, unpeeled
water
½ tsp. soda
2 c. sugar
½ c. vinegar
10 whole cloves
3 pieces stick cinnamon

Cover oranges with soda water and boil 20-30 minutes or until easily pierced with a fork. Drain and cut each orange into eight wedges. Combine sugar, 1¼ c. water, vinegar and spices. Stir over low heat until sugar is dissolved, then boil 5 minutes. Add oranges and simmer 25 minutes. Cool, cover and refrigerate.
Serve with pork, ham, duck, poultry or corned beef and cabbage.

Mrs. H. Alfred Bolton III

OVEN-BAKED PEACHES WITH GINGER

Easy   Serves 4-6   350°
                                                                  15 min.

6 lge. peaches, peeled and
  thickly sliced
¾ c. light brown sugar
3 T. butter
¼ c. slivered crystalized ginger
½ c. light rum

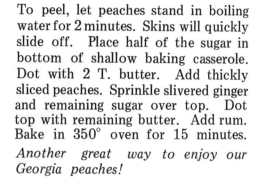

To peel, let peaches stand in boiling water for 2 minutes. Skins will quickly slide off. Place half of the sugar in bottom of shallow baking casserole. Dot with 2 T. butter. Add thickly sliced peaches. Sprinkle slivered ginger and remaining sugar over top. Dot top with remaining butter. Add rum. Bake in 350° oven for 15 minutes.

Another great way to enjoy our Georgia peaches!

Mrs. J. Gordon Dixon

SCALLOPED PINEAPPLE

Easy   Serves 6-8   350°
Do Ahead   1 hr.

3 eggs, well beaten
4 c. fresh bread crumbs,
  cubed
2 c. granulated sugar
1 (1 lb. 4 oz.) can crushed
  pineapple in its own
  juice
½ lb. margarine, cut into
  small pieces

Beat eggs until creamy. Add other ingredients. Put in lightly greased 9 x 13 x 2" or 12 x 12" shallow pan and bake.

Mrs. Lloyd W. Hazleton
Vienna, Virginia

Notes

VEGETABLES and SAUCES

HOW TO PREPARE ARTICHOKES

Wash artichokes under running water, remove tough outer leaves, and trim stems. Have ready in heavy kettle about 2 inches boiling water. Add a dash of salt - sugar and place artichokes stem ends down in water. Cover tightly and cook over low heat about 30 minutes, until an outer leaf can be easily pulled from stem. Time of cooking will depend on the size of artichoke. Drain upside down.

Variation I

Add ¼ c. vinegar to large pot of salted water. Steam covered until leaves pull off easily.

Variation II

Drop prepared artichoke into boiling water to cover, add one coriander seed per artichoke and juice of one lemon for each four artichokes. Simmer, covered, until outer leaves pull off easily.

ARTICHOKE HEARTS

Easy   Serves 3-4   350°
Do Ahead   30 min.

1 (8½ oz.) can drained
   artichoke hearts
1 (10¾ oz.) can cream of
   chicken soup
1 egg yolk
½ lb. fresh mushrooms, or
   4 oz. can, sauteed
1 T. sherry
1 T. lemon juice
1 tsp. grated lemon rind
¼ c. Parmesan cheese

Drain and rinse artichokes. Mix soup, egg yolk, mushrooms, sherry, lemon juice, rind in bowl. Add artichokes and pour into buttered 1 qt. casserole dish. Top with Parmesan. Bake.

Mrs. Douglas Finnegan
Annapolis, Maryland

ASPARAGUS CASSEROLE

Easy   Serves 8   350°
Do Ahead   25 min.

1 (No. 303) can asparagus, drained
1 (10¾ oz.) can mushroom soup
1 (2 oz.) jar pimiento, cut in
   small pieces
3 hard boiled eggs, mashed up
1 sm. onion, chopped
½ lb. cheese, grated
potato chips, crushed
2 T. melted butter

Place ½ can of asparagus on bottom of 2 qt. casserole dish. Add ½ can of soup, ½ jar of pimiento, ½ eggs, ½ onion. Sprinkle this with cheese and potato chips. Repeat layers, sprinkle chips on top and dot with butter. Bake.

Mrs. Lin H. Thompson

IDA BASS' ASPARAGUS

Easy   Serves 6-8   350°
Do Ahead   30 min.

2 (16 oz.) cans asparagus, drained
1 c. olives, green stuffed
½ c. slivered almonds
3 T. butter
2 T. flour
½ - ¾ c. milk
buttered cracker crumbs

Place ½ of the asparagus in bottom of casserole. Sprinkle ½ of olives and nuts on top. Make cream sauce from butter, flour and milk. Pour ½ of sauce on top. Repeat and top with buttered cracker crumbs. Cook at 350° for 30 minutes.

Mrs. Robert Smalley

ASPARAGUS SUPREME

Do Ahead   Serves 8   350°
                                               30-45 min.

2 T. butter
2 T. flour
¾ c. sweet milk, scalded
½ c. chopped onion
2 c. grated American cheese
3 eggs, separated
2 c. cooked or canned
   asparagus tips
salt, pepper and Durkee's
   Salad Dressing to taste

Place butter in pan over low heat, stir in flour slowly. Add scalded milk. When thick and smooth, remove from heat. Add onion and cheese and stir until cheese is entirely melted. Blend in well beaten egg yolks. Carefully add asparagus, cut in small pieces. Season to taste. Fold in well beaten egg whites. Pour into ungreased casserole and bake in 350° oven for 30-45 minutes or until slightly firm.

Mrs. Sam Stacy

FRENCH BEANS

Drop fresh cut beans into pan of lightly salted boiling water.   Cook 3 minutes.   Drain and place beans in ice water to cool quickly.   Drain well and   store in plastic bag or covered container.

To serve: Melt butter and add seasonings (or mushrooms, etc.).   Stir in beans and saute until hot.

FRENCH BEAN CASSEROLE

Do Ahead   Serves 8   375°
                                                                           35 min.

2 (4 oz.) cans sliced mushrooms
1 med. onion chopped
½ c. margarine
¼ c. flour
2 c. warm milk
¾ c. sharp cheese, grated
⅛ tsp. Tabasco sauce
2 tsp. soy sauce
1 tsp. salt
½ tsp. pepper
1 tsp. Accent
3 pkgs. frozen French
   green beans
5 oz. thinly sliced water
   chestnuts (optional)
3 oz. sliced blanched almonds
   (optional)

Saute mushrooms and onion in margarine.   Add flour.   Cook until smooth. Add milk and next 6 ingredients and simmer until cheese melts.   Cook beans, drain and add to above.   Add water chestnuts.   Pour into 2 qt. buttered casserole dish.   Bake 375° for 35 minutes.   Sprinkle almonds on top.

Mrs. LaVerne L. Hinson, Jr.

MARINATED GREEN BEANS

Easy   Serves 8
Do Ahead

2 (16 oz.) cans whole green beans
1 T. salad oil
1 T. vinegar
1 sm. onion, chopped
½ tsp. salt
¼ tsp. pepper
Dressing:
   ½ c. sour cream
   ½ c. mayonnaise
   1 T. lemon juice
   1 T. horseradish
   2 tsp. chopped onions
   1 tsp. dry mustard

Place ingredients in bowl and cover. Let stand overnight.   Next day, drain and add dressing.

Mrs. Jeffrey W. Rowe

SWEET AND SOUR BEANS

Easy   Serves 2-3
Do Ahead

4 slices bacon
1 (16 oz.) can cut green beans
½ c. vinegar
½ c. sugar

Fry bacon until crisp. Crumble and put aside. Into the skillet with the bacon drippings put drained beans, vinegar, sugar. Stir, cover, and simmer 25 minutes. Turn occasionally. When ready to serve, top the drained beans with the crumbled bacon.

Mrs. Louis C. Thacker

LIMA BEAN AND TOMATO CASSEROLE

Do Ahead   Serves 6-8   350°
                                                         30 min.

2-3 lge. onions
1 (29 oz.) can tomatoes
½ c. bacon drippings
2 (10 oz.) pkgs. frozen Ford
   Hook lima beans
buttered bread crumbs

Fry onions in bacon drippings. Add tomatoes and mash as you cook them. Cook separately lima beans (salted) until tender. Combine and put in greased casserole. Cover with buttered bread crumbs. Bake in 350° oven for 30 minutes.

Mrs. James R. Fortune, Jr.

BEETS IN SOUR CREAM

Easy

2 T. sugar
2 T. vinegar
grated or thinly sliced
   onions, to taste
salt and pepper
1 c. sour cream
slices or chunks of beets

In double boiler heat sugar, vinegar, onion, salt and pepper. When thoroughly heated, stir in sour cream and pour over beets.

Mrs. Charlie T. Phillips

BROCCOLI SAUTE

Easy   Serves 4

1 lb. fresh broccoli
3 T. cooking oil
1 tsp. salt
2 T. soy sauce
1 tsp. sugar
1 tsp. gin (optional)

Wash and trim broccoli and slice in thin diagonal pieces 1½ inches long. Cook the broccoli in the hot oil and salt, uncovered, for 5 minutes. Stir and cook for a further 2 or 3 minutes. In a bowl, mix soy sauce, sugar and gin (if used). Add ¼ c. hot water. Pour over broccoli and bring to boiling point, and simmer about 2 or 3 minutes to blend the flavors.

Mrs. Phillip A. Laundy
Ottawa, Canada

BROCCOLI CASSEROLE I *

Easy†   Serves 8   325°
Do Ahead   30 to
                                                45 min.

1 c. mayonnaise
1 can celery soup
2 pkgs. frozen chopped
   broccoli
2 T. minced onion
1 c. sharp Cheddar cheese
2 eggs
1 T. Worcestershire sauce
1 tsp. Accent
salt and pepper to taste
1 c. crumbled Ritz crackers
   (or herb-seasoned stuffing
   mix)
2 T. butter

Mix all ingredients, place in buttered 2 qt. casserole. Top with cracker crumbs and dot with butter. Bake.

Variations: Substitute for 1 can of celery soup:
1 can cream of mushroom soup
        or
1 can cream of chicken soup

BROCCOLI CASSEROLE II

Do Ahead†   Serves 6   350°
                                                        30 min.

4 T. butter
4 T. flour
1 tsp. salt
1/8 tsp. dry mustard
1½ c. milk
½ c. cheese, grated
3 c. (or 2 (10 oz.) pkgs. frozen)
   barely cooked broccoli
Parmesan cheese
paprika

Melt butter in heavy saucepan; add flour, salt and mustard. Cook over low heat until bubbly. Add milk and cook until thick and smooth. Add cheese and stir until completely melted. Add broccoli which has been cooked in boiling salted water until just underdone. Pour into buttered casserole, sprinkle generously with grated Parmesan cheese and paprika. Bake. To serve 18, triple recipe and bake in a 3 qt. Pyrex dish.

Mrs. Andrew Blake

BROCCOLI RING

Do Ahead   Serves 8-10   350°
                                                        25 min.

2 c. cooked finely chopped
   broccoli
1 c. mayonnaise
1 T. melted butter
½ pt. whipping cream
½ tsp. salt
1 T. flour
3 eggs, well beaten

Line a ring mold with waxed paper. Arrange chopped broccoli in mold. Mix remaining ingredients and pour over broccoli. Place mold in pan of water in center of oven and bake for 25 minutes. Turn onto serving plate and carefully peel off waxed paper when cooled slightly. Serve hot.

Mrs. William C. Hewitt

BROCCOLI AND RICE CASSEROLE *

Easy   Serves 6-8   350°
Do Ahead   30-40 min.

1 can cream of chicken soup
4 c. Minute Rice (cooked)
   (2 c. uncooked)
1 pkg. chopped frozen broccoli,
   cooked and drained
1 c. water chestnuts (sliced)
1 sm. jar Cheeze Whiz

Combine all ingredients and pour into greased casserole. Bake at 350° for 30-40 minutes or until thoroughly heated.

BRUSSELS SPROUTS EGG BAKE

Easy   Serves 6-8   350°
Do Ahead   25-30 min.

2 (10 oz.) pkgs. frozen Brussels
  sprouts
3 hard cooked eggs, sliced
1 c. shredded sharp process
  American cheese
¼ c. milk
1 can cream of mushroom soup
½ c. bread crumbs
2 T. butter or margarine, melted

Cook Brussels sprouts according to package directions except omit salt. Drain; halve the large sprouts. Place in 10x6x2" baking dish. Arrange eggs atop sprouts and sprinkle cheese over all. Blend together milk and soup; pour over casserole. If desired, combine crumbs and butter; sprinkle atop. Bake.

Mrs. Don Rainwater

CABBAGE AU GRATIN

Serves 8   375°
                              10-15 min.

2-3 lbs. cabbage (chopped)
bacon fat
2 T. margarine
2 T. flour
1 c. milk
½ c. grated cheese
buttered bread crumbs
¼ c. grated cheese

Boil cabbage in salted water, seasoned with bacon fat, for 7-10 minutes, or until done. Do not overcook. Make white sauce with margarine, flour and milk. Stir in ½ c. grated cheese. In medium baking dish, layer cabbage and cheese sauce. Cover with buttered bread crumbs, dot with grated cheese. Bake until bubbly.

Mrs. Ashley P. Hurt

BRAISED RED CABBAGE

Easy   Serves 8-10

3 lbs. red cabbage
¼ c. butter
¼ c. sugar
1½ tsp. salt
¼ c. cider vinegar
½ c. water

Cut cabbage in half. Wash and drain. Core and shred. Melt butter in pan over low heat. Add cabbage and saute 5 minutes. Add remaining ingredients and toss until mixed. Cover. Cook 1½ hours, stirring occasionally.
This is the traditional Danish accompaniment to Christmas goose. Prepare it ahead and reheat just before serving.

Mrs. H. Alfred Bolton III

GARDEN CHINESE CABBAGE

Easy   Serves 4-6

2 lge. heads Chinese cabbage
4 T. chicken fat or bacon
½ T. cornstarch
2 T. water
½ c. water
1 tsp. sugar
¼ tsp. monosodium glutamate
1½ tsp. salt

Cut cabbage stalks and leaves into 2 inch sections. Mix cornstarch with water. Heat oil in large skillet. Add cabbage to oil as much as can fit. When cabbage is wilted, add ½ c. water. Cover and simmer for 10 minutes or until tender. Stir occasionally. Mix in salt, sugar and monosodium glutamate, then cornstarch. When thickened, serve hot.

Variation: Boil 1 small chopped onion until tender in 1 inch salty (1 tsp.) water. Shred cabbage and cook rapidly in onion water for 6 minutes. Turn into serving dish, pour melted butter over cabbage and sprinkle with chopped parsley.

Mrs. A. M. Oshlag

OMI'S CARROT RING

Do Ahead†   Serves 8   350°
                                                         30 min.

1½ c. bread crumbs
3 c. cooked carrots
¼ c. butter
½ tsp. salt
½ c. sugar
2 eggs beaten
¾ c. milk, sweet
½ tsp. nutmeg

Prepare a 24 oz. or 1 qt. ring mold of your choice. Grease ring and bread with ½ c. bread crumbs. Cook carrots in boiling water until tender. Peel, mash and mix with remaining ingredients. Pack into prepared mold and bake in 350° oven for approximately 30 minutes. Unmold.
Especially pretty filled with parsley or baby lima beans.

Mrs. Clayton Brown, Jr.

MARINATED CARROTS *

Easy
Do Ahead

1 (2 lb.) bunch carrots
1 med. onion
1 green pepper
1 c. tomato soup
¾ c. vinegar
1 tsp. dry mustard
1 tsp. Worcestershire sauce
1 tsp. pepper
½ c. salad oil
1 c. sugar

Slice and cook carrots until just done. Dice onions and green pepper. Add other ingredients, marinate and chill.

CAULIFLOWER CASSEROLE

Easy   Serves 6-8   400°
Do Ahead   20-25 min.

1 cauliflower, broken into
   flowerettes
1 pkg. frozen English peas
   or 1 (16 oz.) can
2 c. white sauce
½ c. grated sharp cheese
1 c. bread crumbs
butter
salt
paprika

Cook cauliflower and peas separately. Drain. Place cauliflower in casserole, dot with butter, a dash of salt and paprika and ⅓ of bread crumbs. Add cheese to white sauce and pour half over cauliflower mixture. Add peas and repeat layers. Top with remaining bread crumbs. Bake.

White Sauce:
   4 T. margarine
   4 T. flour
   2 c. milk
   ¼ tsp. salt

To make White Sauce:
Melt butter and add flour and blend. Add milk and cook over low heat until thick, stirring constantly. Add ¼ tsp. salt.

Mrs. C. Ray Barron

CELERY WITH ALMONDS AU GRATIN

Easy   400°
Do Ahead

1 pt. celery (add a little sugar)
1 pt. cream sauce (medium)
2 oz. almonds (blanched and
   chopped)
2 oz. grated sharp cheese
1 T. bread crumbs

Cut celery into bite size pieces, cover with water and cook about eight minutes. Celery must remain crisp - just barely done. Drain and add to cream sauce mixed with cheese and almonds. Pour into buttered 1½ qt. casserole. Sprinkle bread crumbs on top and bake in hot oven until it bubbles.

Cream Sauce:
  2 T. butter
  3 T. flour
  1½ c. liquid (milk or
    stock)
  ½ c. whipping cream
  salt, pepper, lemon juice

To make Cream Sauce:
Melt butter, add flour and blend. Slowly add liquid, stirring constantly (medium-low heat). Stir in cream, salt, pepper and a few drops of lemon juice.

Mrs. Gerald L. Bilbro

CORN CASSEROLE *

Easy   Serves 6   350°
                                                    45 min.
                                                    to 1 hr.

1 (16 oz.) can creamed corn
1 c. milk, heated slightly
3 T. butter
1 T. sugar
3 T. flour
1 tsp. salt
2 eggs, slightly beaten
dash of pepper

Mix flour in corn. Add all other ingredients, adding eggs last. Pour in greased casserole. Cover and bake until done.

CREOLE CORN PUDDING

Easy†   Serves 6   350°
Do Ahead   45 min.

3 ears fresh corn
1 lb. bacon
¾ c. chopped onion
½ c. diced green pepper
3 T. bacon drippings
2 eggs, beaten
2½ c. milk
½ c. corn meal
dash of pepper

Remove husks and silk from corn. Cut corn from cob and reserve. Cook bacon until crisp - drain and crumble. Saute onion and pepper in 3 T. of bacon drippings. Mix with corn, eggs, milk, corn meal and pepper. Add bacon. Turn into greased 2 qt. casserole. Bake at 350° for 45 minutes.

Mrs. Will Hill Newton II

CORN FRITTERS

Serves 6

2 eggs. separated
2 c. corn, freshly cut from cob
   or 1 (12 oz.) can whole kernel,
   drained
⅛ tsp. Worcestershire sauce
½ tsp. salt
¼ tsp. pepper
¼ c. sifted all-purpose flour
¼ tsp. baking powder
about ¼ c. salad oil

In a small bowl, beat egg whites until stiff but not dry; set aside. In another bowl, beat egg yolks slightly; add corn, Worcestershire, salt and pepper to yolks, combine thoroughly. Stir in sifted flour and baking powder. Fold in beaten egg whites. Heat about 2 T. oil in a large skillet over medium heat. Drop corn mixture by table-spoonfuls into the hot oil and brown about 3 minutes on each side. Remove and keep hot while cooking remaining mixture, adding more oil as needed.

Mrs. William C. Hewitt

BAKED EGGPLANT SLICES

Easy   Serves 6-8   400°
                                                          15 min.

2 med. eggplants, unpeeled and
   cut into ½" - ¾ " crosswise
   slices
6 T. olive oil
2 T. lemon juice
½ tsp. oregano
salt and pepper
Parmesan cheese, grated

Mix olive oil, lemon juice, oregano, salt and pepper. Arrange the eggplant slices in a shallow pan. Spoon ½ of the oil mixture over the eggplant and let stand 15 minutes. Turn pieces and repeat the procedure. Sprinkle gener-ously with cheese and bake 400° for 15 minutes or until tender.

Mrs. Randolph Gilbert

FRENCH FRIED EGGPLANT

Serves 10-12

3 lb. eggplant
4 oz. flour
2 eggs, beaten
¾ c. milk
½ tsp. salt
½ tsp. pepper
¾ c. cracker meal
½ tsp. seasoned salt
2 T. grated Romano cheese

Peel and cut eggplant into French fry size. Dredge in flour, salt and then dip into beaten eggs and milk. Roll eggplant in cracker meal. Fry in deep fat 350° for 5 minutes. Drain on paper towels, dust with seasoned salt and Romano cheese.

Mrs. Jerry Hollberg

EGGPLANT PARMESAN

Serves 6-8   375°
                             20 min.

2 med. eggplants
¼ c. salad oil
2 cloves garlic, finely chopped
2 T. flour
2 (1 lb.) cans stewed tomatoes, undrained
2 tsp. salt
2 tsp. sugar
1 tsp. paprika
⅛ tsp. pepper
⅛ tsp. dried basil leaves
½ c. grated Parmesan cheese

Preheat oven to 375°. Lightly grease a 2 qt. casserole. Wash and peel eggplants; cut into 2 inch cubes. Simmer, covered, in small amount of boiling, salted water for 10 minutes, drain. Meanwhile, in hot oil in skillet, saute garlic until golden - about 3 minutes; remove from heat. Into skillet, stir flour, tomatoes, salt, sugar, paprika, pepper, and basil. Cook, stirring, over medium heat until mixture boils and is slightly thickened. In prepared casserole, layer eggplant cubes alternately with tomato mixture; top with grated cheese. Bake 20 minutes or until top is slightly browned.

Mrs. W. D. Hollberg, Jr.

EGGPLANT SOUFFLE

Easy†   Serves 6   325°
Do Ahead   1 hr.

1 lge. eggplant, peeled and
  cut in cubes
2 T. butter
1 onion, chopped
8 slices bread
1 c. milk
2 eggs, separated
salt and pepper

Boil eggplant in salted water until tender. Drain thoroughly; then add 2 T. butter and mash with potato masher. Add chopped onion. Cut bread into small cubes and add to mixture with milk. Add egg yolks. Salt and pepper to taste. Fold in stiffly beaten egg whites. Pour into greased baking dish and bake until golden brown.

Mrs. William A. Herko

IRANIAN STUFFED EGGPLANT

Do Ahead†   Serves 4-6   400°
                                                           35 min.

1 lge. eggplant
3-4 T. olive oil
¼ c. chopped onions
1 garlic bud, pressed
¼ tsp. pepper
salt to taste
½ lb. ground beef, browned
  and drained
⅔ c. wheat germ
¾ c. drained tomatoes
1 egg
¼ c. wheat germ

Cut eggplant in half and spoon out center. Boil shell in salted water 5 minutes. Chop removed portion and saute in olive oil with onion, pepper and garlic until transparent. Add browned meat, wheat germ, tomatoes, egg and salt to taste. Stuff into shells and top with ¼ c. wheat germ. Bake 400° for 35 minutes.

Mrs. Randolph Gilbert

HOMINY MUSHROOM CASSEROLE

Easy   Serves 6-8   350°
                                                            15-20 min.

2 c. sour cream
1 tsp. salt
½ tsp. dry mustard
1½ c. grated sharp cheese
½ lb. sliced fresh or (4 oz.)
  canned mushrooms
2-3 T. margarine
2 (14½ oz.) cans hominy, well
  drained

Blend sour cream with salt, mustard
and cheese. If fresh mushrooms, saute
in 2 - 3 T. margarine a few minutes.
Drain mushrooms, fold into hominy,
cheese and sour cream. Put into 1½
qt. casserole. Bake 350° 15-20
minutes or long enough to heat
thoroughly.

Mrs. Charlie T. Phillips

HOW TO WASH MUSHROOMS

Put mushrooms in jar with tight-fitting lid. Cover with water and shake
well. Pour off and refill with fresh water, adding 2 T. white vinegar. Shake,
pour off and fill again with fresh water. Shake and pour off. Store in
refrigerator until needed.

HOW TO FREEZE FRESH MUSHROOMS

Select firm, fresh, white mushrooms. Remove any woody portions on
stems. Wash gently in cold water. Dry in terry cloth towel. Either slice or
saute whole in butter or margarine (½ c. to 3 pts.) in a heavy skillet, for
10 to 15 minutes, stirring frequently. Sprinkle lightly with salt. Turn off.
Cover and let cool. Spoon into plastic freezer bags. Pour some broth into
each bag. Secure and freeze. When ready to use, peel off plastic bag and
place in top of double boiler to warm.

OKRA CREOLE

                          Serves 8

¼ c. chopped onion
1 green pepper, chopped
3 T. bacon fat
2 c. sliced okra
2 c. stewed tomatoes
1 c. cut corn
salt and pepper

Saute onion and green pepper in bacon
fat until soft. Add okra and cook
5 minutes. Add tomatoes and corn.
Simmer 15 minutes or until okra and
corn are tender. Season with salt
and pepper to taste.
*Good as side dish; served over rice;
or can and use later in beef and
vegetable soup.*

Mrs. Donald Segars

FRIED OKRA

4 c. cut okra
1 egg, beaten
½ c. corn meal
salt and pepper
½ c. oil

Dip each piece of cut okra into egg, then into meal seasoned with salt and pepper. Fry in medium-hot oil until golden brown, turning once. Serve immediately.

Mrs. Benton Bowen

BARBECUED BRAISED ONIONS

Easy   Serves 4   350°
                                                                1 hr.

4 lge. onions
¼ c. butter or margarine
½ c. honey
½ c. tomato juice
1½ tsp. soy sauce
½ tsp. salt
¼ tsp. pepper
paprika

Cut a thin slice from each end of the onion. Cut each onion in half and remove skin. Place halves, cut side up, in baking dish. Melt butter and add other ingredients except paprika. Spoon over onions, cover tightly with foil. Bake 1 hour at 350°. Sprinkle with paprika before serving.

Mrs. Myrrel Hilger
Blytheville AFB, Arkansas

CREAMED ONIONS WITH PEANUTS

Do Ahead   Serves 5-6   400°
                                                                15 min.

16 whole sm. white onions
  cooked in boiling salted
  water or 1 jar of onions
2 T. butter
2 T. flour
¼ tsp. salt
2 c. milk
¼ c. whole salted peanuts
½ c. buttered bread crumbs
¼ c. salted peanuts, chopped

Preheat oven to 400°. In saucepan, melt butter. Stir in flour and salt. Add milk and cook over medium heat, stirring constantly until smooth and slightly thickened. Put onion in greased 1 qt. casserole and pour cream sauce over them. Sprinkle in whole peanuts. Top with buttered crumbs and chopped peanuts. Bake.

Mrs. Charles L. Smith

ONION PIE

Serves 6-8 · 350° · 45 min.

1½ c. soda cracker crumbs
½ c. melted butter or margarine
2½ c. thinly sliced raw onions
2 T. butter or margarine
1 c. milk
3 eggs, slightly beaten
½ lb. grated Cheddar cheese

Mix crumbs with butter and press into 10" pan. Saute onions in butter and pour into crust. Scald milk and add slowly to eggs. Add grated cheese and stir until cheese melts. Pour into crust and bake 45 minutes at 350°.

Mrs. Lutie C. Johnston

PEAS AND ASPARAGUS CASSEROLE

Easy
Do Ahead

Serves 8 · 350° · 30 min.

1 lge. (17 oz.) can LeSueur peas
2 lge. (15 oz.) cans asparagus
3 chopped hard boiled eggs
1½ cans mushroom soup
4-6 oz. sharp Cheddar cheese

Layer in ungreased casserole in order stated. Top with grated cheese. Bake uncovered at 350° for 30 minutes.

Mrs. Robert A. Parker
Forsyth, Georgia

CREOLE PEAS

Easy†
Do Ahead

350° · 1 hr. 10 min.

3 med. onions, chopped
½ c. celery, chopped
1 bell pepper, chopped
bacon drippings
1 T. vinegar
1 can tomatoes
1½ tsp. salt
red pepper to taste
Worcestershire sauce, to taste
1 can mushroom soup
2 cans green peas, drained

Saute onions, celery and bell pepper in small amount bacon fat until tender. Add vinegar, tomatoes, salt, red pepper and Worcestershire sauce. Simmer 1 hour. Add mushroom soup and peas. Heat and serve. Can be put in casserole, topped with bread crumbs, and put in oven to heat.

Mrs. Robert O. Crouch

HOPPING JOHN

Serves 10   350°
                             15-25 min.

1 c. long-grained white rice,
  cooked
1 pkg. dried black-eyed peas,
  cook according to pkg.
  directions
4 strips of bacon
¼ c. onions
2 (1 lb.) cans tomatoes

Cook rice according to package directions. Also, soak peas and cook as directed. Fry bacon, dice and add onions. Mix rice, peas, bacon, onions and tomatoes (use ½ liquid from tomatoes.) Put in 3 qt. casserole and heat at 350° until bubbly.

Mrs. William Valdon Smith

Editor's note: Hopping John may also be made without tomatoes.

POTATOES AU GRATIN

Easy†   Serves 4   400°
Do Ahead   30 min.

1 c. diced potatoes
2 T. butter
2 T. flour
1 C. milk
½ c. diced sharp cheese
Parmesan cheese
salt, pepper to taste

Boil 1 c. diced potatoes in salted water. While potatoes are cooking, make cheese sauce from butter, flour and milk. Add cheese. Drain potatoes, place in casserole. Pour sauce over. Sprinkle with grated Parmesan. Bake until cheese is melted. Potatoes should be slightly undercooked so they won't get mushy.

Mrs. Thomas W. Fetzer

BACON STUFFED POTATOES

Easy†   Serves 6   400°
Do Ahead   45 min.-1 hr.

8 lge. baking potatoes
¼ c. butter
1 c. commercial sour cream
1 egg
1 tsp. salt
⅛ tsp. pepper
9 crisp bacon slices, crumbled
    fine
paprika

Scrub potatoes and dry. Rub with a little oil and bake directly on oven rack at 400° for 1 hour, or until fork tender. Cut a long oval slice from one side of potato and scoop out in a bowl, add butter, sour cream, egg, salt and pepper. Beat well; stir in crisp, crumbled bacon. Pile back into six potato shells, mounding the potatoes high. Sprinkle with paprika. Bake at 400° until warmed through. To freeze, allow stuffed potatoes to cool. Then wrap each potato individually and freeze. To serve, heat oven to 400°, unwrap frozen potatoes, place on oven rack and bake until heated through - 45 minutes to 1 hour.

Mrs. Donald L. Hutcheson

SOUR CREAM POTATOES

                               Serves 6   300°
                                                           1 hr.

1¼ c. milk
6 med. potatoes
3 eggs
1 (8 oz.) carton sour cream
butter
salt and pepper
bread crumbs

Boil potatoes in jacket until tender. Also, boil eggs. Butter a 1½ qt. casserole and cover with bread crumbs. Mix ¼ c. milk with sour cream. Slice half of eggs and potatoes into casserole and add salt and pepper. Cover with half of sour cream-milk mixture. Repeat. Top with bread crumbs and several pats of butter. Pour 1 c. of milk around sides of casserole. Cook at 300° for 1 hour.

Mrs. William A. Herko

RATATOUILLE

Do Ahead   Serves 8

1 lge. eggplant, diced without
   peeling
1 lge. onion, sliced
½ c. olive oil
2 or 3 garlic cloves, crushed
1 or 2 4" yellow squash
   or zucchini
1 (1 lb. 12 oz.) can tomatoes
   or 6-8 quartered fresh
   tomatoes
½ tsp. oregano
1 tsp. salt

Cook eggplant and onion in the olive oil over very low heat at least 40 minutes or until eggplant is very soft and the onion almost pureed. Add garlic and squash cut in ½" slices, cook about 10 minutes. Add tomatoes and seasonings and simmer uncovered another half hour. Usually served at room temperature but not chilled. Take from the refrigerator at least an hour before serving. Tastes even better 24 hours after first made. Can be eaten hot.
Perfect when your garden's overflowing in the summer.

Mrs. H. Alfred Bolton III

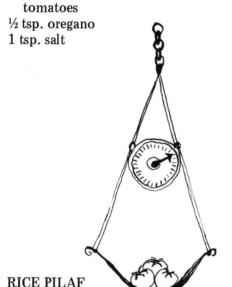

RICE PILAF

Do Ahead   Serves 8   350°
                                                        25 min.

½ c. finely chopped onions
1 clove garlic, minced
⅓ c. butter or margarine
2 c. rice
1 T. chopped parsley
2 tsp. salt
½ tsp. saffron (optional)
¼ tsp. leaf thyme
⅛ tsp. pepper
½ bay leaf
2 (13¾ oz.) cans chicken broth
1½ c. water

Cook onion and garlic in butter until tender, not brown, in 2 qt. flameproof casserole, chicken fryer or 10" fry pan with heat-proof handle. Stir in rice; heat. Add parsley, salt, saffron, thyme, pepper and bay leaf; mix. Combine chicken broth and water; bring to a boil. Pour over rice. Cover, bake in oven at 350° until liquid is absorbed, about 25 minutes. Serve with creole shrimp.

Mrs. Donald L. Hutcheson

WILD RICE AMANDINE

Do Ahead   Serves 12   250°
                                                         1¼ hrs.

2 c. wild rice or 1 c. wild
  rice and 1 c. long grain
  white rice
½ c. olive oil
2 T. chopped onions
2 T. chopped chives
1 tsp. chopped shallots
3 T. chopped green pepper
4½ c. hot chicken broth or
  bouillon
¾ c. almonds, blanched and
  slivered
salt and pepper to taste

Wash and drain rice. Saute vegetables in olive oil. When limp, stir in rice until golden color. Stir in chicken broth. Salt and pepper to taste. Add almonds and turn mixture into casserole. Bake, covered, in 250° oven for 1¼ hours or until done.

Mrs. Marshall R. Sims

SPINACH CASSEROLE

Do Ahead   Serves 6-8   375°
Easy   40 min.

3 pkgs. chopped, frozen
  spinach
1 T. butter
salt to taste
2 jars marinated artichokes
  (drain and reserve juice)
3 (3 oz.) pkgs. cream cheese
4 T. butter
6 T. milk
dash pepper
1/3 c. Parmesan cheese

Cook, drain spinach very thoroughly. Season with salt and 1 T. butter and liquid from 1 jar of artichokes. Cut up artichokes and spread over bottom of 1½ qt. casserole. Spread spinach over this. Beat cream cheese, milk and butter in blender. Pour over spinach. Sprinkle Parmesan cheese over this.
This must be made up 24 hours in advance of cooking.

Mrs. William Lloyd

SPINACH SOUFFLE

Easy   Serves 6-8   350°
Do Ahead   30 min.

2 (10 oz.) pkgs. spinach
1 tsp. salt
½ c. chopped onion
¼ c. margarine
1 can mushroom soup
½ c. grated cheese
2 eggs
bread crumbs
additional butter

Thaw and drain spinach. Add salt. Brown the onion in margarine. Mix spinach, onions, soup and cheese. Beat eggs and fold into mixture. Pour in casserole. Sprinkle with bread crumbs. Dot with butter. Bake.

Mrs. Lewis T. Murphy

BUTTERNUT SQUASH SOUFFLE

Easy†   Serves 6   325°
Do Ahead   45 min.

3 c. cooked butternut squash,
    mashed
sugar to taste
½ c. coconut
½ c. raisins
½ c. chopped pecans
¼ c. margarine
1 tsp. vanilla
1 tsp. lemon extract
2 eggs, beaten
marshmallows (optional)

Combine all ingredients mixing well. Put into greased baking dish and bake 45 minutes at 325° until light brown and firm. Marshmallows may be added to top if desired and lightly browned.

Mrs. Robert Scroggins

SQUASH CASSEROLE I *

Easy†   Serves 10-12   350°
Do Ahead   1 hr.

5 c. warm, cooked squash,
    slightly drained
¼ c. margarine
½ - 1 c. minced onions
1 c. grated cheese
1 tsp. salt or more to taste
½ tsp. pepper
1 c. bread crumbs
3 eggs, slightly beaten
additional buttered bread
    crumbs

Mix ingredients in the order given, pour into an oiled 2 qt. casserole dish and bake 350° for 40 minutes. Top with additional, buttered crumbs and bake 20 minutes longer or until center is firm.

SQUASH CASSEROLE II *

Easy†   Serves 8-12   350°
Do Ahead   30 min.

2 lbs. squash, sliced   Cook squash and onion in small amount
1 med. onion, chopped   salted water until tender. Drain. Add
½ tsp. salt   soup, sour cream and water chestnuts.
1 can cream of chicken soup   Mix melted butter and Herb Dressing.
1 (8 oz.) carton sour cream   Put half of dressing mix in baking
1 sm. can sliced water chestnuts dish. Add squash mixture. Cover with
½ c. butter, melted   remaining dressing. Bake.
1 pkg. Pepperidge Farm Herb
   Dressing

SWEET POTATO AND CRANBERRY CASSEROLE

Easy   Serves 6-8   350°
Do Ahead   55 min.

4 lge. sweet potatoes (cooked)   Arrange ½ of potatoes sliced in greased
   or canned (16-20 oz.) sweet   1½ qt. casserole. Sprinkle with ¼ c.
   potatoes   brown sugar. Dot with margarine.
½ c. packed light brown sugar   Sprinkle with ½ c. cranberries. Repeat
2 T. margarine   layer. Pour orange juice over all.
1 c. fresh cranberries   Cover. Bake 45 minutes. Uncover.
½ c. fresh or frozen orange   Distribute Walnut Topping. Bake
   juice   10 minutes longer.

Walnut Topping:
   ½ c. chopped walnuts   Mrs. Walter E. Jones
   2 T. melted margarine
   1 T. brown sugar
   ½ tsp. cinnamon

GRATED SWEET POTATO PUDDING

Do Ahead†   Serves 6-8   350°
                                                            45 min.

2 c. grated raw sweet potato   Stir all ingredients together, adding the
1 c. sugar   melted butter last. Add a dash of salt.
½ c. cane syrup   Grated orange rind may also be added.
2 T. corn meal   Bake in buttered shallow Pyrex dish
2 eggs   (a pie plate will do nicely).
½ c. evaporated milk
1 tsp. grated fresh nutmeg   Mrs. Andrew Blake
½ c. melted butter or
   margarine
dash of salt
grated orange rind (optional)

SWEET POTATO SOUFFLE

Do Ahead†   Serves 6-8   400°
        40 min.

4 lge. sweet potatoes, baked
2 eggs
1 c. sugar
1 c. milk
2 c. marshmallows
¾ stick butter

Rice potatoes and add eggs, sugar, and milk. Mix well. Melt butter and marshmallows in boiler. Add to potato mixture. Stir. Put in greased baking dish and add topping. Bake.

Topping:
    ¾ stick butter
    ½ c. chopped nuts
    ½ c. brown sugar
    1 c. crushed cornflakes or
      wheat germ

Heat topping in boiler until butter is melted. Pour over potatoes.

Mrs. C. E. Williams, Jr.

BAKED CHEESE-STUFFED TOMATOES

        Serves 6   350°
        25 min.

6 med. tomatoes
2 c. grated Swiss cheese
½ c. light cream
2 egg yolks, slightly beaten
2 T. snipped chives
3 T. grated onion
½ tsp. dried marjoram
1 tsp. dry mustard
1½ tsp. salt
⅓ c. packaged bread crumbs
2 T. butter (melted)

Halve tomatoes crosswise. Scoop out pulp. Save shells. Combine coarsely chopped tomato pulp with remaining ingredients except crumbs and butter. Mix well and spoon into tomato shells. Toss crumbs with butter and sprinkle over stuffed tomatoes. Bake in greased dish.

Mrs. Warren K. Wells

TOMATO TOP PATTIES

Easy†
Do Ahead

Serves 6

350°
20-30 min.

1 pkg. frozen spinach
1 c. Pepperidge Farm Herb
   Stuffing
1 lge. onion, chopped fine
3 eggs, beaten
6 T. butter, melted
¼ c. Parmesan cheese
½ tsp. garlic salt
¼ tsp. thyme
½ tsp. black pepper
½ tsp. Accent
tomatoes

Cook spinach - salt to directions. Drain. Combine all ingredients and mix. Make into small patties to fit on top of ½ tomato. Put on cookie sheet, freeze, then bag. To serve, place pattie on tomato and put in oven. Bake 30 minutes if frozen, 20 minutes if thawed.

Mrs. James F. Lewis
Savannah, Georgia

VEGETABLES AND EGG CREOLE

Do Ahead†

Serves 10-12

325°
45 min.

1 lge. bunch celery, chopped
2 med. onions, chopped
3 med. green peppers, chopped
1 (1 lb. 4 oz.) can tomatoes
1 (1 lb. 4 oz.) can peas
¼ lb. butter plus 2 T.
1 glass Old English cheese
1 pt. milk
1 doz. boiled eggs, sliced
1 lb. grated Cheddar cheese
½ pt. cream
1 c. cracker crumbs

Cook celery, onions, peppers with tomatoes and liquid from drained peas until tender. Make cream sauce of ¼ lb. butter, Old English cheese and 1 pt. milk. Arrange in 3 qt. baking dish, layering vegetables, eggs, cream sauce, grated cheese. Add cream over all. Dot with remaining butter and cracker crumbs. If you freeze, grate the eggs and mix rather than layer.
This is an excellent vegetable dish for a dinner party. Good with country ham.

Mrs. Paul McCubbin
Campbellsville, Kentucky

ZUCCHINI CASSEROLE

Easy

Do Ahead

400°

45 min.

butter
zucchini
tomatoes
onions
salt
freshly ground pepper
grated Parmesan
bread crumbs

No precise measurements here. Butter an oven proof casserole. Wash zucchini and slice thinly. Place layer of zucchini, top with layer of sliced tomatoes and sliced onions. Sprinkle with salt and pepper and cheese. Repeat layer until casserole is full. Top with bread crumbs. Cover with foil and bake 45 minutes at 400°. Remove foil for last 10 minutes to brown top. (Yellow squash or shredded cabbage may be used instead of zucchini).

Mrs. A. M. Oshlag

ZUCCHINI ITALIANE

Easy

Do Ahead

Serves 6

350°

15-20 min.

1 sm. chopped onion
margarine
1 lb. sliced zucchini
1 can stewed tomatoes (or
 fresh tomatoes, green pepper
 and celery)
salt and pepper
bread crumbs
1 slice Mozzarella cheese
 (or grated Parmesan cheese)

Heat margarine over medium heat in a Corning Ware 1½ qt. casserole. Add onion. Slice in squash; stir fry for 5 minutes. Add tomatoes, salt and pepper. Top with bread crumbs and cheese cut into ½" strips. Put into oven to melt cheese and brown crumbs 15-20 minutes at 350°.

Mrs. Charles B. Wynne

STUFFED ZUCCHINI

Serves 6

400°
15-20 min.

6 med. zucchini (or 1 or 2 lge.)
6 bacon slices
¾ c. chopped onion
1 clove garlic (minced)
1 (4 oz.) can mushroom stems
  and pieces (drained)
⅔ c. seasoned bread stuffing
  mix
⅓ c. wheat germ
2 T. grated Parmesan cheese
1 T. catsup
¾ tsp. basil
½ tsp. salt
⅛ tsp. pepper

Cook zucchini in boiling water 5-10 minutes or until tender. Drain. Cool. Cook bacon until crisp, drain and crumble. Reserve 3 T. drippings. Set aside. Saute onion and garlic in drippings. Add mushrooms and cook 5 minutes, stirring occasionally. Slice zucchini lengthwise. Scoop out and chop center. Add chopped centers and all other ingredients (except bacon) to mushroom mixture. Mix well. (Can add 1-2 T. water if too dry.) Fill zucchini shells with mixture and sprinkle bacon over top. Place in large shallow baking pan. Bake at 400° for 15-20 minutes.

Mrs. H. Alfred Bolton III

SAUCES

BLENDER BEARNAISE SAUCE

Easy

3 egg yolks
2 T. lemon juice
¼ tsp. salt
1 thin slice of onion
2-3 sprigs of parsley
½ tsp. dried tarragon
½ c. butter

Mix all but butter in blender for a few seconds (low). Melt butter, add slowly, while beating until thick - about 3 minutes. Serve immediately.

Mrs. James H. Cobb III

"NEVER FAIL" HOLLANDAISE

Easy   Yield: ¾ cup

4 egg yolks
½ tsp. salt
½ tsp. dry mustard
1 T. fresh lemon juice
½ c. butter, melted

Put egg yolks, salt, dry mustard and lemon juice in blender. While above is processing, slowly pour melted butter in a steady stream. May be left in blender in a pan of hot water until ready to serve.

Mrs. Warren K. Wells

HORSERADISH SAUCE

Easy
Do Ahead

¼ c. melted butter
1 tsp. wine vinegar
1 tsp. (scant) pepper
  vinegar
1 sm. onion
1 tsp. salt
1 tsp. sugar
1 tsp. Dijon mustard
1 T. cream style horseradish
  (½ T. extra may be added
  if stronger horseradish
  flavor desired)
1½ c. mayonnaise

Place melted butter, both vinegars and peeled and quartered onion in blender or in Cuisinart with chopping blade. Blend until onion is of grated consistency. Add remaining ingredients and blend only until well mixed. Store in a tightly covered jar in the refrigerator and use as needed.
*If doubled, 1 c. of the mayonnaise will need to be stirred in so as not to overflow the Cuisinart or blender.

Mrs. Paul J. Mitchell, Jr.

QUICK HOT VEGETABLE SAUCE

Easy

1 c. mayonnaise
2 T. seasoned mustard
(Gulden's)

Mix and pour over hot vegetables.

TOMATO SAUCE

Easy
Do Ahead

1 (16 oz.) can tomatoes or
equivalent from the
garden
1 c. brown sugar
¾ c. vinegar
2 med. onions, chopped
½ tsp. salt
¼ tsp. allspice
black pepper to taste
dash Tabasco sauce

Simmer for a long time with top
off until thick. Stir often to keep
from sticking.
Wonderful over vegetables.

Mrs. Charlie T. Phillips

PESTO SAUCE

Easy†
Do Ahead

2½ c. fresh washed basil
leaves
3 cloves garlic, peeled
3 T. lightly toasted pine
nuts or almonds
¾ c. olive oil
½ c. freshly shredded
Parmesan cheese

Place first four ingredients in the
blender and blend until the leaves
are pulverized. Add cheese and
blend a few seconds longer. Use at
once or freeze (drop by small mounds
on a foil covered baking sheet and
freeze. When solid peel from foil
and package.) Makes about 1¾ c.
Serve on hot egg noodles, over sliced
tomato, hot corn on the cob, cooked
zucchini or green beans, steak, ham-
burgers, or in a green salad with oil
and vinegar dressing.

Mrs. Allen J. Brock
Atlanta, Georgia

Notes

MEATS

BEEF WELLINGTON

Serves 8-10   425°-400°
                               30 min.-30 min.

4 - 4½ lb. beef tenderloin
salt and pepper to taste
Butter Pastry
Duxelles
1 egg
1 T. water

Place beef on rack in shallow baking pan. Sprinkle with salt and pepper. Roast at 425° for 30 minutes. Let stand until cool, then trim off the fat. Roll butter pastry on a floured surface to rectangle about 3" longer than roast and 12 to 13" wide. Press duxelles into pastry, leaving 1" uncovered on all edges. Place beef on pastry. Moisten pastry edges and enclose beef, pressing edges firmly together. Trim off excess pastry from ends so single layer covers ends of roast. Place roll, seam side down, in a shallow baking pan. Cut decorations from pastry trimmings and place on top. Brush pastry with egg beaten with 1 T. water. Bake at 400° for 30 to 35 minutes (until browned). Let stand 15 to 20 minutes before slicing. Serve immediately.

Butter Pastry:
Follow exactly
   3¾ c. sifted flour
   1 tsp. salt
   1 c. cold butter
   2 T. shortening
   ¾ c. (about) ice water

Combine the flour and salt in a bowl and cut in the butter and shortening until particles are fine. Add water 1 T. at a time to make stiff dough. Cover and chill.

Duxelles
   1 lb. fresh mushrooms,
      finely chopped
   ¼ c. fresh green onions,
      chopped
   ¼ c. butter
   ½ tsp. salt
   2 tsp. flour
   dash of coarse ground
      pepper
   ¼ c. beef broth
   2 T. chopped fresh parsley
   ½ c. finely chopped cooked
      ham

Saute the mushrooms and onions in butter in a saucepan until liquid evaporates. Stir in salt, flour, pepper and broth. Cook, stirring constantly, until mixture comes to a boil and thickens. Remove from heat and stir in parsley and ham. Cool.

Mrs. Roberto Oviedo

LONDON BROIL

Easy   Serves 4   Broil
                                                        10 min.

2 lbs. flank steak
1 T. salad oil
2 tsp. chopped parsley
1 clove crushed garlic
1 tsp. salt
1 tsp. lemon juice
1/8 tsp. pepper

Trim fat from meat - lay on cutting board - score top. Combine all other ingredients and brush half of mixture over one side of meat. Set aside for 20 minutes. Lightly grease broiler - broil steak oil side up - 5 minutes. Turn and brush on rest of oil mixture - broil 5 minutes. Slice very thin on the diagonal.

Mrs. J. Thomas Grayson

GRILLED CORNED BEEF

Easy   Grill
Do Ahead

corned beef
1/3 c. prepared mustard
1/4 c. packed brown sugar
1/4 tsp. nutmeg
freshly ground pepper
   to taste

Fully cook corned beef (by simmering about 1 hour per pound or in oven wrapped in foil or as directed on package). Coat with mustard mixture and brown on grill until crusty.

Mrs. Robert Caswell

FILET JOSEPH

                            Serves 4

1/2 lb. mushrooms, sliced
3 T. butter
salt and pepper to taste
1 T. brandy, warm
1 T. sherry, warm
1 T. Madeira, warm
1/4 c. butter
1 tsp. flour
1 T. Dijon-style mustard
4 tenderloin filets, 3/4"
   thick
butter

Saute mushrooms in 3 T. butter for about 5 minutes. Add salt and pepper and warm brandy, sherry and Madeira. Ignite the spirits - shake the pan until the flames die out. Stir in 1/4 c. butter creamed with flour and mustard. Cook the sauce until slightly thickened. Pan broil 4 slices tenderloin of beef in butter. Spread sauce on filets.

Mrs. John H. Cheatham

BEEF KABOBS

Do Ahead   Serves 4   Grill
                 15-20 min.

Marinade:
 ½ c. burgundy or other
  dark red wine
 1 tsp. Worcestershire sauce
 1 clove garlic or ¼ tsp.
  garlic powder
 ½ c. salad oil
 2 T. catsup
 1 tsp. sugar
 ½ tsp. salt
 ½ tsp. Accent
 1 T. vinegar
 ½ tsp. marjoram
 ½ tsp. rosemary

3 lbs. sirloin

Combine all ingredients for marinade. Marinate sirloin (cut in 1 - 1½" pieces) overnight. Put meat on skewers along with any or all of the following: tomato wedges, green peppers (cut up), canned onions, canned whole potatoes, bacon strips, fresh mushrooms. Cook on grill to desired doneness (15-20 minutes).
It is fun to let everyone "build" his own kabob with items set out on tray.

Mrs. Doug Wheeless
Korea

SWEET-SOUR KABOBS

Do Ahead   Serves 4   Grill
                 25-30 min.

Sauce:
 1 c. margarine
 1 c. catsup
 3 T. vinegar
 1 T. lemon juice
 1 T. Worcestershire sauce
 1 tsp. prepared mustard
 1 tsp. Tabasco sauce
 ½ tsp. garlic salt
 1 med. onion, chopped
 dash thyme
 parsley

1 - 2 lbs. sirloin tip steak
 (cut in 1" cubes)
1 (15 oz.) can chunk pineapple
10-12 slices bacon (slightly
 cooked)

Make sauce and simmer for 25-30 minutes. Remove from heat, add meat cubes. Cover and refrigerate overnight. Before cooking on charcoal grill, skewer with chunks of pineapple and pieces of bacon (cut each piece in thirds). Spread additional sauce over everything on skewers and baste while cooking.

Mrs. John Umstead
Chapel Hill, North Carolina

DILL ROAST BEEF

Easy
Do Ahead

Serves 6

350°
3-4 hr.

3 to 5 lb. chuck roast
1 (10¾ oz.) can Golden
    Mushroom soup
2 T. dill weed
1 (8 oz.) carton sour cream

Sear meat in a hot dutch oven (on top of stove) until brown all over. Add soup, 2 cans water, dill weed, salt and pepper to taste. Cover and place in oven. Check to see when additional water is needed and turn at least once. For gravy - add sour cream to juices.

Mrs. O. E. Anderson

SAUERBRATEN

Do Ahead

Serves 8-10

450° - 300°
30 min.-3 hrs.

3 c. water
3 c. cider vinegar
1 onion, sliced
3 bay leaves
1 tsp. peppercorns
¼ c. sugar
4 - 5 lb. pot roast
flour
seasoning
1 c. sour cream

Heat to just below boiling the water and vinegar. Add onion, bay leaves, peppercorns and sugar. Pour this mixture while hot over beef, so that it is more than half covered. Cool, and put into refrigerator, covered, for two to seven days. The longer you leave it, the sourer the meat will get (I usually leave mine about 3 days). Drain, saving the marinade and put meat in greased dutch oven and place in 450° oven for 20-30 minutes to brown. Add enough marinade to cover meat, cover and bake at 300° for 3 hours. Add more marinade if necessary. Turn meat occasionally. When the meat is tender, remove from the pot, strain stock and thicken with flour. Season and add 1 c. sour cream. Serve with potato dumplings and red cabbage.

Mrs. Eugene F. Robbins, Jr.

RARE ROAST BEEF

2 - 4 Ribs (4½ - 12 lbs.)

Cooking chart:

Ribs	lb.	Min.
2	4½ - 5	25-30
3	8 - 9	40-45
4	11-12	55-60

Have roast at room temperature. Preheat oven to 500°. Put roast in shallow pan, fat side up and rub with flour, salt and pepper. Put no water in pan. Place pan in oven.

When cooking time is finished, turn off heat and leave in oven 2 or 3 hours until lukewarm. DO NOT OPEN OVEN UNTIL THEN.

Mrs. Robert Smalley

ROULADEN

Do Ahead

sirloin tip roast, sliced thin
    approximately 5 rolls per
    lb.
seasoned salt
pepper
mustard
bacon
dill pickle, sliced thin
onion, sliced
oil
bouillon cube (beef)
1 c. water

On each slice of meat: sprinkle salt and pepper, spread a coating of mustard, place 1 strip of bacon, several pickle slices, and several onion slices. Roll jelly roll fashion; secure with a toothpick. Brown rolls in hot oil; add bouillon and water; simmer about 20 minutes or to desired degree of doneness.

Mrs. Rolf Duerr
Newport News, Virginia

SOUTHERN BAR-B-QUE STEAK

Serves 6

Broil
20 min.

Seasoned butter:
    ¼ c. soft butter or margarine
    2 T. dry mustard
    2 tsp. salt
    2 tsp. sugar
    ¾ tsp. paprika
    ¼ tsp. pepper

2 lbs. 1" sirloin steak
Sauce:
    ¼ c. olive oil
    2 T. Worcestershire sauce
    2 T. catsup
    ¾ tsp. sugar
    ¾ tsp. salt

Mix seasoned butter ingredients; spread half on one side of steak. In large skillet brown meat butter side down. As this browns, spread remaining butter over top; turn and brown. Remove to broiler pan. Mix remaining ingredients and add skillet drippings. Brush sauce on steak. Broil 5" from heat about 5-7 minutes on each side, brushing frequently with sauce.

Mrs. Gerald Lawhorn

COUNTRY FRIED STEAK

Easy
Do Ahead

Serves 5

5 pieces cubed steak
shortening
flour
salt and pepper to taste
approximately 1 c.
   boiling water

In a large heavy pan melt small amount of shortening. Coat steak in flour and season with salt and pepper. When shortening is hot, add steak and brown. When browned evenly on both sides, pour in boiling water. Cover and reduce heat to low. Continue cooking until tender. If gravy is not thick enough, add a little more flour.

Mrs. Ronnie Cain

ITALIAN STUFFED STEAK

Serves 4-6

2 lbs. round steak ½" thick
½ tsp. salt
½ tsp. dried basil, crushed
½ tsp. dried oregano,
   crushed
¼ tsp. pepper
2 oz. salami, chopped
   (about ⅔ c.)
2 T. shortening
½ c. tomato juice
1 T. flour
½ c. cold water

Remove bone and excess fat from round steak; cut into serving pieces. Blend seasonings; sprinkle seasonings and salami over meat. Roll each steak as for jelly roll. Tie. In a 10" skillet, brown meat rolls in hot shortening; add tomato juice. Cover; simmer for 1 hour or until tender. Remove meat rolls to platter. Pour pan juices into large measuring cup; skim off excess fat. Return ½ c. juices to skillet. Combine flour with water; add to juices. Cook and stir until thickened and bubbly. Serve over meat.

Mrs. Allen J. Brock
Atlanta, Georgia

SWISS CREAM STEAK

Easy   Serves 4-6   350°
Do Ahead   1 hr.

2 lbs. round steak
salt, pepper, flour
¼ c. margarine or butter
2 med. onions,
    chopped
½ c. water
½ c. sour cream
6 T. grated Swiss cheese
1 tsp. paprika

Cut meat into serving portions; dust with salt, pepper and flour. Melt butter, add onions and heat until golden. Remove from pan. Add meat, browning on both sides. Mix onions and other ingredients and add to steak. Place in casserole, cover, bake at 350° for about 1 hour or until tender.

Mrs. William Valdon Smith

TENDERLOIN ROYALE

Do Ahead   Serves 10   300°
                                                      1½ hr.

5 lbs. beef tenderloin
6 oz. soy sauce
4 oz. burgundy wine
1 clove garlic, minced
1 tsp. salt
½ tsp. pepper
1 T. salad oil
½ tsp. monosodium glutamate
¾ tsp. lemon juice
½ tsp. ground ginger

Remove all fat from tenderloin. Mix all other ingredients and marinate beef 24 hours, turning after 12 hours. Water may be added to marinade if needed to make enough to cover lower half of meat. After 24 hours, grill and brown meat on all sides. Put browned meat back in marinade and cover with foil. Bake at 300° for 1½ hours. Use marinade from pan as gravy.

Mrs. Paul J. Mitchell, Jr.

BARBECUED BEEF BRISKET

Do Ahead   Serves 8   325°
                                                        4 hrs.

1 - 5 lb. fresh beef brisket
1 T. salt
½ tsp. garlic powder
¼ c. barbecue sauce
¼ tsp. pepper
¼ tsp. paprika

Sauce:
    1 can beef broth
        (consomme)
    ¼ c. barbecue sauce
    ¼ c. prepared mustard
    1 c. catsup
    3 T. brown sugar
    2 T. Worcestershire sauce
    ½ tsp. garlic powder

The night before roasting rub seasonings into meat, cover and refrigerate. Place meat in a shallow pan, fat side up. Roast uncovered without water for 2½-3 hours. Heat the sauce ingredients and pour over meat. Cover with foil. Bake 1 more hour, basting several times. Let meat stand about 15 minutes before slicing. Slice thin. May be served with strained sauce from the pan.

Mrs. Sid Esary

BEEF CONTINENTAL

Serves 4-6

2 T. shortening
1½ lbs. sirloin tip or round
    steak cut into strips
    2 x ¼ x ¼"
2 med. onions, thinly
    sliced
1 clove garlic, minced
1 tsp. salt
⅛ tsp. pepper
1½ T. flour
1½ c. water
½ - ¾ c. dry red wine
½ c. tomato catsup
¼ tsp. basil leaves
¼ tsp. ground thyme

Melt shortening in large skillet; saute meat, onions, and garlic until lightly browned. Sprinkle with salt, pepper and flour; blend well. Stir in water and next four ingredients. Cover and simmer 45 minutes or until meat is tender, stirring occasionally. Serve over or in saffron rice ring.

Mrs. LaVerne L. Hinson, Jr.

BEEF AND PEPPERS

Serves 4

4 T. soy sauce
1 T. cornstarch
1 T. sherry
1 tsp. sugar
¼ tsp. monosodium glutamate
1 lb. flank steak 1" thick, cut
   into 2" cubes on the diagonal

Mix soy sauce, cornstarch, sherry, sugar, and monosodium glutamate. Marinate steak in this mixture for as long as possible, at least 30 minutes.

2 lge. peppers cut into 1"
   squares
4 T. cooking oil
1 c. onion or 1 slice
   ginger root

Cook peppers, stirring constantly, in 2 T. hot oil. Drain. Add 2 more T. oil. Add onions or ginger and beef. Cook 2 minutes, stirring over high heat constantly. Return peppers and warm quickly. Serve immediately.

Mrs. William S. McDaniel

Editor's note: Any crisp green vegetable or combination of several can be used in this versatile stir-fry dish.

PEPPER STEAK

Do Ahead

Serves 6

2 sirloin steaks, ½" thick
   (approx. 1½ lbs. each)
Make following up twice -
   once for each steak

   ¼ c. flour
   ½ tsp. salt
   ¼ tsp. pepper

¼ c. Crisco
3 c. hot water
4 beef bouillon cubes
1 c. chopped onion
2 cloves garlic minced
1 (16 oz.) can whole tomatoes
1 can sliced mushrooms
2 lge. bell peppers
3 tsp. Worcestershire sauce

Cut steak into 2" thin strips. Place flour, salt and pepper in bag, add strips from one steak, shake to coat lightly. Repeat for second steak. Brown strips in Crisco. Dissolve bouillon cubes in hot water. Drain tomatoes. Add juice from tomatoes, garlic, onion, bouillon to steak strips - turn flame down to simmer and cook 1 hour. Stir occasionally to prevent sticking. Cut tomatoes (remove seeds) and bell pepper into strips. Add tomatoes, pepper strips, mushrooms and Worcestershire. Cook additional 15 minutes. Serve over rice.

Mrs. Carl H. Cartledge

BEEF STROGANOFF

Do Ahead   Serves 6

2 onions, chopped
3 T. butter
2 T. flour
1 c. stock or consomme
1 T. tomato paste or
  catsup
1 tsp. Worcestershire sauce
½ tsp. salt
⅛ tsp. pepper
1½ lbs. sirloin, cut in thin
  strips
½ lb. mushrooms
1 c. sour cream

Saute onions in butter until yellow. Stir in flour, then gradually add other liquids. Cook and stir until smooth and thickened. In hot frying pan, saute beef strips until brown. Add beef to sauce and salt and pepper. Saute mushrooms in frying pan, adding additional butter if needed. Add mushrooms to meat and sauce. Just before serving, add sour cream and heat. Do not let boil.
This dish is good to make the day before a dinner party. Always add sour cream just before re-heating.

Mrs. Lester L. Luttrell

Variation: For tomato paste and Worcestershire sauce, substitute ⅓ c. sauterne and 1 tsp. Dijon mustard.

Mrs. Louis C. Thacker

BEEF-N-BEER STEW

Do Ahead   Serves 5-6

2 lbs. stew beef or chuck,
  cut in 1" cubes
¼ c. shortening or bacon
  grease
1 tsp. salt
½ tsp. black pepper
½ tsp. marjoram leaves
¼ tsp. tarragon
½ tsp. basil
2 bay leaves
1 (10½ oz.) can beef consomme
1 (12 oz.) can or bottle of
  beer
4 carrots
4 potatoes
6 onions
¼ c. flour
¼ c. water

Brown meat in hot shortening. Add seasonings, beef consomme and beer. Cover and simmer approximately 1½ hours or until meat is almost tender. Cut peeled carrots into 1" pieces. Peel and quarter potatoes. Peel onions. Add vegetables to stew and continue cooking for about 40 minutes to 1 hour or until vegetables are tender. Salt to taste. Make a smooth paste by mixing together the flour and an equal amount of water; stir into stew and cook stirring until thickened.

Mrs. Lutie C. Johnston

ELEPHANT STEW

Do Ahead   Serves 3,800   465°
                                                4 weeks

1 elephant - medium size
2 rabbits, optional
salt and pepper to taste
brown gravy (lots)

Cut elephant into bite size pieces. This should take about 2 months. Reserve the trunk, you will need something to put the pieces in. Add enough brown gravy to cover. Cook on kerosene stove for about 4 weeks at 465°. This will serve 3,800 people. If more are expected, the 2 rabbits may be added. Do this only if necessary, as most people do not like to find "hare" in their stew.

STEW BEEF CASSEROLE

Easy   Serves 4-5   300°
Do Ahead   2 hrs.

1 lb. stew beef (bite size)
1 (10¾ oz.) can mushroom
   soup
1 envelope Lipton's dehydrated
   onion soup
1 (3-4½ oz.) can mushrooms
   and stems
½ c. burgundy wine

Place ingredients in casserole. Cook 2 hours in 300° oven. Cook covered with foil. Serve over rice.

Mrs. Grady Norton

GROUND BEEF DISHES

WESTERN BARBECUE BEANS

Easy   Serves 8   325°
Do Ahead   40-45 min.

1½ lb. ground beef
1½ tsp. salt
¼ tsp. pepper
1 clove minced garlic
3 T. cooking oil
¼ c. chopped onion
½ c. tomato juice
⅓ c. chili sauce
¼ c. sweet pickle, diced
3 drops Tabasco sauce
½ tsp. Worcestershire sauce
2 cans pork and beans
onion rings
catsup

Combine ground beef, salt, pepper and garlic. Saute in cooking oil in large skillet over medium heat until lightly browned. Add onion and brown for few minutes until onion is golden. Remove from heat and add remaining ingredients. Pour into bean pot and garnish with onion rings and catsup. Bake at 325° for 40-45 minutes.

Mrs. Tom Lockhart

CALICO BEANS

Easy†   Serves 6   350°
Do Ahead   35-40 min.

1 lb. ground beef
½ lb. bacon
1 c. onion (if you don't
    like a heavy onion taste,
    cut to ½ c.)
2 T. mustard
2 T. molasses
½ c. catsup
1 c. brown sugar
1 (16 oz.) can lima beans
1 (16 oz.) can kidney beans
1 (16 oz.) can pork and
    beans

Brown beef, brown bacon. Pour off excess grease, combine onions and brown. Add to meat mixture. Add mustard, molasses, catsup and sugar and mix well. Drain beans and add to above. Heat in 350° oven until bubbly.
A great winter supper, served in bowls with bread and salad.

Mrs. William S. Colvin

BEER BURGERS

Easy

2 lbs. ground beef
2 T. minced onion
½ can beer
2 T. Worcestershire sauce
½ c. catsup
½ tsp. salt
2 T. vinegar
dash pepper
2 drops Tabasco sauce
1½ T. sugar

Form ground beef into patties and brown. Combine remaining ingredients and simmer. Pour over patties, and serve on French bread slices.

Mrs. James F. Lewis
Savannah, Georgia

STUFFED CABBAGE ROLLS

Do Ahead†

350°
1 hr.

1 lge. head of cabbage
1½ lbs. ground beef
chopped onion
salt
pepper
2 c. cooked rice
1 lge. can or jar of
    sauerkraut
1 lge. can of tomatoes
    (whole or chopped)
1 med. size can tomato
    sauce
bacon
1 sliced onion

There are no exact proportions, adjust to your needs.

Place whole head of cabbage in boiling water until you can peel outer leaves off and they will roll without tearing. After taking off softened leaves, return cabbage to water.

Mix ground beef, onion, rice, salt and pepper. Place small amount of meat mixture in center of each cabbage leaf and roll, tucking in sides. Start rolling with thick end of cabbage leaf.

In a large roasting pan, spread sauerkraut and place cabbage rolls (seam down) on top. Pour tomato sauce and canned tomatoes over rolls. Lay strips of bacon and slices of onion on top. Cover and bake at 350° for 1 hour or until done.

Mrs. R. Lee Pfrogner

CHILI

Easy†
Do Ahead

Serves 15-20

5 lbs. finely ground chuck
2 qts. hot water
1½ tsp. cumin
8 oz. mustard
16 oz. catsup
1½ tsp. salt
5 T. chili powder
1½ tsp. garlic powder
1½ tsp. black pepper
1½ tsp. red pepper
3-4 (15 oz.) cans red
    kidney beans

Combine all ingredients in large pan.
Stir frequently. Simmer 3 - 4 hours.
Good as main dish with saltines or to
embellish hot dogs. For thicker chili,
use 1 - 1½ qts. water.

Mrs. Arthur K. Bolton

CHILI CON CARNE

Easy†
Do Ahead

Serves 6

2 T. salad oil
1 lb. ground beef
1 tsp. salt
2 T. chili powder
1 onion, chopped
1 (8 oz.) can tomato sauce
1 (15 oz.) can Stokely Van
    Camp's New Orleans (style)
    Red Kidney Beans, and
    all of liquid
2 T. apple cider vinegar

Brown beef and onions in salad oil.
Add remaining ingredients. Cover and
simmer 45 minutes.

Mrs. Flynt Langford

CHINESE BEEF

Easy   Serves 6   350°
Do Ahead   1 hr.

2 c. chopped onions
1 c. chopped celery
oil
1½ lbs. ground chuck
⅓ c. uncooked rice
1 (10¾ oz.) can mushroom
     soup
1 can water
¼ c. soy sauce
1 med. can mushrooms,
     chopped
1 tsp. pepper
1 can bean sprouts,
     drained
water chestnuts, drained

Brown onions and celery in small amount of oil. Set aside. Brown chuck and stir. Add onions and celery; mix in soup, mushrooms and pepper. Toss in bean spouts and chestnuts. Pour in casserole and cook ½ hour covered and ½ hour uncovered.

Mrs. O. R. Butler

BEEF AND BEAN ENCHILADAS

Do Ahead   Serves 6   350°
                                                        15 min.

1½ lbs. ground beef,
     crumbled
1 med. onion, chopped
1 (1 lb.) can refried beans
1 tsp. salt
⅛ tsp. garlic powder
⅓ c. taco sauce
1 c. quartered pitted ripe
     olives
2 (10 oz.) cans enchilada sauce
salad oil
12 corn tortillas
3 c. shredded Cheddar
     cheese (about 10 oz.)
sliced pitted ripe olives for
     garnish
sour cream
hot green chili sauce

In a frying pan saute ground beef and onions until meat is browned and onions are soft. Stir in beans, salt, garlic powder, taco sauce and olives; heat until bubbly. Heat enchilada sauce, pour about half into an ungreased shallow 3 qt. baking dish. Pour oil to a depth of about ¼" in a small frying pan. Heat. Dip tortillas, one at a time, in hot oil to soften; drain quickly. Place about ⅓ c. of ground beef filling on each tortilla and roll to enclose filling. Place, seam side down, in sauce in baking dish. Pour remaining enchilada sauce evenly over tortillas; cover with cheese. Bake, uncovered, at 350° for about 15 minutes or until thoroughly heated. Before baking, if preferred, the dish may be covered and refrigerated overnight.

Mrs. Newton Crouch

LASAGNE

Do Ahead†   Serves 8-10   350°
                            20-30 min.

2 lbs. ground beef
2 cloves garlic
2 (6 oz.) cans tomato paste
1 to 1½ (1 lb.) cans tomatoes
   (use juice so that sauce will
   spread easily but not be
   watery)
1 tsp. salt
generous dash pepper
1 tsp. oregano
6-8 long strips of wide
   Lasagne noodles
8 oz. sliced Swiss cheese
¾ lb. crumbled Mozzarella
   cheese
12 oz. carton cottage cheese
   mixed with 1 egg, beaten
Parmesan cheese

Lightly grease bottom of 3 qt. casserole. Brown beef and garlic; add tomato paste, tomatoes, salt, pepper, oregano; cover and simmer 20 minutes. Cook noodles according to package directions, drain and separate noodles. Build Lasagne layers by first spreading a very thin layer of sauce on bottom of dish then a layer of noodles, Swiss cheese, Mozzarella cheese, cottage cheese mixture. Repeat each layer. Cover finally with layer of sauce, then dust with Parmesan.
Lasagne is much better if prepared a day ahead. Do not cook before freezing. Lasagne cuts much better if allowed to stand 10 minutes after removing from oven.

Mrs. Allen W. Marshall III

MORE - MORE

Easy†   Serves 20   350°
Do Ahead   1 hr.

2 T. salt
4 to 6 qts. boiling water
1 lb. medium egg noodles
1 c. chopped onions
1½ c. chopped green
   pepper
2 T. chili powder
salt to taste
2 T. margarine
4 lbs. ground beef (chuck)
6 (8 oz.) cans tomato sauce
1 lb. can corn, drained
1 lb. Cheddar cheese,
   grated

Cook noodles in salted water. Drain. Saute onions until soft. Add meat. Cook until brown. Add green pepper, tomato sauce, corn, chili powder and salt. Combine with noodles and top with cheese in 2 - 3 qt. baking dishes.

Mrs. John R. Carlisle

KOENIGSBERGER KLOPS
(Meatballs in Wine Sauce)

Do Ahead   Serves 10-12

4 anchovy fillets
1½ c. chopped onion
2 T. melted margarine
2 tsp. salt, divided
½ c. evaporated milk
2 eggs, slightly beaten
¼ tsp. pepper
2 T. chopped parsley
1 lb. ground chuck
½ lb. ground veal
½ lb. ground pork
¾ c. uncooked quick-cooking
  oats
¾ c. sauterne or dry white
  wine
2¼ c. water, divided
1 bay leaf
4 whole cloves
4 whole peppercorns
3-4 T. flour
¼ c. water
1 lemon, thinly sliced
1 T. capers
hot cooked noodles

Soak anchovies in cold water 20 minutes; drain and chop. Saute onion in margarine until tender. Combine anchovies, onion, 1½ tsp. salt, evaporated milk, eggs, pepper, parsley, meat and oats; mix well and shape into 24 large meatballs. Combine sauterne, 2 c. water, bay leaf, cloves and peppercorns in a dutch oven. Bring to boil. Add meatballs; cover and simmer 25-30 minutes. Remove meatballs with slotted spoon, and strain cooking liquid. Return liquid to dutch oven and thicken with paste of flour and ¼ c. water, stirring constantly until smooth and thickened. Add lemon slices, capers, ½ tsp. salt and meatballs; stop here and refrigerate if preparing ahead. Cook 2 minutes. Serve over hot noodles.

Mrs. Eugene F. Robbins, Jr.

DUTCH MEAT LOAF

Easy†   Serves 6   400°
Do Ahead   1 hr.

1½ lbs. ground chuck
1 med. onion, chopped
½ c. bread crumbs
1 egg
½ can tomato sauce
salt and pepper to taste

Sauce:
  ½ can tomato sauce
  ½ c. water
  1 tsp. prepared mustard
  ¼ c. vinegar
  1 T. Worcestershire sauce
  cooked noodles

Mix ingredients together in a loaf shape. Pour sauce over the loaf. Bake at 400° for about 1 hour. Serve over a bed of noodles.

Mrs. T. M. Furlow, Jr.

ONION SOUP MEAT LOAF

Easy†
Do Ahead

Serves 6-8

350°
1½ hr.

2 lbs. lean ground beef
2 eggs, beaten
1½ c. torn bread (in very
   small pieces)
1 pkg. Lipton Onion Soup
   Mix
½ to ¾ c. catsup
½ c. chopped green
   pepper (optional)
1½ c. scalded milk

Mix all ingredients thoroughly. Mold into 9 x 5" loaf tin. Top loaf with more catsup if desired. Bake. Remove promptly from oven to keep moist taste.

Mrs. James H. Cobb III

MEXICALI MEAT PIE

Easy
Do Ahead

Serves 6

425°
30 min.

9" unbaked pie shell

1 egg
1 lb. lean ground beef
1 (7 oz.) can whole kernel
   corn with sweet peppers,
   drained
½ c. soda cracker crumbs
½ c. chili sauce
2 T. sweet pepper flakes
1 T. instant minced onion
½ tsp. oregano
4 stuffed green olives,
   sliced
6 slices crisp, crumbled
   bacon (or Baco's)

Beat egg slightly in mixing bowl. Add ground beef, corn, cracker crumbs, chili sauce, sweet pepper flakes, onion and oregano. Mix well. Press meat mixture firmly into pie crust. Bake at 425° for 20-25 minutes. Spread topping on filling. Top with olives and bacon. Bake additional 5 minutes until cheese melts. Let stand 10 minutes before serving.

Topping:
   1 egg slightly beaten
   2 T. milk
   ½ tsp. salt
   ½ tsp. dry mustard
   ½ tsp. Worcestershire sauce
   1 c. shredded Cheddar cheese

Combine egg and milk; add salt, dry mustard, Worcestershire and cheese.

Mrs. Jerry Hollberg

ONION-BEEF MACARONI CASSEROLE

Easy†   Serves 6   400°
Do Ahead   15 min.

1½ lbs. ground beef
1 envelope Lipton dehydrated
  onion soup mix
1 T. flour
1 (8 oz.) can tomato sauce
2 c. water
1 c. raw macaroni, cooked
¼ c. grated Cheddar cheese

Brown meat in large skillet; drain off excess fat. Stir in onion soup mix, flour, tomato sauce and water. Simmer, covered, for 5 minutes. Stir in macaroni. Turn into 1½ qt. casserole. Sprinkle with cheese. Bake 15 minutes at 400°.

Mrs. Herman Swint
Orchard Hill, Georgia

PICADILLO

Easy†   Serves 6
Do Ahead

1 T. margarine
1 med. onion, chopped
1 sweet pepper, chopped
1 clove garlic
1 lb. ground beef
1 (16 oz.) can tomato sauce
1 tsp. capers
½ c. raisins
1 small bottle stuffed
  olives

Fry onion, sweet pepper and garlic in a little fat slowly. When tender add ground beef and brown. Add tomato sauce, capers and raisins and let simmer slightly. Just before serving add stuffed olives. Serve on yellow rice.

Mrs. Walker Cook, Jr.

Editor's note: Very colorful and delicious. Would make a great volume dish for party.

CHILI SKILLET SUPPER

Easy   Serves 6
Do Ahead

1 lb. ground beef
1 (16 oz.) can kidney beans
1 (16 oz.) can whole kernel
  corn
1 c. regular rice
1 (16 oz.) can tomatoes
1 (1¾ oz.) pkg. dry chili mix

Brown ground beef in skillet. Pour off excess fat. Add the rest of the ingredients and simmer on low until rice is done - approximately 20-25 minutes. Add water when needed to keep from sticking.

Mrs. David G. Cummins

TOOTUM'S SPAGHETTI SAUCE

Easy†   Serves 6
Do Ahead

2 lge. onions, chopped
2 lbs. ground chuck
1 can tomato soup
1 (8 oz.) can tomato sauce
1 (6 oz.) can tomato paste
1 c. catsup
½ c. water
1 T. Worcestershire sauce
½ - 1 tsp. Tabasco sauce
1 T. Heinz 57 sauce
several garlic cloves

Cook onions in a little oil until
opaque. Add beef and brown. Add
remaining ingredients and cook for
4 to 6 hours.

Mrs. James Searcy

SPAGHETTI SAUCE

Do Ahead†   Serves 8

4 T. olive oil
3-6 cloves garlic, crushed
3 med. onions, chopped
2 med. green peppers,
    chopped
2 lbs. very lean ground round
¾ lb. pepperoni, chopped
1 qt. tomatoes
2 (6 oz.) cans tomato paste
2 c. beef stock, hot
1 T. oregano
1 T. basil
1 T. dry mustard
1 tsp. chili flakes or
    ½ tsp. chili powder

Saute garlic, onions and peppers in hot
olive oil until soft and light brown.
Add crumbled beef and pepperoni.
Cook until browned. Set aside; pour
off fat. Pour ingredients into 4 to 6
qt. pot.   Add tomato paste and
tomatoes. Rinse frying pan with hot
stock and add to pot. Add seasonings.
Stir and bring to boil. Cover and
simmer 6 to 8 hours, stirring occasionally. Uncover last hour.

Mrs. Don Segars

LAMB

ROAST LAMB

Do Ahead

Serves 12-14

350°
15-20 min.
per lb.

6-8 lb. leg of lamb, preferably
  boned and rolled
garlic slivers
salt and pepper
juice of 2 lemons
¼ c. melted butter

Insert slivers of garlic under skin, rub
roast with salt and pepper. Squeeze
the lemon juice over the roast. Drizzle
with butter. Roast in 400° oven for
15 minutes, reduce heat to 350° and
bake 15-20 minutes per pound, depending on degree of doneness desired.

potatoes cut in $\frac{1}{8}$ths
1 c. water

Add potatoes (cut lengthwise) and
water at the start of roasting; baste
with pan juices.

Mary Hazleton
Vienna, Virginia

ACCOMPANIMENT FOR ROAST OR LAMB

1 jar currant jelly
horseradish

Whip jelly with whisk, add horseradish
to taste.

BASTING SAUCE FOR LAMB

Easy
Do Ahead

3 T. olive oil
2 T. white wine or
  vermouth
½ tsp. finely chopped fresh
  thyme (dry may be
  substituted, but use
  ½ as much)
2 tsp. finely chopped mint
½ tsp. salt
freshly ground black pepper

Mix together. Use as a basting sauce
or increase amounts and use as a
marinade for lamb roast or chops.

Mrs. Robert Caswell

PORK

MAPLE-FLAVORED HAM

Easy
Do Ahead

325°
15 min.
per lb.

1 boneless, precooked baking
    ham (not canned) size depends
    on number being served
1 (18 oz.) bottle maple syrup

Have butcher slice entire ham and tie for baking. Place ham on enough foil to completely close, pour entire bottle of maple syrup over. Close foil and bake. Let ham cool in juices and reheat in closed foil before serving (if made the day before) or bake and serve.

Mrs. Warren K. Wells
Mrs. Taylor B. Manley, Jr.

HAM AND SPINACH GRATINE

Do Ahead   Serves 4-5   350°
                                                         20 min.

2 c. croutons (I use Brownberry
    Seasoned)
¼ c. melted butter (no
    substitute)
1 (10 oz.) pkg. frozen,
    chopped spinach
⅓ c. sour cream
1 tsp. onion flakes
1 tsp. Worcestershire sauce
8 thin slices cooked ham
1 c. cream of chicken soup
1 c. mayonnaise
2 T. lemon juice
sauteed mushrooms
    (4 oz. canned or ½ lb.
    fresh)

Mix croutons with melted butter and spread on bottom of flat casserole. Cook, drain spinach and mix with sour cream, onion flakes and Worcestershire. Spoon portion on ham slice, roll and place seam down on croutons. Continue to fill remaining ham slices and arrange. Combine soup, mayonnaise and lemon juice and pour over ham-rollups. Garnish with sauteed mushrooms. Bake at 350° for 20 minutes or until bubbly.

Mrs. Douglas A. Finnegan
Annapolis, Maryland

GLAZED HAM-RAISIN BALLS

Do Ahead†   Serves 5-6   350°
                                                           50 min.

½ lb. ground ham
½ lb. ground fresh pork
1 c. Raisin Bran Flakes cereal
1 (6 oz.) can evaporated milk
  (⅔c.)
1 egg
1 T. finely chopped onion
dash salt
dash pepper
dash dried thyme, crushed

Combine all ingredients and mix thoroughly. Shape into 8 to 10 meatballs, using about ¼ c. meat mixture for each ball. Place in an 11 x 7 x 1½" baking pan. Bake uncovered, in a moderate oven 350° for 30 minutes. (Mixture will be very sticky and wet.)

Glaze:
  ¼ c. brown sugar
  ¼ c. corn syrup
  1 T. vinegar
  ½ tsp. dry mustard

In a small saucepan, combine brown sugar, corn syrup, vinegar and dry mustard; bring to boiling. Pour over ham balls and bake 20 minutes more, basting with the sauce once or twice during baking.

Mrs. R. Lee Pfrogner

TAHITIAN HAM ROLL

Serves 8   325°
                            1 hr. 30 min.

1 lb. ground smoked ham
1 lb. ground fresh pork
⅔c. coarse cracker crumbs
  (saltine type)
½ c. chopped onion
½ c. milk
1 slightly beaten egg
1 T. parsley
  (fresh or dried)
dash pepper
8 slices pineapple (save
  juice for glaze)

Combine first 8 ingredients and shape into 9 patties the size of the pineapple slices. In a 13 x 9" pan line up a row of alternating patties and pineapple, starting and ending with a ham pattie. Bake uncovered 30 minutes. Combine brown sugar, pineapple juice, vinegar and mustard. Pour over ham patties and pineapple and continue baking 1 hour longer, basting every 20 minutes.

Mrs. R. Lee Pfrogner

Glaze:
  1 c. brown sugar
  ¼ c. pineapple juice
  2 T. vinegar
  1 tsp. mustard

BAKED PORK CHOPS

Easy   Serves 8   350°
Do Ahead   1½ hrs.

8 - 1" thick pork chops
1 c. catsup
½ c. brown sugar
2 onions
2 lemons

Place 1" thick pork chops in a shallow baking dish. On top of each put the following: 2 T. catsup, 1 T. brown sugar, 1 slice of onion, and 1 slice of lemon. Cook 45 minutes covered and then cook 45 minutes uncovered. If not sufficiently brown when done, run under broiler.

Mrs. Donald L. Hutcheson

ROAST PORK

Easy   325°
Do Ahead   25 min.
                                              per lb.

pork roast (approximately
    4-7 lbs.)
garlic powder
cumin powder
salt
1 c. red wine vinegar
½ c. water

Lightly rub outside of the roast with seasonings. Place in oven bag. Add wine vinegar and water. Bake at 325° allowing 25 minutes per pound. Remove. Slice. Heat liquid for gravy.

Mrs. Roberto Oviedo

PORK PICNIC ROLLS

Do Ahead†   Serves 4   350°
                                                         25 min.

1 (1 lb.) loaf - frozen bread
   dough
salad oil
1 onion, thinly sliced
melted margarine
1 lb. boneless pork (butt
   or shoulder cut in ½"
   cubes)
1 garlic clove, minced
   or mashed
¼ tsp. caraway seed
1 T. soy sauce
1 T. honey
⅓ c. dried apricots
3 oz. diced cream cheese
2 T. lemon juice
salt
pepper

Take bread dough from package, brush lightly with salad oil, cover, let thaw at room temperature until pliable - as per package directions. Fry onion in 1 T. margarine until limp. Remove onions, add pork, stir in garlic, caraway seed, soy sauce and honey. Cook, stirring over medium high heat until pork is well browned - about 10 minutes. Stir in apricots, cream cheese, onion and lemon juice. Season with salt and pepper. Divide dough into 10 equal portions on a floured board. Roll each portion into 4" x 6" oval. Put ¼ c. filling across the length of the oval to within about ½" of each end. Pull long ends together over filling, push to seal, fold up remaining ends, pinch to seal. Place rolls seam side down on greased sheet. Brush with melted margarine. Bake at 350° for 25 minutes. Serve warm, cooled, or reheated. To reheat frozen buns, place uncovered on a sheet and bake at 350° for 15 minutes.

Mrs. H. Alfred Bolton III

SAUSAGE CASSEROLE

                             Serves 6   400°
                                                         20-25 min.

1 lb. sausage
1 med. onion
1 (No. 2) can corn
1 chopped green pepper
chili peppers to taste
1 c. cornmeal
2 tsp. baking powder
¼ tsp. salt
1 egg
½ c. milk
⅛ c. oil
1 c. grated Cheddar cheese

Saute sausage, onions, corn, pepper and chili peppers until sausage is done. Pour off grease. Place meat mixture in 8 x 8" greased baking dish. Mix corn bread recipe (next 6 ingredients). Pour over meat. Bake. Just before done, sprinkle cheese over top.

Mrs. Joe Hollingsworth
Bowling Green, Kentucky

SAUSAGE MACARONI CASSEROLE

| Easy | Serves 5-6 | 425°-375° |
| Do Ahead | | 60-75 min. |

1 onion, chopped
1 bell pepper, chopped
2 cloves garlic, minced
1 lb. bulk sausage
1 c. bow-shaped macaroni,
  uncooked
3 fresh tomatoes, chopped or
  1 (16 oz.) can tomatoes,
  drained and chopped
1½ c. buttermilk
4 oz. Neufchatel cheese
  (or cream cheese)
4 oz. shredded Monterey Jack
  or mild Cheddar cheese
  (a generous cup)

Saute onion, green pepper and garlic with sausage until the sausage is browned. Pour off fat. Mix with the macaroni, tomatoes, and buttermilk. Pour into greased shallow 2½ qt. baking dish. Dot with Neufchatel, sprinkle with shredded cheese, cover and refrigerate until needed. When ready to bake, set in cold oven set at 425° for 20 minutes. Reduce heat to 375° and bake 55 minutes, or until macaroni tests tender with a fork. If baking at once, use a temperature of 375° for 1 hour.

Mrs. H. Ray Simonton

"TIP"

Sprinkle salt in frying pan before frying meat to prevent fat from splashing.

SAUSAGE AND RICE CASSEROLE

| Easy† | Serves 6 | 350° |
| Do Ahead | | 1½ hrs. |

1 lb. bulk sausage
1 c. onion, chopped
1 clove garlic, chopped
1 c. celery, chopped
1 green pepper, chopped
1 c. rice, uncooked
1 can cream of mushroom
  soup
2 cans cream of chicken
  soup

Brown sausage in frying pan and pour off grease. Add chopped onion, garlic, celery and green pepper to sausage and simmer until tender. Wash rice and add to mixture in Pyrex baking dish along with the soups. Bake 1½ hours at 350°, stirring occasionally.

Malvina M. Beal

TUCKERMAN SPECIAL

Do Ahead†   Serves 5-6   350°
                                                          1½-1¾ hrs.

1 c. dry lima beans
1 lb. bulk sausage meat
¾ c. onion, finely chopped
¼ c. pepper, finely chopped
    (may be omitted)
2 T. molasses
1 T. brown sugar
2 tsp. salt
¼ tsp. pepper
1 can tomato soup, do not
    dilute
¼ tsp. dry mustard
½ c. sharp cheese, grated

Soak lima beans overnight; then boil until semi-done. Brown sausage, remove from pan and brown onion and pepper in remaining fat. Combine all ingredients except cheese. Bake 1 hour at 350°. Top with cheese, add more tomato soup if desired, and bake 30-45 minutes longer. The flavor improves on standing, so I often make it one day and bake 1 hour and complete it the next day or after taking it from the freezer.

Mrs. Lloyd W. Hazleton
Vienna, Virginia

SCRAPPLE

Do Ahead†

3 to 4 lb. fatty pork roast
1 sm. onion, chopped
3 to 4 stalks celery,
    greens too
salt and pepper to taste
dash Worcestershire sauce
2 beef bouillon cubes
cornmeal
dash monosodium glutamate

Cover pork roast with water and add onion, celery, salt and pepper and bouillon cubes. Simmer for 3 to 4 hours until meat falls off bone. Remove meat and cool - save water. After trimming excess fat from meat, grind up meat to medium texture. Remove celery stalks from water and bring to a boil. Add ground meat and monosodium glutamate and enough cornmeal to thicken the mixture to the consistency of thick paste, Pour mixture into loaf pans and chill. When firm remove from pans and slice about ½" thick. Wrap in waxed paper in individual slices and store in the refrigerator for a few days, or can be frozen for 2 months. When ready to serve scrapple, fry in grease for breakfast and serve with eggs. Should be browned on both sides, but not fried hard.

Mrs. Richard Barnes
Plattsburg, Missouri

MAGGIE'S BARBECUED RIBS

Easy

Do Ahead

Serves 6

300°

2½-3 hrs.

3 lbs. country style spare
  ribs
3 T. Worcestershire sauce
2 T. vinegar
½ c. catsup
1 tsp. salt
1 tsp. black pepper
1 tsp. Tabasco sauce

Rinse ribs with warm water. Pat
dry with paper towel. Sprinkle with
salt and pepper. Place ribs in shallow
baking pan. Pour Worcestershire sauce,
vinegar, catsup and Tabasco sauce
evenly over ribs. Cover with tin foil
and bake approximately 2½ hours.
Remove foil and brown.

Mrs. Clayton Brown, Jr.

SWEET AND SOUR SPARE RIBS

Easy

Do Ahead

Serves 4

450°-350°

2¼ hrs.

3 to 4 lbs. spare ribs, cut
  in pieces

Sauce:
  3 T. vinegar
  ½ c. orange juice
  ½ c. brown sugar
  1 T. cornstarch
  1 T. water
  1 tsp. salt

Salt ribs; place in shallow roasting
pan and roast at 450° oven about
45 minutes. Drain excess fat from
pan. Make basting sweet and sour
sauce and pour over ribs. Reduce
oven to 350° and bake another 1½
hours. Baste frequently.

Mrs. Jack L. Austin

VEAL

VEAL AND ARTICHOKES

Serves 8

2 cloves garlic
oil (olive oil, if
  preferred)
2 lbs. veal round (have
  butcher flatten to ¼")
flour seasoned with salt
  and pepper
1 (1 lb.) can tomatoes
½ c. sherry or sauterne
¼ tsp. oregano
2 (10 oz.) pkgs. frozen
  artichoke hearts

In a heavy skillet, saute garlic in oil.
Dust veal with flour; brown in oil.
Add tomatoes, wine, oregano; mix
well.   Add frozen artichoke hearts.
Cover.   Simmer 45 minutes to 1
hour or until meat is tender. Serve
with or over rice.

Mrs. Warren K. Wells

VEAL SCALLOPINE

Serves 6

1½ lbs. veal cutlet, sliced
  thin
⅓ c. flour
1 tsp. salt
¼ tsp. pepper
⅓ c. oil
1 med. onion, chopped
2 T. chopped green pepper
1 (10¾ oz.) can condensed
  tomato soup
½ c. water
½ c. grated cheese

Roll veal slices in flour, salt and
pepper.   Heat oil in large skillet.
Fry onion and green pepper until
tender. Remove. Add veal, brown
on both sides. Pour off excess oil.
Add soup mixed with water. Return
onion and green pepper. Cover,
simmer 10 minutes or until meat
is tender. Sprinkle with cheese. Heat
until melted.

Mrs. Thomas W. Fetzer

WIENER SCHNITZEL
(Breaded Veal Cutlets)

Serves 6

2 lbs. veal (cut in
   6 slices)
flour
2 eggs, well beaten
1 c. bread crumbs
1 c. cooking oil
   (Crisco will be fine)
lemon wedges or slices
salt and pepper

Trim all fat, pound each slice as thin as possible. Salt and pepper to taste. Dredge veal first in flour, then in egg (you may use a little milk to stretch it), then bread crumbs, press on crumbs firmly, shake off excess. Fry in oil, deep enough to cover well 2-5 minutes each side or until golden brown.   Drain.   Serve with lemon slices or wedges on hot platter.

Mrs. James D. Goodwin
Baton Rouge, Louisiana

MEAT SAUCES

BARBECUE SAUCE

Do Ahead

¼ c. vinegar
½ c. water
2 T. brown sugar
1 T. prepared mustard
1½ tsp. salt
½ tsp. black pepper
juice of 1 lemon
1 lge. onion, sliced
¼ c. butter
½ c. catsup
2 T. Worcestershire sauce

Mix together first nine ingredients, adding ¼ tsp. cayenne pepper, if you like a hotter sauce. Bring to a boil and simmer 20 minutes. Strain. Discard onion. Add catsup and Worcestershire sauce. Good on chicken and pork. If barbecuing chicken on outside grill, baste with melted butter until last 10-15 minutes, then baste with barbecue sauce.

Mrs. H. Ray Simonton

H. P.'S BAR-B-Q SAUCE

Do Ahead   Yield: 2½ gallons

1 gal. cider vinegar
1 c. red pepper
2 c. chili powder
2 c. sugar
3 (46 oz.) cans tomato juice
1 pt. Wesson Oil
juice of 6 lemons

Mix all ingredients. Boil slowly for 2 hours uncovered. Makes approximately 2½ gal. Store in jars sealed tightly. The sauce will keep 1 year easily. Store jars in cool area.
This is Tennessee Bar-B-Q at its finest.

Mrs. Richard L. Mullins

MARINADE FOR BEEF TIPS

Easy

6 oz. unsweetened pineapple
   juice
½ c. soy sauce
½ c. water
1 tsp. ground ginger
1 tsp. pepper - regular
   or Lawry's seasoned
garlic - 1 clove put through
   press or ½ tsp. garlic
   powder

Mix all ingredients. Pour over beef tips and marinate 4 to 5 hours - turn meat several times.

Mrs. Charles L. Smith

MUSHROOM SAUCE FOR BEEF

†

Brown sauce:
   1½ T. butter
   1½ T. flour
   1 can consomme plus
      enough water to make
      2 c.

Melt butter, blend in flour. Cook over low heat until browned. Stir in brown stock (consomme plus water to make 2 c.). Bring to a boil and cook 3 to 5 minutes. Reduce heat and simmer 30 minutes stirring occasionally.

½ - ¾ lb. fresh mushrooms,
   cleaned and sliced
4 T. butter
½ tsp. salt
dash ground pepper
1 onion, finely chopped
⅓ c. Madeira or dry
   sherry
1 c. brown sauce
1 tsp. chopped parsley

Brown mushroom slices in butter. Add salt and pepper and cook until mushrooms are golden brown. Add onion, wine and brown sauce. Bring to a boil. Reduce heat and cook for 5-6 minutes. Add parsley
Also delicious served over filet mignon.

Mrs. Lutie C. Johnston

SAUCES FOR MEAT FONDUE

CUCUMBER DIP

Do Ahead

Serves 4-6

1 - 8 oz. and 1 - 3 oz. pkg.
   cream cheese
1 sm. onion, chopped fine
   or grated
1 sm. or half a regular
   cucumber - remove seeds
   and chop fine or grate
1 T. Worcestershire sauce
   (use less for milder flavor)
1 T. mayonnaise
1-2 tsp. vinegar
good shake of celery salt

Let cheese get to room temperature. Add ingredients and mix very well. Flavor best at room temperature - needs to be soft to dip.

Mrs. Fred Omundson

MUSTARD SAUCE

Do Ahead   Yield: 1⅓ cups

1 T. cornstarch
2 tsp. sugar
1 tsp. dry mustard
½ tsp. salt
1 c. water
1 tsp. butter
¼ c. vinegar
2 tsp. horseradish
2 beaten egg yolks

In top of double boiler, mix together cornstarch, sugar, mustard and salt. Add water and stir over direct low heat until mixture thickens and boils 1 minute. Remove from heat and mix in butter, vinegar and horseradish. Add egg yolks. Cook and stir over boiling water until sauce thickens slightly.

Mrs. Thomas W. Fetzer

SOUR CREAM SAUCE

Easy   Serves 4-6
Do Ahead

1 c. sour cream
1 tsp. prepared salad mustard
1 tsp. horseradish

Mix together well. Can add more mustard or horseradish if "hotter" dip is desired.

Mrs. Fred Omundson

GAME

BAKED DOVE IN SAUCE

Easy
      350°
      30-45 min.

dove (I use only the
   dove breast)
celery salt, pepper
butter
1 can cream of mushroom
   soup
½ c. cooking sherry
parsley

Season birds with celery salt and pepper. Brown in a little butter. Make sauce with cream of mushroom soup and sherry; add parsley. Place in baking dish and pour sauce over birds. Bake at 350° for ½ hour or until tender, basting frequently. *A delicious, moist recipe for this game bird.*

Mrs. Douglas Hollberg

DOVE I

2 hours

dove
salt and pepper
flour
Per Dove:
   1 T. A-1 sauce
   1 T. Worcestershire
     sauce
   1 tsp. lemon juice

Salt and pepper cleaned dove. Flour well. Sear in deep fat. Put into roasting pan or casserole with lid. Pour off excess grease. Rinse frying pan to get dregs. Pour this water over dove. Have at least ½" water in pan. Cook 1 hour. Add 1 T. A-1, 1 T. Worcestershire sauce and 1 tsp. lemon juice per dove. Cook 1 additional hour. Serve with wild rice. Use gravy that the birds were cooked in.

Mrs. Charlie T. Phillips

DOVE II

Serves 3-4
      450° - 325-350°
      Brown - 1 hr.

6 to 8 dove
salt and pepper
¼ c. margarine, melted
1½ c. water
½ c. sherry
flour and water to make
   paste
canned mushrooms
   (if desired)

Salt and pepper dove. Arrange in baking dish. Pour melted margarine over them. Brown in 450° oven. Add water and bake at 325° - 350° until tender, 1 hour or more. Last ½ hour add sherry and mushrooms with juice. Baste occasionally. Remove birds and add paste of flour and water to thicken the drippings. Reheat the birds in the gravy.

Mrs. E. Herben Turner

DOVE OR QUAIL

Serves 4   350°
                           1 hr. 20 min.

6 quail or 8 dove
½ c. butter
salt and pepper
1 c. water
1 c. whipping cream
1 c. sherry

Salt and pepper birds. Brown in melted butter in heavy dutch oven. Pour water over birds. Cover and bake in 350° oven for 1 hour and 10 minutes. Add whipping cream and sherry and return to oven for 10-15 minutes.

Mrs. Dick Slade

QUAIL BAKED WITH HONEY

Do Ahead   Serves 4   350°
                                     45 min.

salt
⅓ c. butter, melted
8 quail
⅓ c. flour
1 onion, finely chopped
rosemary
8 tsp. honey
1 (10¾ oz.) can chicken
   broth

Salt quail lightly and roll in flour, then brown lightly in melted butter. Remove to a casserole and cook the onion in butter until done but not brown. Sprinkle rosemary over each quail, pour a tsp. of honey over each one - then put the onions on top. Pour the can of undiluted chicken broth around quail. Cover and bake at 350° for ¾ hour. Baste occasionally.

Mrs. Jack L. Austin

MOUNT VERNON QUAIL

Do Ahead   Serves 4   250°
                                                     2-3 hrs.

8 quail, cleaned (or 2 per person)
flour, salt, pepper
½ c. margarine
½ - 1 c. water
Worcestershire sauce

Roll quail in seasoned flour; brown in skillet. Place on rack in pan. Add water for steam. Dash with Worcestershire sauce. Cover with foil and place in oven at 250° for 1 to 2 hours, until tender. Make gravy from drippings and serve with game over wild rice.

Mrs. James K. Duffes
Mrs. E. Herben Turner

Variation: Omit Worcestershire sauce and add burgundy wine to taste just before serving.

Mrs. Joe G. Hunter
Opelika, Alabama

WILD DUCK WITH CURRANT SAUCE

Do Ahead   Serves 4   350°
                                                     2 hrs.

4 wild ducks
¼ c. salt
¼ c. vinegar
water to cover

Mix vinegar, salt, water and let ducks soak overnight. Drain. Place each duck in individual foil to cover.

8 orange sections
1 med. onion, (quartered)
4 strips bacon
8 T. Grand Marnier
4 T. fresh lemon juice

Stuff each duck with orange sections and 1 onion quarter. Lay strip of bacon on top. Pour 2 T. Grand Marnier and 1 T. lemon juice over each. Salt and pepper to taste. Cook 30 minutes with foil open. Cook 1½ hours with foil closed.

2 T. red currant jelly
1 c. cream

Drain juice from duck into pan. Add jelly and cream and heat (do not boil). Thicken if necessary.

Mrs. Warren K. Wells

ROASTED WILD DUCK

Serves 3-4   450° - 325-350°
                                Brown - 3 hrs.

3 or 4 ducks
salt and pepper to taste
onion
celery
¼ c. margarine, melted
1½ c. water
½ c. sherry
flour and water to
    make paste

Salt and pepper picked, dressed ducks. Place piece of onion and celery in each cavity. Arrange ducks in roasting pan. Pour melted margarine over them. Bake in 450° oven until slightly brown. Pour water over ducks; cover. Reduce heat to 325° or 350° and bake until fork tender, about 3 hours. Add water as needed. Last ½ hour add sherry. Remove duck from pan. Thicken gravy with paste of flour and water. Reheat duck in the gravy.

Mrs. E. Herben Turner

WILD DUCK OR GOOSE

Do Ahead†   350°
                                3 hrs.

wild duck or goose
water
2 tsp. vinegar
salt
apple
orange
potato, peeled
onion
salt and pepper
bacon
red or rose wine
water

Soak game overnight in water, vinegar and salt. Wash game; dry. Salt and pepper cavity, stuff with apple, orange, potato and onion. Lay a strip of bacon on each. Cover with ¾ wine and ¼ water. Cover and bake. When done, take out stuffing and carve. Make gravy with some of the juices and flour. Can freeze cooked whole game in juices.

Mrs. Andy Austin

ROAST GOOSE AND APPLE-PRUNE STUFFING

Serves 6-8   400°-325°
                               15 min.-4 hrs.

8-10 lb. goose
2 lb. red cooking apples,
   pared, cored and cubed
2 c. dried prunes, cooked,
   cooled, pitted and halved
white wine
coarse salt
pepper
½ lemon
thyme
butter
currant jelly

Thaw goose if frozen. Soak apples and prunes in white wine for several hours. Remove fat from cavity. Remove neck and giblets. Rinse goose in cold water, wipe dry. Rub neck and body cavities with salt and freshly ground black pepper. Rub outside of body with the cut lemon, sprinkle with salt, pepper and thyme. Heat the oven to 400°. Stuff the goose with the apples and prunes, then truss. Lay the goose breast up on a rack in roasting pan and place in the oven for 15 minutes or until fat begins to run. Prick fatty parts of the goose with a fork to help draw out remaining fat and reduce oven temperature to 325°. Baste occasionally with a little white wine, butter and dried thyme. Spoon off fat as it gathers in the pan. An 8 lb. goose will take 4 hours to roast. Test by moving drumstick up and down - it should move freely. Make gravy from pan drippings; stir currant jelly into the gravy.

Mrs. H. Alfred Bolton III

ARCHER'S SURPRISE (VENISON)

Do Ahead   Serves 4   350°
2½-3 hrs.

¼ c. flour
¾ tsp. salt
¹⁄₁₆ tsp. red pepper
dash of thyme
dash of cloves
dash of nutmeg
16 to 18 ribs of venison
2 T. oil
3 large onions, thinly sliced
2 c. of fresh tomatoes,
    quartered
1½ T. Worcestershire sauce
4 drops of Tabasco sauce
1½ c. burgundy
½ small clove of garlic
salt and pepper to taste
1 sm. can mushrooms

Dredge meat in flour and seasonings. Heat oil - brown ribs and onion. Add tomatoes, Worcestershire sauce, Tabasco sauce, burgundy and garlic. Cover pot tightly and cook 2½ hours at 350°. Add salt and pepper to taste. Stir in mushrooms.

Mrs. T. W. Gary

206

Notes

POULTRY

CHICKEN AND ARTICHOKES

Do Ahead   Serves 16-18   375°
                                                            40 min.

10 lbs. chicken breasts
salt and pepper
butter
2 lbs. fresh mushrooms
4 pkgs. frozen artichokes
1 c. dry sherry
1 c. Parmesan cheese
paprika

Bone chicken and cut in large chunks. Season with salt and pepper and fry in butter until brown and tender; remove from pan. Slice mushrooms and saute in butter. Partially cook artichokes and drain. Place layers of chicken, mushrooms and artichokes in casserole. Pour sherry over all. Make cream sauce and pour over. Sprinkle with Parmesan cheese and paprika. Bake in 375° oven 40 minutes.

Cream Sauce:
   12 T. butter
   12 T. flour
   1 T. Worcestershire
      sauce
   salt and pepper to
      taste
   6 c. half and half

Cream Sauce: Melt butter and mix flour stirring until smooth. Add Worcestershire and salt and pepper to taste. Pour in half and half and cook, stirring until smooth.

Mrs. William C. Hewitt

CHEESY CHICKEN

Easy   Serves 4   350°
                                                            1 hr.

6 chicken breast halves
mayonnaise
Parmesan cheese

Place chicken in pan. Spread top with mayonnaise. Cover with Parmesan cheese. Bake.

Mrs. John R. Carlisle

CHICKEN CORDON BLEU

Do Ahead†   Serves 8   400°
                                                        40 min.

8 chicken breasts, boned
  and skinned
8 thin slices of ham in
  strips
8 strips of Swiss cheese
½ c. butter
1 c. bread crumbs
1 tsp. salt
1 tsp. pepper
1 tsp. paprika

Wash and dry chicken breasts. Put on waxed paper and place another layer of waxed paper on top, and roll with rolling pin to flatten the breasts. Place one slice of ham and one slice of cheese in middle of each chicken breast. Roll up and secure with toothpicks. Make bread crumbs out of thin Pepperidge Farm white bread. Put on cookie sheet and let melba in oven at 250° until crisp. Then put between foil, or waxed paper, and roll into crumbs. Season the crumbs with salt, pepper and paprika. Melt butter in pan and then roll chicken in butter then in crumbs. Put in buttered baking dish and store in refrigerator overnight. Bake uncovered at 400° for 40 minutes.

Mrs. C. Whitten Walter
Birmingham, Alabama

Variation: Substitute 8 triangles (1 oz. each) process Gruyere cheese, sliced for Swiss cheese.

Mrs. Thomas W. Fetzer

CHICKEN DIVAN

Do Ahead†   Serves 6   350°
                                                                    20 min.

2 (10 oz.) pkgs. frozen
   broccoli
¼ c. margarine or butter
¼ c. flour
1 c. chicken broth
½ c. heavy cream
3 T. sherry
½ tsp. salt
1 c. grated sharp cheese
3 chicken breasts, cooked
   and sliced thin
sliced peaches

Cook broccoli until tender. Drain.
Arrange crosswise in 13 x 9 x 2" (3 qt.)
baking dish. Melt butter, add flour,
broth and cream. Cook until thick.
Stir in cheese and sherry and salt.
Pour half of the sauce on broccoli.
Arrange chicken slices on top of
broccoli. Then pour on the remaining
sauce. Bake 20 minutes at 350° or
until hot. Then broil just until sauce
browns. Trim with sliced peaches.
Can be made a day ahead of time and
refrigerated until ready to use.

Mrs. Olin Hunter

CHICKEN DISH DINNER

Easy   Serves 4   350°
                                                                    1 hr.

4 onions, sliced
6 deboned chicken breasts
4 potatoes, sliced
1 pkg. broccoli, frozen or
   fresh
2 c. Cream Sauce:
   4 T. butter
   4 T. flour
   salt and pepper
   2 c. half and half
½ lb. sharp cheese, grated

In square baking dish, layer chicken,
onions and potatoes. Make cream
sauce with cheese and pour over.
Bake 45 minutes, add broccoli around
edge. Sprinkle with cheese and bake
15 minutes more.

Mrs. J. Taylor Wynne

ELEGANT CHICKEN

Easy   Serves 6-8   275°
Do Ahead   3 hrs.

4 whole boned chicken
   breasts
8 slices bacon
4 oz. chipped beef
1 (10¾ oz.) can cream of
   mushroom soup
½ pt. sour cream (1 c.)
almond slivers

Halve chicken breasts and wrap each
half in a slice of bacon. Cover the
bottom of a greased 8 x 12" baking
dish with chipped beef. Arrange
chicken on top of this. Blend soup
and sour cream, and pour over chicken
breasts. Sprinkle with almond slivers.
Refrigerate at this point, if desired.
Bake uncovered at 275° for 3 hours.
*The gravy is good over rice. If this is
too salty, scald the beef with boiling
water, drain well and line the dish.*

Mrs. Eugene F. Robbins, Jr.
Mrs. Louis C. Thacker

JADE CHICKEN

Do Ahead   Serves 4

2 whole chicken breasts, boned
   and skinned
2 tsp. cornstarch
2 T. dry sherry
1 T. soy sauce
½ c. water
2 T. corn oil
1 tsp. salt
½ tsp. monosodium glutamate
¼ c. chopped scallions
2 c. fresh broccoli, cut in
   1" pieces

Cut each chicken breast half in 10 to
12 crosswise strips. Dissolve cornstarch in sherry and soy sauce in small
bowl; add water. Heat oil in large
skillet over high heat. Add chicken,
sprinkle with salt and monosodium
glutamate, stir over high heat until
white - about 3 minutes. Add cornstarch mixture, scallions and broccoli.
Cook over high heat, stirring
constantly, for 3 minutes or until
chicken is tender, broccoli is crisp-
tender and sauce is thickened.
*The preparation of this dish can be
done several hours in advance leaving
only the short cooking time until the
last minute. The broccoli can be
left out and the chicken served over
rice.*

Mrs. James Whitmire

CHICKEN JUBILEE

†   Serves 8   325°
                                           1 hr. 45 min.

8 fryer breasts
2 tsp. salt
¼ tsp. pepper
½ c. melted margarine
1 c. water
½ c. brown sugar
½ c. raisins
1 tsp. garlic salt
1 med. onion,
   sliced
12 oz. bottle chili sauce
1 c. sherry
16 oz. can bing cherries,
   pitted and drained

Place chicken in roasting pan, skin
side up. Season with salt and pepper.
Drizzle with melted margarine and
brown in broiler. Combine remaining
ingredients except wine and cherries.
Mix thoroughly. Pour over chicken.
Cover with foil. Bake 1¼-1½ hours
at 325°. Remove foil. Add sherry
and cherries. Continue baking 15
minutes longer.

Mrs. Walter E. Jones

OVEN-FRIED LEMON CHICKEN

Easy†   Serves 6   400°
                                                                   1 hr.

¼ c. butter
flour
salt, pepper, paprika
3 chicken breasts, split and
  deboned
2 T. chopped onions
¼ c. salad oil
¼ tsp. garlic powder
½ c. lemon juice
salt and pepper
½ tsp. thyme

Melt butter in shallow pan in oven. Flour chicken; turn in butter. Place skin side down in pan. Sprinkle with salt, pepper and paprika. Bake at 400° for 30 minutes. Turn, combine remaining ingredients with ½ tsp salt, and pepper to taste. Pour over chicken. Bake 30 minutes longer.

Mrs. Joe Joiner
Thomaston, Georgia

Mrs. Charlie T. Phillips

FILETTI DI POLLO PARMIGIANA
(Chicken Parmesan)

Serves 6   350°
                                   40 min.

3 whole chicken breasts, split,
  skinned and boned
2 eggs slightly beaten
1 tsp. salt
⅛ tsp. pepper
¾ c. Italian flavored bread
  crumbs
½ c. olive oil
2 c. tomato sauce
¼ tsp. basil
⅛ tsp. garlic powder
1 T. butter or margarine
½ c. grated Parmesan cheese
8 oz. Mozzarella cheese, sliced
  and cut into triangles

Pound chicken breasts until about ¼" thick. Combine eggs, salt and pepper. Dip chicken into egg mixture, then crumbs. Heat oil until very hot in large skillet. Quickly brown chicken on both sides. Remove to shallow 2 qt. baking dish. Pour excess oil from skillet. Stir tomato sauce, basil, and garlic powder into skillet; heat to boiling. Simmer 10 minutes or until thickened. Stir in butter. Pour over chicken; sprinkle with Parmesan cheese. Cover. Bake for 30 minutes. Place Mozzarella over chicken. Bake 10 minutes longer.

Mrs. Lutie C. Johnston

PICNIC CHICKEN

Do Ahead   Serves 3

3 double chicken breasts
    (about ½ lb. each) boned,
    skinned and split
1 T. butter
1 (4 oz.) can mushroom stems
    and pieces, well drained
2 T. chopped chives
1 T. sherry or lemon juice
1 egg slightly beaten with
    1 T. water
⅓ c. all-purpose flour
salad oil for frying

Pound chicken breasts to ½" thickness.
Set aside.   Melt butter in a skillet.
Add mushrooms and chives.   Cook
over medium heat for 1 minute. Add
sherry and continue to cook until
moisture evaporates, cool slightly.
Sprinkle each chicken breast with salt
and pepper.   Spread them with the
mushroom mixture.   Roll up breasts
and secure with skewers or strings.
Dip in egg then flour.   Heat salad oil
in a large skillet with light fitting
cover.   Brown chicken in hot oil -
turning to brown all sides.   Cover
and cook slowly for 20-25 minutes
or until tender, turning occasionally.
Drain on paper towels. Remove strings.
Serve hot or chill in refrigerator.

Mrs. William L. Wages

POULET A DEUX

Serves 8   375°
                            30 min.

8 halves boned chicken
    breasts
salt and pepper
1 lb. (approx.) pre-cooked
    ham, sliced thin
½ c. Parmesan cheese
1 (15 oz.) can tomato
    sauce
2 tsp. sugar
½ tsp. salt
½ tsp. Tabasco sauce
½ tsp. garlic powder
1 (6 oz.) pkg. sliced Mozzarella
    cheese

Pound   chicken   breasts to   flatten.
Sprinkle with salt and pepper; cover
with slices of ham.   Place 1 T.
Parmesan cheese in center of each.
Roll and secure with toothpicks;
arrange in baking dish.   Combine
tomato sauce, sugar, salt, Tabasco and
garlic powder; pour over chicken.
Cover and bake at 375° for 30
minutes.   Remove toothpicks, place
slice of Mozzarella cheese over each
roll.   Return to oven until cheese
melts.   Garnish with pimiento and
parsley.

Mrs. Marshall R. Sims

TARRAGON CHICKEN

Serves 6   Broil
                             350°
                             10-30 min.

1 lemon
6 med. chicken breasts
salt and pepper
1 T. Beau Monde seasoning,
   if desired
2 T. butter plus
   ½ c. butter
1 tsp. dried tarragon

Halve the lemon and rub each piece of chicken with rind. Season with salt, pepper and Beau Monde seasoning. Place chicken in shallow pan, skin side down; dot with 2 T. butter. Brown lightly under broiler - 5 minutes to side. In a saucepan, melt stick of butter with tarragon. Simmer for 10 minutes and pour over chicken. Turn oven to 350° and cook another 30 minutes.

Mrs. Thomas W. Fetzer

WAIKIKI BEACH CHICKEN

Serves 4   350°
                             1 hr.

2 whole chicken breasts
2 whole chicken legs
½ c. flour
⅓ c. salad oil or
   shortening
1 tsp. salt
½ tsp. pepper
1 (1 lb. 4 oz.) can sliced
   pineapple
water
1 c. sugar
2 T. cornstarch
¾ c. cider vinegar
1 T. soy sauce
¼ tsp. ginger
1 chicken bouillon cube
1 lge. green pepper,
   sliced

Wash chicken, pat dry, dredge in flour. Heat oil in large skillet. Add chicken; brown. Remove as browned to shallow roasting pan, skin side up. Sprinkle with salt and pepper. Preheat oven to 350°. Make sauce: Drain pineapple, saving liquid. Add water to pineapple liquid to make 1¼ c. In medium saucepan combine sugar, cornstarch, pineapple syrup, vinegar, soy sauce, ginger and bouillon cube. Bring to a boil for 2 minutes and pour over chicken. Bake uncovered for 30 minutes. Add pineapple slices and green pepper and bake 30 more minutes or until done. Serve over rice.

Mrs. Frank Jolly

APRICOT CHICKEN CASSEROLE

Easy   Serves 4-6   350°
Do Ahead   1 hr.

1 whole chicken or parts   Skin chicken and place in a Pyrex
  if preferred   dish. Pour the mixture of dressing,
1 (8 oz.) bottle French   soup, preserves, and sherry over the
  dressing   chicken and let stand until ready to
1 jar apricot preserves   cook. Bake 60 minutes at 350°.
  (at least 10 oz.)   Serve over rice or thin noodles.
1 pkg. Lipton Onion Soup
¼ c. sherry   Mrs. James R. Fortune

BARBECUED CHICKEN

Do Ahead†   Serves 8   350°
                                                                      1 hr.

Sauce:
  2 T. flour   Mix flour and sugar. Add remaining
  2 T. sugar   sauce ingredients. Sprinkle pieces of
  2 sm. cans tomato sauce   chicken with paprika. Heat shortening
  ¼ c. chopped onion   (not butter) and brown chicken. Pour
  ½ bell pepper, chopped   off excess shortening. Season chicken
  ½ c. melted butter   with salt. Pour sauce over chicken
  ¾ c. catsup   and cook 20 minutes in pressure
  2 T. vinegar   cooker or bake in covered roaster in
  2 tsp. Worcestershire 350° oven about 1 hour.
    sauce
  1 T. water   Mrs. Malcolm Hemphill
  ⅛ tsp. red pepper
  ¼ tsp. black pepper
  1 tsp. salt

8 chicken breasts
paprika
shortening
salt

BARBECUED CHICKEN VERMOUTH

Serves 4

2 or 3 garlic cloves
½ tsp. curry powder
2 tsp. salt
1 T. salad oil
2 T. dry vermouth

2 broilers (no more than
  5 lbs.)

Mix:
  ¼ c. melted butter
  ¼ c. dry vermouth

mayonnaise

Crush garlic cloves through a press, combine with curry powder, salt, salad oil and vermouth. Brush chickens well with marinade. Let stand in the refrigerator overnight. Broil chicken on grill - brushing while they broil with the butter and vermouth mixture. Blend any remaining marinade (or make another recipe) with enough mayonnaise to make a creamy sauce. Serve over the chicken.

Mrs. H. Alfred Bolton III

CHICKEN CACCIATORE

Do Ahead†

Serves 6

2½ lb. chicken, cut up, or
  5-6 chicken breasts
¼ c. flour
¼ c. oil
1 med. onion, coarsely
  chopped
1 med. green pepper,
  chopped
1 clove garlic, minced
1¼ tsp. salt
⅛ tsp. pepper
2 bay leaves
1 (16 oz.) can tomatoes
1 (8 oz.) can tomato sauce
¼ c. dry white wine
2 T. parsley, chopped

Coat chicken with flour - preheat electric frying pan to 340° (or heat regular frying pan on top of stove). Heat oil, add chicken and cook until lightly brown, turning as needed. Remove chicken. Add onion, green pepper and garlic; cook 3 minutes. Add chicken, seasonings, tomatoes, tomato sauce, and wine. Cover, reduce to simmer and cook 1 hour or until tender. Turn occasionally as cooking. Add parsley and serve. Can be served over or with spaghetti.

Mrs. Donald A. Chiofolo
Rock Hill, South Carolina

Mrs. John Umstead
Chapel Hill, North Carolina

CHICKEN SCAMPI

Do Ahead†   Serves 6

2½ lb. fryer, cut in pieces
   or 3 lb. chicken breasts
¼ c. butter
3 sm. onions, chopped
2 cloves garlic
½ tsp. pepper
1 T. salt
3 T. parsley
1 tsp. basil
1 (8 oz.) can tomato sauce
½ c. Port wine
1½ lb. shrimp, shelled
   and cleaned

Brown chicken pieces in melted butter. Remove chicken. In remaining drippings, saute onions and garlic. Add chicken and all other ingredients except wine and shrimp; simmer 1 hour. Add wine and shrimp; continue cooking 5 minutes. Serve over rice. *Delightfully easy and as elegant as desired.*

Mrs. Mark Kapiloff

COUNTRY CAPTAIN SUPREME

†   Serves 6   325°
                                          1 hr.

1 frying chicken, cut up
salt and pepper
salad oil
flour
1 green bell pepper,
   chopped
1 med. onion, chopped
2 (No. 2) cans tomatoes
1 tsp. salt
½ tsp. white pepper
1 tsp. curry powder
1 tsp. thyme
1 tsp. parsley
¼ lb. blanched almonds
1 T. black currants or
   raisins

Salt and pepper chicken and roll in flour. Fry in salad oil until golden. Remove from fat. In same fat, brown onion and pepper. Add tomatoes and cook 10 minutes. Add seasonings, almonds and currants. Cook 5 minutes longer. Place chicken in deep casserole, pour sauce over it. Cover and bake 325° for 45 minutes. Serve on platter lined with steamed rice. Sprinkle a few more currants on top.

Mrs. H. Coleman Jackson, Jr.

CHINESE CHICKEN CASHEW CASSEROLE

Do Ahead†   Serves 4-6   350°
                                                                   20 min.

2 c. diced cooked chicken
   breasts
1 c. chopped celery
¼ c. chopped onion
1 T. margarine
1 can cream of chicken
   soup

1 T. soy sauce
½ c. cashew nuts
1 sm. can Chinese noodles

Simmer ingredients a few minutes,
then pour into a casserole and cover
with Chinese noodles, soy sauce, and
cashew nuts. Bake 20 minutes at 350°.
Serve on rice.   Add a few crisp
noodles on top.

Mrs. Robert C. Patterson
Decatur, Georgia

CLUB CHICKEN CASSEROLE

Do Ahead†   Serves 8-10   350°
                                                                   30 min.

4 T. butter
4 T. flour
1 c. chicken broth
1 (14 oz.) can evaporated
   milk
½ c. water
1 tsp. salt
3 c. cooked rice
   (or egg noodles)
1½ - 2 c. diced cooked
   chicken
1 (3 oz.) can mushrooms
¼ c. chopped pimiento
⅓ c. chopped green pepper
½ c. blanched almonds
   (optional)

Melt butter.   Add flour and blend.
Add broth, milk and water.   Cook
over low heat until thick.   Stir
constantly. Add salt to taste. Alternate
layers of rice, chicken, vegetables and
sauce in a greased casserole.   Pour
remaining sauce over; sprinkle almonds
on top.   Bake in moderate oven (350°)
30 minutes.

Mrs. William Woodward

*Variation: Add 1 T. onion juice and
8 oz. Old English Cheese to white
sauce.   Top   with   toasted bread
crumbs   and   paprika.*

Mrs. Robert W. Brandon

EAST INDIAN CURRY

Do Ahead†   Serves 4-6

½ c. margarine
1 lge. onion, chopped
1 clove garlic, chopped
sprig of parsley
1 stalk celery, diced
½ bay leaf
¼ tsp. dry mustard
1 tart apple, peeled and
   diced
2 T. flour
½ tsp. mace
2 tsp. curry powder
2½ c. chicken broth
2 c. cooked chicken
   (or lamb)

Cook together for 8 minutes, stirring often: margarine, onion, garlic, celery, bay leaf, parsley, mustard and apple. Add flour, mace and curry powder and cook 4 minutes longer. Add broth and simmer 1 hour. Add meat and serve over rice with condiments. Curry condiments: chutney, grated coconut, chopped almonds, raisins, grated egg white, grated egg yolk, crumbled bacon, chopped onion, etc. *Sauce without meat can be made and frozen, then leftover chicken or lamb added for a gourmet treat.*

Mrs. John J. Flynt, Jr.

CHICKEN ENCHILADAS

Do Ahead†   Serves 8
                                               250°
                                             45 min.

3 tsp. butter
1 med. onion, chopped
1 sm. can green chilies
¾ c. chicken broth
1 can cream of mushroom
   soup
1 can cream of chicken
   soup
1 (5 oz.) can evaporated milk
1 chopped cooked chicken
12 tortillas
½ lb. Cheddar cheese, grated

Brown onion and chilies in butter. Add next 5 ingredients. Simmer about 10 minutes. Line the casserole with 6 tortillas, add layer of sauce and layer of grated Cheddar cheese. Repeat. Bake 45 minutes at 250°. Can be made the day before you bake it or freeze until needed.

Mrs. Louis C. Thacker

FRENCH CHICKEN

Do Ahead†   Serves 14

6 lbs. chicken breasts or
  5-6 lb. hen
2 c. onion, chopped
2 c. green pepper,
  chopped
2 bunches of celery
1 garlic clove, chopped
  fine
1 lb. wide noodles
1 (6 oz.) can pitted ripe
  olives, drained
2 (4 oz.) cans mushrooms,
  drained
2 cans tomato soup
1 small bottle
  Worcestershire sauce
1 c. fresh parsley, chopped

Cover chicken with water, seasoned well, and cook until chicken falls off bone. Cut in bite size pieces and save broth (about 8 c.). Cook onions, pepper, celery and garlic in half of broth until tender. Cook noodles in rest of broth adding water if necessary. Do not overcook. Drain. Add noodles to mixture above and add olives, mushrooms and tomato soup. Add Worcestershire sauce and parsley. Freeze at this point in casserole dishes or heat thoroughly, to serve at once. If frozen, thaw and heat in 300°-325° oven until bubbly. Serves 14 generously.

Mrs. Robert Smalley

CHICKEN MEXICAINE

Serves 6   350°
                            30-40 min.

5 lbs. boiled chicken
flour
salt, paprika
½ c. butter
1 lge. onion, grated
1 clove garlic, grated
1 green pepper, chopped
1 c. tomatoes, strained
1 lb. sauteed mushrooms
parsley

Remove meat from the bones in large pieces. Dredge with flour mixed with salt and paprika. Brown in hot butter and place in casserole. Simmer onion, garlic and green pepper in the same butter until tender. Mix with tomatoes and sauteed mushrooms. Season and pour over chicken. Cover and bake at 350° for 30-40 minutes. When ready to serve, sprinkle with minced parsley.

Mrs. Newton Crouch

HOT CHICKEN SALAD

Serves 8-10   350°
                               30 min.

2 c. diced cooked chicken
1 can cream of chicken
  soup
1 T. onion juice
1 tsp. salt
1 c. celery, diced
1 c. slivered toasted
  almonds
1 c. mayonnaise
4 hard cooked eggs,
  diced
potato chips

Mix first 8 ingredients and pour into casserole. Top with crushed potato chips. Bake 30 minutes at 350°.

Mrs. Dick Slade

Variation: Add 1 T. Worcestershire sauce and substitute 2 T. grated onion for the onion juice.

Mrs. E. Herben Turner

Variation: Add 1 T. lemon juice and ½ tsp. monosodium glutamate and substitute 2 tsp. grated onion for the onion juice.

Mrs. William Valdon Smith

HOT CHICKEN SOUFFLE

Do Ahead†   Serves 8   325°
                                                   1 hr.

6 slices white bread
2 c. diced cooked chicken
½ c. chopped onion
½ c. chopped green pepper
¼ c. chopped pimiento
½ c. chopped celery
½ c. mayonnaise
¾ tsp. salt
dash pepper
2 beaten eggs
1½ c. milk
1 can condensed cream of
  mushroom soup
½ c. shredded sharp cheese

Cube two slices bread, place in bottom of 8 x 8 x 2" square baking dish. Combine chicken, vegetables, mayonnaise and seasonings and spoon over cubed bread. Trim crust from remaining four slices and arrange on top of chicken mixture. Combine eggs and milk, pour over all. Cover and chill 1 hour or overnight in refrigerator. When ready to bake, spoon soup on top and cook in slow oven (325°) for 1 hour or until set and lightly browned. Sprinkle cheese over top last few minutes of baking. This will serve eight. May be cut in squares or served from dish for buffet.

Mrs. Bruce M. Morgan

PUFFED CHICKEN BAKE

Easy   Serves 8   350°
Do Ahead   50 min.
†(omitting egg mixture
until baking time)

1 pkg. frozen French style
   green beans or 1 can
1 box chicken flavored Stove
   Top Stuffing Mix
1 (10½ oz.) can cream of
   mushroom soup
⅓ c. water
4 eggs, separated
1½ c. cooked chicken, cut
   into large cubes (or more
   to taste)
1 (4 oz.) can French fried
   onions

If using frozen green beans, prepare according to directions. Prepare stuffing mix according to directions, adding ½ c. more water. Heat mushroom soup with ⅓ c. water. Beat egg yolks until light. Beat egg whites until stiff. Fold egg whites into yolks. Place green beans in 2 qt. baking dish. Cover beans with chicken. Pour soup over top of this mixture. Use a fork to push down in several places to be sure soup gets to the beans. Spread dressing mix on top of this. Spoon egg mixture over top and bake at 350° for 45 minutes. Top with French fried onions, bake 5 minutes longer. Serve hot.

Mrs. F. Ted Wilder, Jr.

Editor's note: This is really an entire meal in one dish and a popular one with all ages. It adapts well to quantity cooking. We've prepared it for the sixty members of the Senior Citizens' Club which the Utility Club sponsors and it was a big success.

CHICKEN TETRAZZINI

Do Ahead†   Serves 10-12   350°
                                                            1 hr.

large hen: stuff cavity of hen with celery ribs and quartered onions. Cover with water and cook until tender. Add salt, 2 whole bay leaves and 4 whole allspice to water. Cool hen, remove bones, discard skin. Chop hen in bite size pieces. Reserve stock.

½ c. butter
⅛ tsp. garlic powder
½ tsp. salt
¼ tsp. cumin powder
¼ tsp. black pepper
½ c. onions, minced
3 stalks of celery, chopped
   fine
1 lb. fresh mushrooms,
   sliced
½ c. green pepper, chopped
½ c. flour
2 c. half and half
1½ c. chicken stock
1 chicken bouillon cube
1 (4 oz.) jar pimientos,
   chopped
10 large ripe olives, sliced
1 (8 oz.) pkg. spaghetti
   (vermicelli) broken into
   2" pieces and cooked
3½ c. cubed chicken
½ c. sherry
grated Parmesan cheese

Heat butter in large heavy frying pan. Add garlic, salt, cumin, pepper and cook until blended. Saute onion, celery, mushrooms and green pepper. Blend flour, half and half, and chicken stock and pour slowly into frying pan mixture, stirring carefully. Add bouillon cube and cook to slight boil. Remove from heat. In a large casserole combine pimientos, olives, cooked spaghetti and cooked chicken. Pour entire frying pan mixture over this; add sherry and mix well. (At this point you may refrigerate or freeze.) When ready to bake, sprinkle generously with cheese and bake for 1 hour. I usually freeze this recipe in small casseroles to serve 2 or 4.

Mrs. Arthur K. Bolton

CHICKEN LIVERS

CHICKEN LIVER RAGOUT

Easy†
Do Ahead

Serves 4

1 lb. chicken livers
4 T. butter or margarine
2 T. chopped onion
2 beef bouillon cubes,
  dissolved in 2 c. hot
  water
3 T. flour
1 (4 oz.) can drained
  mushroom pieces
2 T. sherry
salt and pepper

Saute livers in 2 T. butter. Remove and cut into bite sized pieces. Saute onion in remaining 2 T. butter. Add livers and bouillon to saucepan. Add flour (stirred into a little cold water to keep from lumping). Add mushrooms and sherry and simmer, stirring, for about 15 minutes over low heat. Serve over rice or toast points.

Mrs. John J. Flynt, Jr.

CHICKEN LIVER SAUTE

Easy

Serves 6

½ c. butter or margarine
½ c. frozen or fresh chopped
  onion
¼ tsp. garlic powder
1½ lbs. chicken livers
2 (4 oz.) cans sliced mushrooms,
  drained
¼ tsp. Tabasco sauce
¼ tsp. dried basil
1 T. flour
½ c. beer

Melt butter in skillet; add onions and cook over moderate heat until tender. Add garlic powder, chicken livers, mushrooms, Tabasco, and basil; cook until chicken livers are lightly browned. Stir in flour. Gradually add beer; cook and stir until sauce is thickened. Serve over hot rice.

Mrs. Don Segars

Editor's note: Sherry can be substituted for beer if desired.

CREAMY CHICKEN LIVERS

Serves 4

8 oz. chicken livers, cut
  in large pieces
2 T. butter or margarine
1 (6 oz.) can sliced mushrooms,
  drained or 1 pt. fresh
  mushrooms, sliced
¼ c. chopped green onion
½ c. sour cream
1½ tsp. soy sauce
1½ tsp. chili sauce
pepper
dill
parsley

Cook livers in butter in a covered skillet until almost tender, about 10 minutes. Add mushrooms and onion and cook until onion and liver are tender. Combine sour cream, soy sauce, chili sauce, pepper and dill (to taste) and add to liver mixture. Heat and stir just until sauce is hot; don't boil. Serve over toast points; dust with parsley.

Mrs. Allen J. Brock
Atlanta, Georgia

CORNISH HENS

CORNISH HENS ON ITALIAN RICE

Easy
Do Ahead

Serves 4

350°
1 hr. 30 min.

1 c. long grain rice
1 envelope Italian Salad
  dressing mix
2½ c. boiling water
1 can cream of chicken
  soup
2 Cornish hens
seasonings to taste

Brown rice by spreading in a 3 qt. shallow baking dish and bake at 375° for 15 minutes. Remove from oven. Combine salad dressing mix with boiling water and the chicken soup. Stir into rice. Cut hens in half lengthwise. Season. Put hens cut side down on top of rice mixture. Cover tightly with foil. Bake 1 hour covered - uncover and bake 30 minutes more.

Mrs. Robert W. Brandon

STUFFED CORNISH HENS

Serves 6   350°
                                                1 hr. 15 min.

6 Cornish hens
salt
pepper
6 oz. pkg. Uncle Ben's Wild
  Rice
onion slices
orange rind
¼ c. melted butter

Sauce:
  6 oz. jar currant jelly
  2 T. lemon juice
  ½ tsp. mustard
  1½ T. cooking wine

Thaw hens, wash and rub with salt and pepper. Cook rice according to package instructions, adding orange rind and onion slices. Tie legs together after stuffing with rice. Brush with melted butter. Bake. (Cover with foil if browning too quickly at last). Baste with sauce before serving. Serve sauce with hens at the table.

Mrs. Ashley P. Hurt

CORNISH HENS WITH PORT SAUCE

Serves 6   400°
                                                35-45 min.

6 Cornish hens
½ lb. sausage
livers of hens (chopped)
2 T. butter
1 c. toasted bread
  crumbs
1 T. chopped parsley
pinch thyme and freshly
  ground black pepper
6 slices bacon
½ c. chicken stock
½ c. Port
1 tsp. flour
1 tsp. butter
½ c. hot heavy cream

Saute sausage, drain fat, add next 6 ingredients. Stuff birds. Sprinkle with salt and pepper, cover breasts with bacon. Place in roasting pan, add stock and port, bake - basting several times with pan juices. Discard bacon. Remove birds. Skim excess fat from pan juices. Mix flour and butter, add to juices, stir in cream. Pour sauce over birds to serve.

Mrs. Warren K. Wells

Editor's note: Delicious too using 1 c. Pepperidge Farm Herb Stuffing in place of bread crumbs.

TURKEY

TURKEY HAWAIIAN

Do Ahead†   Serves 6-8

1 lge. onion, chopped
2 T. salad oil
1 pkg. frozen green peas
1½ c. sliced celery
2 envelopes instant chicken
   broth
¾ c. water
2 T. cornstarch
1 T. soy sauce
1 (14 oz.) can pineapple
   tidbits
1 (4 oz.) can sliced mushrooms
1 can water chestnuts
½ c. whole almonds
3 c. cooked turkey,
   chopped

Saute onion in salad oil. Stir in frozen peas, celery, broth and water. Cover, heat to boiling; simmer 5 minutes. Blend cornstarch in soy sauce in 2 c. measure. Drain and stir in syrup from pineapple and liquid from mushrooms. Stir into vegetable mixture. Cook, stirring often, until sauce thickens and boils 3 minutes. Stir in pineapple, mushrooms, water chestnuts, almonds and turkey. Cover; heat slowly until hot. Serve over hot rice.

Mrs. Don Segars

TURKEY ON GRILL

Do Ahead   Grill
                                     3-4 hr.

10 - 12 lb. turkey
2 chicken bouillon cubes
2 c. water, boiling
1 c. white wine
salt
rosemary
oil
disposable foil pan

Wash and dry turkey. Rub cavity with salt and small amount crushed rosemary. With ice pick punch 6 or 8 holes in bottom of pan. (Be sure pan will fit on your grill.) Place turkey on pan and brush lightly with oil. Cook turkey on preheated gas grill at low setting with lid closed. Dissolve bouillon cubes in 2 c. water. Add wine. Baste turkey with mixture about every 20 minutes. Cook 3-4 hours or until done.

Mrs. Douglas J. Brown

Notes

SEAFOOD

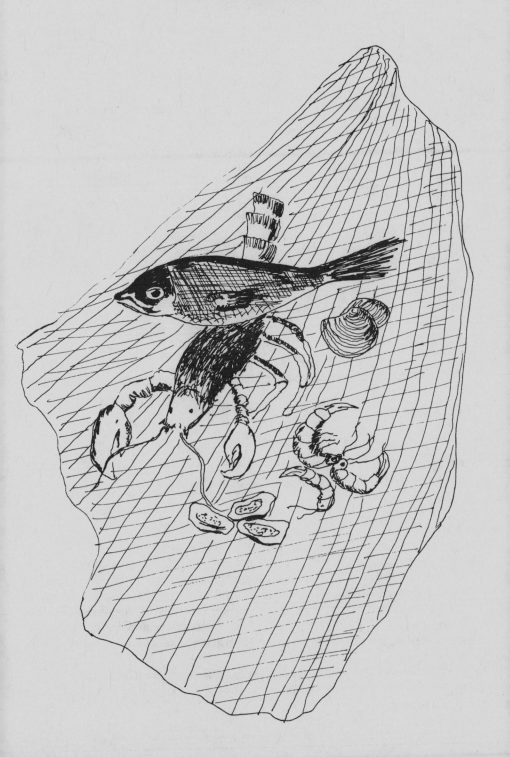

CRAB CASSEROLE

Do Ahead   Serves 6-8   350°
                                                         15-20 min.

5 T. butter
3 T. flour
2 c. milk
½ tsp. celery salt
2 T. minced onion
1 T. grated orange rind
1 T. minced parsley
1 T. minced green pepper,
    optional
1 pimiento, minced
2 T. sherry
1 egg, beaten
dash of hot sauce
1 tsp. black pepper
1 lb. fresh crabmeat
bread crumbs
1 T. butter

Make white sauce of butter, flour
and milk. Add next 6 ingredients
and remove from heat. Add sherry.
Add a little hot sauce to egg, then add
egg to rest of sauce. Add hot sauce,
salt, pepper and crab. Put into 1½ qt.
casserole. Sprinkle top with bread
crumbs mixed with 1 T. melted butter.
Bake.

Mrs. Franklin P. Lindsey, Jr.

DEVILED CRAB

Easy   Serves 6   350°
Do Ahead   25-30 min.

1 (6½ oz.) can claw crabmeat,
    drained
1 c. finely grated Waverly
    cracker crumbs
1 c. mayonnaise
3 hard boiled eggs,
    minced
¼ c. grated onion
¾ tsp. salt
¼ tsp. garlic powder
butter

Empty crabmeat into bowl. Sort
through to find any shell pieces.
Combine ingredients, saving about ⅓
cracker crumbs to sprinkle over top.
Dot with butter and bake. This may
be put in one casserole or 6 shells.

Mrs. Charles L. Smith

MARYLAND CRABCAKES

Easy†   350°
Do Ahead

1 lb. crabmeat - Chesapeake   Mix together lightly. Shape into
   Bay   cakes. Fry at 350° until pale golden
1 c. bread crumbs   brown.
2 eggs
2 T. mustard   Mrs. Russell Duncan
2 T. melted butter or   Huntington, Maryland
   margarine
pinch red pepper
salt and pepper
parsley flakes

CRAB SANDWICHES

Easy   Serves 6   325°
Do Ahead   1 hr.

12 slices thin sliced, trimmed,   Place 6 slices bread, buttered side up,
   buttered bread   in a buttered dish. Spread crabmeat
1 (7½ oz.) can crabmeat   and cover sandwich fashion with
½ lb. Cheddar cheese, grated   remaining bread slices. Put cheese
4 eggs, beaten   on top. Mix eggs with milk and
3 c. milk   seasoning and pour over all. Let
½ tsp. curry powder   stand in refrigerator overnight. Bake
½ tsp. salt   until puffy and brown, about 1 hour.

                                     Mrs. Ralph King
                                     Columbus, Georgia

CRAB SUPREME

Do Ahead   Serves 6   325°
                                                   1½ hrs.

1 lb. fresh crabmeat   Combine all ingredients except bread
2 c. cooked rice   crumbs in casserole. Sprinkle with
1 c. sliced mushrooms   buttered crumbs. Bake at 300-325°
⅔ c. mayonnaise   for 1½ hours.
½ c. milk
1 c. tomato juice   Mrs. William S. Colvin
1 grated bell pepper
1 grated onion
2 tsp. chili powder
salt and pepper
buttered bread crumbs

POACHED FISH IN THE DISHWASHER

Put washed fish into a large roasting-cooking bag. Add one to two cups dry white wine and seasoning to taste. Tie the open end of the bag securely.

Put the fish in the bag on the top rack of the dishwasher. Don't put soap in the dishwasher! Close the door and start the wash cycle. For a 1-3 lb. fish, one wash, rinse, and dry cycle is enough. For 3-8 lb. fish use 2 wash, rinse, and dry cycles.
Great conversation piece at the dinner table!

Editor's note: Try it, it really works.

Mrs. William S. Conner

STUFFED FISH A LA DIXIE

Serves 2-3   350°
1 hr. 15 min.

2-3 lb. flounder, trout, red
fish or bass
½ c. chopped celery
¼ c. green pepper, chopped
¼ c. onion, chopped
2 T. margarine
¼ c. mayonnaise
1 T. snipped parsley
dash cayenne
2 T. melted margarine
salt and pepper
1½ c. Pepperidge Farm Herb
Stuffing, prepared as directed
on package

Lay fish side down in the middle of a large piece of foil placed in a baking dish sufficiently large to hold fish. Cut a pocket to the bone in the upper side of the fish about 1" up from midline ½" from the gill section to ½" of the tail, then enlarge this pocket by cutting toward the backbone up the rib cage.* Salt and pepper fish slightly. Saute the celery, onion and green pepper in 2 T. margarine until transparent. Add the prepared stuffing, snipped parsley, mayonnaise and cayenne. Mix well and use to stuff pocket. Seal the fish in the foil and bake 350° for 50 minutes. Break the foil and pull it back. Brush the fish with 2 T. melted margarine and bake 20-25 minutes longer. Remove to serving dish and garnish with parsley. Serve immediately. For a special touch, shrimp, crabmeat or both may be mixed with the stuffing and white wine may be substituted for water in preparing the stuffing.
*Fold in the natural cavity. Do not stuff cavity, only pocket.

Mrs. Randolph Gilbert

PARTY SALMON STEAKS

Easy   Serves 4   400°
Do Ahead   15 min.

4 fresh salmon steaks
   (1" thick)
2 lemons
seasoning salt
8 T. mayonnaise
nutmeg
1 c. sliced fresh mushrooms
   (uncooked)
4 T. Parmesan cheese

Place steaks in greased oblong pan (not touching). Squeeze juice of ½ lemon over each steak and sprinkle generously with seasoning salt. Spread 2 T. mayonnaise over each, lightly sprinkle with nutmeg, top with mushrooms and 1 T. Parmesan cheese on each. Bake.

Mrs. Warren K. Wells

BAKED SHAD

Do Ahead   250°
                                   4-5 hrs.

1 4-5 lb. shad
lemon juice
butter
bacon strips
salt and pepper

First remove the roe (which is broiled in lemon butter in the oven). Score the fish, salt and pepper. Squeeze ½ lemon juice over fish. Place bacon strips over the scores. Place on a roaster rack for 30 minutes in 450° oven. Add small amount of water (which must not touch fish). Cover and bake at 250° for 4 or 5 hours. Brush with butter and more lemon juice before serving.

Mrs. J. Lamar Wells
Mt. Vernon, Georgia

SPICY OYSTERS

Easy   Serves 4   Broil
                                   3 to 5 min.

1 qt. select oysters
juice of 1 lemon
¼ tsp. oregano
¼ tsp. basil
¼ tsp. thyme
¼ tsp. pepper
2 c. bread crumbs (fine)
¼ c. butter

Drain oysters and pat dry. Place in single layer in buttered 2 qt. shallow casserole dish. Sprinkle with lemon juice. Mix 4 spices together and put over oysters. Put crumbs on, then top with melted butter. Broil for 3 to 5 minutes. Serve at once.

Mrs. W. J. Kendrick

ARTICHOKE-SHRIMP CASSEROLE

Do Ahead   Serves 4   375°
                                                        20 min.

1 (No. 2) can artichoke hearts
¾ lb. med. sized cooked shrimp
   (or 1 lb. fresh)
¼ lb. fresh mushrooms
4 T. butter
4 T. flour
1½ c. milk
1 T. Worcestershire sauce
¼ c. dry sherry
salt and pepper
¼ c. grated Parmesan cheese
paprika
chopped parsley

Drain artichokes and arrange in a buttered, flat baking dish. Spread the cooked shrimp over artichokes. Saute sliced mushrooms in 2 T. butter for 6 minutes; add to baking dish. Make a cream sauce of 2 T. butter, flour and milk. Add Worcestershire, sherry, salt and pepper to the cream sauce. Pour over contents of baking dish. Sprinkle the top with Parmesan; dust with paprika. Bake. Dust dish with chopped parsley just before serving.

Mrs. Eugene F. Robbins, Jr.

BARBECUED SHRIMP

                            Serves 6

2 lbs. lge. shrimp in shell
1 c. salad oil
1 c. lemon juice
2 tsp. Italian salad dressing
   mix
2 tsp. seasoned salt
2 tsp. seasoned pepper
4 T. brown sugar
2 T. soy sauce
½ c. chopped green onions

Wash shrimp and drain on paper towel. Mix oil, lemon juice, dressing mix, salt and pepper. Stir and mix in shrimp. Marinate in refrigerator 2-4 hours, stirring occasionally. Cook shrimp over grill (about 6" from coals) for 10 minutes on each side or until pink. Pour marinade in a pan and add brown sugar, soy sauce and onion. Boil for several minutes. Pour into individual serving cups. Peel shrimp and dunk in sauce.
Hint: If shrimp are small, put a piece of wire mesh over grill.

James H. Cobb III

SHRIMP CASSEROLE

Serves 6   325°
45 min.-1 hr.

3 lbs. shrimp (cleaned)
1 box Uncle Ben's Wild Rice
   with Herbs
4 T. chopped green peppers
4 T. chopped onions
4 slices bacon cooked and
   crumbled
4 T. bacon drippings
2 cans cream of mushroom
   soup
4 T. lemon juice
1 c. sharp cheese, cubed
1 tsp. Tabasco sauce
1 T. Worcestershire sauce
1 c. chopped celery
1 can French onion rings
salt and pepper to taste

Saute onions and peppers in bacon drippings. Add mushroom soup and cheese. Cook over low heat until all cheese is melted. Add bacon, lemon juice, celery, Tabasco, Worcestershire sauce and salt and pepper. Cook rice very dry. Mix with sauce and add shrimp. Heat in slow oven until bubbles. Add onion rings 5 minutes before serving. (Cooking time will depend on depth of container.)

Mrs. W. Evans Bruner
Atlanta, Georgia

CREOLE SHRIMP

Do Ahead   Serves 8

4 c. sliced onion
2 cloves garlic, minced
¼ c. olive oil
4 c. coarsely chopped and
   peeled tomatoes (about 4
   med. tomatoes)
3 c. coarsely chopped green
   pepper (about 3 med. peppers)
1 c. sliced fresh mushrooms
2 (8 oz.) cans tomato sauce
¼ c. dry white wine
2 tsp. salt
½ tsp. leaf thyme
⅛ to ¼ tsp. pepper
1 bay leaf
few threads saffron
   (optional)
2 lbs. raw shrimp, cooked
   and cleaned or 1 lb. cleaned
   cooked shrimp

Add onion and garlic to oil in large fry pan. Cook until tender, not brown. Add tomato, green pepper, mushrooms, and tomato sauce; stir and cook 5 minutes. Add wine, salt, thyme, pepper, bay leaf and saffron; mix well. Simmer uncovered to cook vegetables and blend flavors, about 20 minutes. Add shrimp; heat well. Serve over Rice Pilaf.
A wonderful dish for summer when tomatoes and peppers are plentiful!

Mrs. Donald L. Hutcheson

SHRIMP AND CRAB NEWBURG

Serves 15

¾ c. margarine
8 T. flour
1 pt. half and half
1 c. milk
¾ c. cooked celery
2 T. cooked onion
1 can shrimp soup (frozen
    or canned)
4 T. catsup
2 T. Worcestershire sauce
little ground black pepper
¼ tsp. red hot sauce
1 T. lemon juice
½ c. mayonnaise
2 T. cooking sherry
1 tsp. paprika
1 (6½ oz.) can white crabmeat
1 (20 or 24 oz.) pkg. shrimp,
    cooked and drained
1 c. grated cheese

Using large skillet, melt margarine. Blend in flour. Stir in half and half and milk. When thickened, start adding other ingredients. Stir until well heated. Be sure shrimp is pre-cooked and drained. If frozen, thaw and drain. Will be too soupy if not drained and thawed. May be served on regular type toast, in patty shells, on toasted English muffins, or over rice.

Mrs. Lewis T. Murphy

CURRIED SHRIMP

Easy

Serves 4

1 sm. onion, chopped
2 T. butter
1 clove garlic, crushed
2 tsp. curry powder
1 can cream of mushroom
    soup
1 lb. shrimp, cooked slightly
8 lge. mushrooms, sliced
4 oz. sour cream

Saute onion and garlic in butter. Add curry powder and mushroom soup, mushrooms and shrimp. Simmer slowly. Can be thickened with cornstarch, sherry or milk. Add 4 oz. sour cream.

Mrs. William L. Wages

SHRIMP AND LOBSTER THERMIDOR

3 (7 oz.) pkgs. frozen lobster
   tails
3 lbs. fresh shrimp
juice of 3 lemons
1 sm. onion
celery leaves
parsley
4 to 5 T. butter or margarine
6 T. flour
1 pt. half and half
1 c. heavy cream
½ c. sherry
1 c. milk
1 tsp. salt
⅓ tsp. white pepper
4 to 5 T. cracker crumbs to
   thicken (if needed)
1 (14 oz.) pkg. rice

Cook lobster and shrimp the day before.   To cook shrimp; wash in colander, put in heavy boiler, squeeze juice of 3 lemons over shrimp, add 2 T. salt, a small onion cut into rings, celery tips, and parsley to flavor.   Bring to a full boil, stirring. Cook 8 to 10 minutes and let cool in liquid. (You may use "shrimp and crab boil" and follow directions on package.)   Peel and devein shrimp. If shrimp are large, cut in half. Cook lobster according to package instructions and remove meat; cut into bite size pieces.   Store shrimp and lobster in covered container in refrigerator overnight. To make the sauce cook over medium heat in heavy utensil. Melt the butter, add flour and stir to paste; gradually add half and half, milk and cream, stirring constantly until it thickens. Do not let it boil. Add sherry, salt and pepper. Add seafood. Add cracker crumbs if the sauce needs thickening. It should be the consistency of a medium white sauce. Cook rice according to package directions.   Keep warm in top of double boiler. Serve thermidor over the hot rice.

Mrs. Ron Franklin

MY OWN SHRIMP

Serves 4

cleaned raw shrimp
   (amount depends on number
   to be served)
For 2 lbs. shrimp:
   2 T. butter
   ¼ c. sherry
   ¼ tsp. grated nutmeg
   red pepper to taste

Saute shrimp in butter until pink - add sherry. Let sherry boil away. Add nutmeg and pepper. Serve immediately as an hors d'oeuvre or may be served on rice as main dish.
This is a bit tricky - as it must be done at last minute and too little or too much cooking spoils it. It is different and very popular at small parties.

Mrs. H. McCall Freeman
Petersburg, Virginia

SHRIMP WITH WILD RICE

Serves 4

2 lbs. cooked shrimp
2 c. raw wild rice
1 lge. onion, chopped
1 green pepper, chopped
½ c. butter
1 c. chili sauce
1½ c. cream
½ c. sherry
salt and pepper

Prepare the shrimp. Cook wild rice as per package directions. While rice is cooking, saute onion and green pepper in butter. When soft, add chili sauce, cream and sherry. Season with salt and pepper. Add the rice and shrimp to the sauce. Heat well and serve immediately.

Mrs. Thomas F. Jones

PLAYBOY PAELLA

Serves 12

1½ lbs. pork loin, center cut
2 chicken breasts (4 halves),
  boned and skinned
1 lb. sliced leg of veal,
  pounded thin as for scallopini
2 sweet red peppers or canned
  pimientos
2 green peppers
1 lb. raw shrimp
1 lb. fresh peas or 10 oz. pkg.
  frozen
olive oil
½ lb. chorizo sausage, ¼" slices
½ lb. fresh mushrooms, thinly
  sliced
3 lge. cloves garlic, minced
1 lge. Spanish onion, minced
¼ tsp. saffron powder
½ tsp. oregano
2 c. long grain rice
4 to 5 c. chicken broth,
  canned or fresh
½ lb. bay scallops
salt and pepper to taste

Remove bone and fat from pork. Cut into 1" squares, ¼" thick. Cut chicken crosswise into 1" chunks. Cut veal into 1" squares. Cut pepper into ½" squares, discarding stem ends, seeds and membranes. Clean and peel shrimp. Shell fresh peas. Heat ½ c. oil in paella pan. Saute pork until deep brown; remove from pan. Saute chicken, chorizo, veal until light brown; remove from pan. Wash and dry pan. Add ½ c. oil and heat over low flame. Add garlic, onion, saffron, oregano and rice and stir well. Saute, stirring constantly, 5 minutes. Add chicken broth, pork, chicken, chorizo, veal, scallops, peppers, mushrooms and shrimp. Bring to boil. If chicken broth is unseasoned, add 1 to 2 tsp. salt. Reduce heat; simmer 10 minutes. Add peas and simmer 15 to 25 minutes longer, stirring gently but as little as possible, to keep ingredients from sticking to pan. Sprinkle with salt and pepper.

Mrs. William C. Hewitt

SHRIMP PILAU

Do Ahead   Serves 6

4 slices raw bacon
1 c. raw long-grain rice (not
  par-boiled or converted)
1¾ c. water
1 tsp. salt
2 c. (12 oz.) raw, shelled and
  deveined shrimp or frozen
  deveined shrimp
1 tsp. Worcestershire sauce
1 T. flour
3 T. butter or margarine
½ c. finely chopped celery
2 T. finely chopped, seeded
  green pepper
½ tsp. salt
⅛ tsp. pepper
2 T. butter or margarine

Cook bacon over moderately high heat until lightly browned; drain. Add to bacon fat in saucepan the rice, water and the 1 tsp. of salt and bring to a boil over moderately high heat; boil uncovered 10 to 15 minutes, until all the water is absorbed. Reduce heat to very low, cover saucepan and continue cooking rice 45 minutes, stirring occasionally with a fork. About 15 minutes before rice is done, sprinkle shrimp with Worcestershire sauce and dredge with flour. In a large skillet heat 3 T. of butter over moderate heat; add celery and green pepper and cook, stirring occasionally, 2 to 3 minutes. Add prepared shrimp to the skillet and cook 3 to 4 minutes, turning shrimp once or twice. Sprinkle shrimp with the ½ tsp. salt and the pepper. Add cooked rice to shrimp and toss lightly, adding the 2 T. of butter if desired. Crumble bacon and sprinkle over the pilau. Makes 6 servings.

Mrs. Tascar Williams

QUICK SEAFOOD FROM THE SHELF

Serves 4

1 can cream of mushroom soup
1 c. shredded Cheddar cheese
dash Worcestershire sauce
2 cans shrimp, drained
1 can mushrooms, drained
½ can pimiento

Combine soup, cheese and Worcestershire sauce. Heat until the cheese melts and add shrimp, mushrooms, and a sprinkling of chopped pimiento. Heat thoroughly and serve over hot rice or toast points.

Mrs. Donald A. Chiofolo
Rock Hill, South Carolina

SOLE AUX CHAMPIGNONS

Serves 8   350°
                        30 min.

3 lbs. fresh or frozen sole
1½ lbs. fresh mushrooms
2 lbs. cooked shrimp
½ lb. grated Parmesan cheese
salt
pepper
paprika
1 tsp. basil
1 tsp. parsley
1 T. grated onion
milk
5 T. flour
6 T. butter
⅓ c. sherry
⅓ tsp. cayenne
1½ tsp. monosodium glutamate
dash Tabasco sauce
additional grated cheese

Saute 3 lbs. frozen or fresh filets of sole in butter - 1 minute on each side. Place in large oblong Pyrex dish. Salt, pepper, and paprika. Wash and dry 1½ lbs. fresh mushrooms. Reserve 12 caps. Saute in butter and salt. Place in layers over sole. Make a sauce in double boiler of 5 T. flour, 6 T. butter and 2 c. of liquid (juices from frying pan plus ⅓ c. sherry plus milk to make 2 c. of liquid). Add grated onion, basil, parsley, cayenne, mono-sodium glutamate and Tabasco. When thick add ½ lb. grated Parmesan cheese and 1½ lb. cooked shrimp cut in half. Reserve 10-12 large shrimp. Salt to taste and cook until cheese melts. Pour sauce over sole and mushrooms in casserole. Sprinkle with grated cheese. Garnish with shrimp and mushroom caps.

Mrs. J. Denny Hall

CAPTAIN'S CASSEROLE

Easy   Serves 4-6   375°
Do Ahead   20-25 min.

1 can cream of mushroom soup
½ c. milk
⅔ c. grated Cheddar cheese
1⅓ c. Minute Rice
½ tsp. oregano (optional)
dash pepper
1 lb. can whole tomatoes
1 sm. onion, thinly sliced
water and juice drained from
    tomatoes to make 1½ c.
    liquid
2 (6½ oz.) cans tuna
¼ c. sliced stuffed olives
½ c. crushed potato chips or
    bread crumbs

Heat soup, milk and cheese until cheese is melted, stirring occasionally. Combine rice, oregano and pepper in greased 1½ qt. shallow baking dish. Drain tomatoes, reserving juice. Combine juice with water to measure 1½ c. Stir into rice. Arrange tomatoes, broken in large pieces, over rice. Make a layer of onion, then tuna, and then olives. Pour sauce over and sprinkle with potato chips or bread crumbs. Bake at 375° for 20 to 25 minutes or until heated through. (Baking time will be longer if prepared ahead and refrigerated.)

Mrs. W. Barron Cumming

SOUR CREAM TUNA CASSEROLE

Easy†
Do Ahead

Serves 4-6

400°
20 min.

1 can mushroom soup
½ pt. sour cream
¼ c. dry white wine
¼ c. chopped celery
½ tsp. garlic salt
1 tsp. onion salt
½ tsp. lemon juice
1 (6½ oz.) can tuna
1 (5 oz.) pkg. thin noodles,
    cooked
grated cheese
bread crumbs

Combine first 7 ingredients in 2 qt. casserole.   Stir well and add well-drained tuna.   Add noodles and mix well.   Top with cheese and bread crumbs. Bake at 400° for 20 minutes. If you like, fresh mushrooms may be added.

Mrs. William Valdon Smith

TURBOT PARMESAN

Easy
Do Ahead

Serves 4

350°
25-30 min.

2 lbs. turbot filets (or any
    white fish)
2 oz. dry vermouth
⅓ c. Parmesan cheese
1 T. lemon juice
1 T. grated onion
½ tsp. salt
½ tsp. Tabasco
1 c. sour cream
paprika

Cut filets into serving size and place in single layer in greased baking dish. Sprinkle vermouth and lemon juice over fish. Combine remaining ingredients except paprika and spread over fish.   Before baking sprinkle with paprika.   Done in 25-30 minutes or when flakes with fork. Do not over-cook.

Mrs. Robert P. Shapard III

SEAFOOD SAUCES

LOUIS DRESSING

Easy
Do Ahead

Serves 4

1 c. mayonnaise
⅓ c. chili sauce
1 sm. onion, grated
1 T. chopped parsley
½ tsp. horseradish
dash cayenne
1 T. tarragon vinegar
2 T. chopped stuffed
   olives
½ tsp. Worcestershire sauce

Combine ingredients. Chill. Serve dressing separately.

Mrs. Thomas W. Fetzer

SEAFOOD COCKTAIL SAUCE

Easy
Do Ahead

1 c. tomato catsup
2 T. lemon juice
1 tsp. salt
¼ tsp. Tabasco sauce
4 tsp. horseradish
1 tsp. Worcestershire sauce

Mix together. Makes about 1 cup sauce. Use with any seafood.

Mrs. J. Henry Walker III

DESSERTS and COOKIES

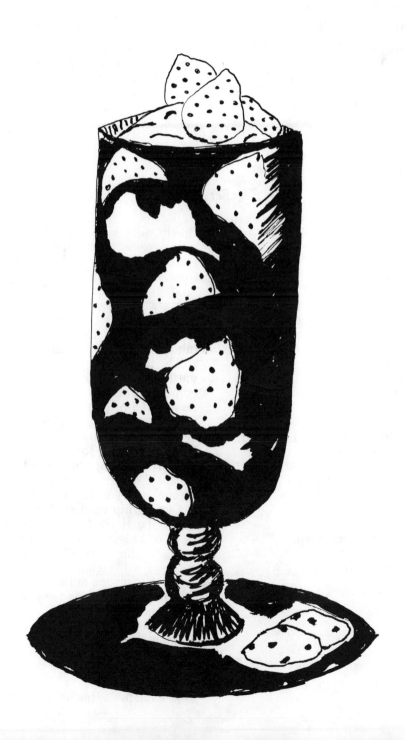

INTERNATIONAL CHRISTMAS DESSERTS

AMBROSIA

Do Ahead   Serves 10-12

24 oranges
1 coconut
½ - ¾ c. sugar (to taste)

Peel, section and seed oranges, removing all traces of membrane. Grate coconut and add to orange sections. Add sugar to taste and refrigerate until ready to serve.

Mrs. Benton Bowen

BLACK FOREST TORTE

Do Ahead†   Serves 12-16   350°
                                                15-18 min.

1¾ c. flour (all purpose)
1¾ c. sugar
1¼ tsp. soda
1 tsp. salt
¼ tsp. baking powder
⅔ c. chiffon type margarine
4 squares unsweetened
  chocolate (melted and
  cooled)
1¼ c. water
1 tsp. vanilla
3 eggs

Chocolate Filling:
  1½ bars (4 oz. each) German
    sweet chocolate
  ¾ c. chiffon type margarine
  ½ c. chopped toasted
    almonds

Cream Filling:
  2 c. whipping cream
  1 T. sugar
  1 tsp. vanilla

Brush sides and bottom of four 9" round cake pans with chiffon type margarine. Bake only 2 layers at a time if desired. Measure into large mixing bowl the first 9 ingredients. Beat 2 minutes at medium speed scraping sides of bowl. Add 3 eggs; beat 2 minutes more. Pour ¼ batter (about 1 c.) into each pan. Layers will be thin. Bake 15 to 18 minutes or until wooden pick inserted in center comes out clean. Cool slightly and remove from pan. Cool thoroughly. Chocolate Filling: Melt 1½ bars sweet chocolate over hot water. Cool. Blend in ¾ c. soft type margarine. Stir in ¼ c. chopped toasted almonds. Cream Filling: Beat 2 c. whipping cream with 1 T. sugar and 1 tsp. vanilla. Whip until stiff; do not overbeat. To finish torte: Place bottom layer of cake on serving plate. Spread with ½ chocolate filling; next layer with ½ of cream filling. Repeat layers, having cream filling on top. Do not frost sides. Using vegetable peeler, make chocolate curls with remaining ½ bar sweet chocolate. Decorate top completely. Wrap with Saran wrap. Refrigerate until ready to serve. This torte freezes nicely.

Mrs. William C. Hewitt

FLAN

325-350°
1 hr.

6 eggs
9 T. sugar
3 c. milk
½ tsp. salt
½ tsp. vanilla
2 T. cornstarch

Caramel:
1 c. sugar
2 T. water

Beat eggs; add all ingredients and strain through sieve. Prepare caramel: mix sugar and water on medium high heat; watch carefully; stir after it turns golden brown. Pour caramel mixture into pie pan or individual molds; fill with egg mixture. Place in shallow container of hot water; bake for 1 hour in moderate oven. Refrigerate and invert to serve.

Mrs. H. Ciordia

FRENCH YULE LOG

375°
15-20 min.

4 eggs (room temperature)
¾ c. sifted sugar
½ c. cake flour (sifted)
½ tsp. baking powder
¼ tsp. salt
1 tsp. vanilla
2 squares unsweetened
  chocolate, melted
2 T. sugar
¼ tsp. soda
3 T. cold water

confectioners sugar
1 c. cream, whipped
  (slightly sweetened)

Preheat oven. Sift sugar over eggs in large bowl. Beat until thick and light. Fold in flour, baking powder, salt and vanilla all at once. Add sugar, soda and water to melted chocolate and fold into above. Turn into greased and waxed paper lined 15 x 10 x 1" jelly roll pan. Bake 15 to 20 minutes or just until cake springs back when pressed gently. While cake bakes, sift thick layer of confectioners sugar onto clean dish towel. When cake is done invert onto towel, peel off paper and cut crisp edges from cake. Cool 5 minutes only. Roll cake gently from long end, rolling towel up in it. Cool on wire rack about 1 hour. Just before serving, carefully unroll cake, quickly spread with whipped cream to within 1" of edge. Roll cake as before; lay open edge on bottom. For serving garnish with whipped cream or slice and serve with ice cream.

Mrs. W. Evans Bruner
Atlanta, Georgia

ENGLISH PLUM PUDDING

Do Ahead†

Yield: 2 molds or
4 - 2 lb. coffee cans

300-325°
2½ - 3 hrs.

1 lb. bread crumbs
1 pt. milk
salt (pinch)
2 eggs (beaten)
1 lb. dark brown sugar
2 lbs. mince meat
2 c. chopped nuts
1 c. flour (scant cup mixed
   together with nuts)
1 c. white or dark seedless
   raisins
½ c. currants
1 T. soda
1 T. cinnamon
1 T. cloves
2 T. butter

Mix bread crumbs and milk together and add a pinch of salt. Let stand about 5 minutes. Mix beaten eggs with sugar, add crumb and milk mixture. Add mince meat and floured nuts to the remaining dry ingredients and add butter. Mix all together. Grease mold well with solid shortening. Fill ¾ full and seal well with lid or aluminum foil. Place in roaster, add 2 to 3 inches of water (more if mold is a high one). Cover and place in oven at 300°-325°. Steam until pudding begins to leave sides of mold, about 2½ - 3 hours. Length of time will depend on size of mold. Do not let water all boil out while cooking. When done the pudding will spring back when pressed. Store in refrigerator or freezer until ready to use. Heat covered with foil in slow oven until hot. Serve with Sherry Sauce.

Sherry Sauce:
   1 c. brown sugar
   1 c. white sugar
   2 T. flour (mixed with
      sugar
   1 c. butter
   2 eggs (beaten separately)
   sherry

Cream butter and sugar thoroughly, add egg yolks, then stiffly beaten egg whites. Cook in double boiler until thickens, stirring constantly. Remove from stove. When begins to cool, season heavily to taste with sherry. Store in refrigerator. Heat before serving.

Mrs. Edward C. Hammond
Atlanta, Georgia

DANISH RICE PUDDING

Serves 8

1 c. regular long-grain rice
6 c. milk (1½ qts.)
3 T. sugar
½ tsp. salt
1 whole blanched almond
½ tsp. ground cinnamon
¼ c. sugar
butter
cream
Marzipan Pig

Rinse rice in water. Place rice, milk, sugar and salt in heavy large saucepan. Heat over medium heat, stirring constantly until bubbles form around edge of pan. Cover. Reduce heat to low. Cook 1 hour or until rice is soft and thick, stirring occasionally. Ladle into tureen. Place almond in pudding. Combine cinnamon and sugar in small bowl. Top pudding with lump of butter. Sprinkle with some cinnamon-sugar; save remainder for each person to use on pudding. Pass a pitcher of cream.

Danish legend says that whoever finds the almond wins a prize - the marzipan pig - and will enjoy good luck in the coming year.

Mrs. H. Alfred Bolton III

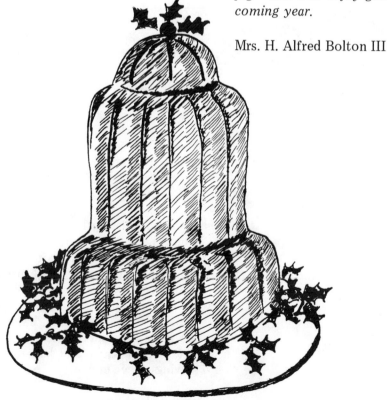

APPLE STRUDEL

Do Ahead   Serves 8   375°
                                                        1 hr.

6 lge. or 8 med. apples   Peel and slice apples, placing in a
1 c. sugar   buttered 2 qt. baking dish. Sprinkle
1 tsp. cinnamon   1 c. sugar mixed with the cinnamon
½ c. brown sugar   over apples. Cream brown sugar and
½ c. butter   butter; add flour gradually and mix
1 c. flour   until smooth. Add chopped nuts. Pat
1 c. chopped nuts   mixture in a thin crust over apples and
                           bake at 375° for 1 hour.
                           *This is good served hot with vanilla
                           ice cream.*

                           Mrs. W. B. Smith
                           Athens, Georgia

BANANAS FOSTER

                           Serves 4

2 ripe bananas, peeled   Slice bananas in half lengthwise. Brush
1 T. lemon juice   with lemon juice. Melt butter and
¼ c. dark brown sugar   sugar in a flat chafing dish or 10"
2 T. butter   skillet. Add bananas, saute until just
⅛ tsp. cinnamon   tender. Sprinkle with cinnamon.
2 T. banana liqueur   Remove from heat; add liqueur and
¼ c. white rum   rum. Immediately ignite and baste
1 pt. vanilla ice cream   bananas with warm liquid until flame
                           burns out. Divide sauce and bananas
                           over 4 servings of ice cream.

                           Mrs. Enrique Montero

BANANA SPLIT CRUMB CAKE

Do Ahead   Serves 10-12

½ c. margarine, softened
½ c. sugar
2½ c. graham cracker crumbs
16 oz. cream cheese
2 c. sugar
4 lge. bananas
1 (20 oz.) can crushed
   pineapple, drained
1 (9 oz.) Cool Whip
½ c. pecans, chopped
½ c. maraschino cherries

Mix together margarine, ½ c. sugar and graham cracker crumbs. Reserve ¼ c. of this mixture. Press remaining mixture into 2 qt. oblong cake pan. Bake at 350° for 5 minutes. Cool. Cream together cream cheese and sugar. Spread over cracker crumbs. Slice bananas over cheese mixture. Spread pineapple over bananas. Cover with Cool Whip mixed with pecans and cherries and remaining crumb mixture. Chill.

Mrs. David Rumph
Mineral Wells, Texas

NANIE'S BREAD PUDDING

          Serves 6   300°
                                30-40 min.

6-8 slices of bread
milk, enough to cover
3 eggs, beaten
½ c. sugar
1 tsp. baking powder
1 tsp. vanilla
raisins, optional

Sauce:
   1½ c. brown sugar
   ⅛ c. margarine

Soften bread in milk. Place sliced bread in greased 9 x 9" or 9 x 11" pan, sprinkling raisins between slices if desired. Mix well eggs, sugar, baking powder and vanilla and pour over bread mixture. Bake for 30 to 45 minutes until lightly browned and set.

Heat ingredients for sauce over low heat until well blended. Pour over each serving of bread pudding while hot.

Mrs. Jack Moore

BROKEN GLASS DESSERT

Do Ahead | Serves 12

1 pkg. each lime, cherry and
   orange Jello
4½ c. hot water
24 graham crackers, crushed
½ c. margarine, melted
½ c. sugar
1 pkg. unflavored gelatin
¼ c. cold water
1 c. hot pineapple juice
2 pkgs. Dream Whip
¼ c. sugar
1 tsp. vanilla
1 c. milk

Prepare each package of Jello in 1½ c. hot water. Let set in ice cube trays until very firm. Jello may be made the day before. Mix graham cracker crumbs with melted margarine and sugar. Line bottom of 9 x 13" pan with crumb mixture, saving a little for use on top. Dissolve gelatin in cold water. Combine with 1 c. hot pineapple juice. Chill but do not gel. Whip 2 pkgs. Dream Whip with sugar, milk and vanilla. Fold in gelatin mixture. Cut colored Jello into little squares; fold into topping mixture. Put in pan and top with remaining crumbs.
Looks very pretty and festive at Christmas.

Mrs. Herbert Carley
Freemont, Ohio

CHARLOTTE RUSSE

Serves 8

2 eggs
2 c. milk
1 c. sugar
1 tsp. vanilla
1 envelope unflavored
   gelatin
¼ c. water
½ pt. whipping cream
8-10 ladyfingers
sherry, optional

Beat eggs well, stir in milk and sugar. Cook in top of double boiler until mixture coats spoon, add vanilla. Cool. Sprinkle gelatin over cold water in small saucepan. Stir constantly over low heat until gelatin dissolves. Add to above mixture. When mixture is completely cooled, fold in whipped cream. Line 2 qt. casserole with split ladyfingers. Sherry may be sprinkled over ladyfingers before the custard is poured. Pour custard slowly over ladyfingers. Ladyfingers will tend to float to the top. For looks only, you may want them all up or all down. Refrigerate several hours. May serve with whipped cream on top.

Mrs. Louis C. Thacker

Editor's note: This is also delicious with 2 oz. sherry stirred into the custard.

CHEESECAKE I

Do Ahead   Serves 12   350°
                                                         55 min.

Crust:
    12 crushed graham crackers
    ½ c. melted butter

Filling:
    24 oz. cream cheese
    5 eggs
    1 c. sugar
    1 tsp. vanilla

Topping:
    ¼ c. sugar
    1 c. sour cream

Preheat oven to 350°. Pour butter over crumbs in a spring-form pan. Mix well and press crumbs to pan. Set aside. Separate eggs and beat egg whites until stiff. Combine other filling ingredients in mixing bowl and mix until smooth. Gently fold in egg whites. Pour into pie crust and bake 50 minutes. Mix sugar and sour cream and pour over top of cake. Bake 5 additional minutes. Serve chilled.

Mrs. William L. Wages

CHEESECAKE II

Do Ahead   Serves 12   250°-300°
                                                         50 min.

1 (6 oz.) box Zwieback,
    crushed
5 T. butter, melted
3 (8 oz.) pkgs. cream cheese
1¼ c. sugar
4 eggs
1 tsp. vanilla
1 pt. sour cream
½ c. sugar

Line a spring-form pan with butter and Zwieback. Cream cheese very well and add sugar, eggs and vanilla. Pour in pan. Bake in slow oven (250°-300°) for 30-40 minutes. Remove from stove. Mix 1 pt. sour cream with ½ c. sugar. Spoon gently on cake. Return to oven for 10 minutes. Turn oven off. Let remain in oven until oven cools. Remove. Place in refrigerator until ready to serve.

Mrs. John Lerner

STRAWBERRY GLAZE FOR CHEESECAKE

3 c. strawberries
1 c. sugar
3 T. cornstarch

Mash berries with sugar and let stand 30 minutes. Mix with cornstarch and cook until thick and clear. Strain and cool. Pour over cheesecake.

Mrs. James B. Dunaway

BRANDIED CHERRIES FLAMBE

Easy
Do Ahead

Serves 4

1 c. canned pitted dark cherries
¼ c. cognac
2 T. sugar
½ tsp. cinnamon
¼ tsp. cloves
2 T. Kirsch or Cointreau
1 - 2 T. cognac

Combine cherries, ¼ c. cognac, spices and Kirsch in pint glass jar. Refrigerate. To serve, turn mixture into chafing dish and heat. Pour 1 - 2 T. cognac on top of mixture and light with match. Stir. When flame goes out, spoon over vanilla ice cream or pound cake.

Mrs. W. Evans Bruner
Atlanta, Georgia

CHOCOLATE ALMOND FLUFF

Do Ahead

Serves 8-9

1 (3 oz.) pkg. chocolate pudding mix (not instant)
2¼ c. milk
¼ tsp. coriander or mace
½ tsp. cinnamon
1 T. plain gelatin
¼ c. brown sugar, packed
½ tsp. vanilla
1 (4 oz.) pkg. small ladyfingers or 10 large ladyfingers
1 c. whipping cream
½ c. toasted slivered almonds

Combine chocolate pudding mix, 2 c. milk and spices. Cook, stirring constantly, until mixture boils fully. Remove from heat. Soften gelatin with remaining ¼ c. milk and blend into pudding mixture. Stir in brown sugar and vanilla. Cool. Line bottom and sides of a buttered 8" square pan with ladyfingers. Whip cream, then fold into pudding mixture; pour into pan over ladyfingers. Sprinkle almonds over top. Chill thoroughly.

Mrs. Herman Swint
Orchard Hill, Georgia

CHOCOLATE FONDUE *

Easy

2 - 3 T. honey
½ c. light cream
8 oz. semi-sweet chocolate
2 T. Cointreau (optional)

Melt all ingredients together on low heat. Serve with the following for dipping:

bananas	apple wedges
pound cake	seedless grapes
maraschino cherries	strawberries
pineapple chunks	angel food cake
mandarin orange sections	
marshmallows	

POT - DE - CREME

Easy   Serves 4
Do Ahead

6 oz. pkg. chocolate bits   Mix all ingredients in blender until
1 T. brandy   smooth, adding milk for the last 60
¾ c. hot milk   seconds. Chill. This is pretty served
1 T. sugar   in demi-tasse or smallest ramekins
¼ tsp. salt   with a dab of whipped cream and bit
                                  of shaved chocolate on top.

                                  Mrs. William C. Hewitt

CHOCOLATE PUDDING

Easy   Serves 4
Do Ahead

2 c. whole milk   Mix all ingredients, except vanilla, in
½ c. sugar   saucepan and cook over medium heat
2 T. cornstarch   until it begins to thicken and just
2 T. flour   comes to a boil. Remove from heat,
dash of salt   and stir in vanilla. Pour into ½ c.
1 tsp. vanilla   glass pudding cups. Let cool, then
3 T. cocoa   chill in refrigerator. May be served
                                  warm or cold.

                                  Mrs. Arthur Lesser III

                                  *Editor's note: Also good in a pie shell
                                  with whipped cream on top.*

COFFEE CREME

Do Ahead   ·   Serves 8

2 envelopes unflavored   Mix gelatin, sugar and salt in medium
   gelatin   saucepan. Gradually stir in water. Heat
⅔ c. sugar   over medium heat, stirring constantly,
¼ tsp. salt   until gelatin is dissolved; remove from
1 c. water   heat. Add ice cream, lemon juice and
1 qt. coffee ice cream,   rum. Stir until ice cream is melted.
   softened   Pour into 5 or 6 cup mold. Refriger-
2 T. lemon juice   ate at least 8 hours. Unmold on
¼ c. golden rum or   serving plate; decorate with whipped
   1 T. rum flavoring   cream and chocolate curls.
sweetened whipped cream
chocolate curls   Mrs. Jerry Hollberg

COFFEE MOUSSE

Do Ahead   Serves 12

1½ pt. whipping cream
32 lge. marshmallows
3 pkgs. unfilled, split
  ladyfingers
1½ T. instant coffee, melted
  in ¼ c. water

Melt marshmallows in double boiler adding a few drops of water if necessary. Cool slightly. Whip cream. Add coffee to marshmallows and mix well. Fold into cream. Line spring-form pan (9" diameter) with ladyfingers. Pour ½ cream mixture; add 1 layer of ladyfingers and rest of cream. Refrigerate. (Can be made the night before serving.)

Mrs. William S. Colvin

Editor's note: Can also be served frozen.

STRAWBERRY CREPES

Yield: 12-16 crepes

Crepes:
  1 c. cold milk
  1 c. water
  4 whole eggs
  ½ tsp. salt
  4 T. melted margarine
  2 c. sifted all-purpose flour

whipped cream
fresh strawberries

Blend first 6 ingredients in blender for 1 minute. Scrape down and turn on again for few seconds. Pour about ¼ c. in hot slightly greased skillet (or use crepes skillet). Immediately pour excess back. When edges begin to come away clean with spatula, turn crepe. Can be done ahead and re-warmed in oven before serving. Put strawberries in center, spoon on whipped cream, roll up and pour Apricot Sauce on top.

Apricot Sauce:
  ½ stick butter
  1 can apricot nectar
  1 c. orange juice
  ¾ c. brown sugar,
    packed
  cornstarch

Cook on top of stove all ingredients until thick like a sauce. (Thicken with small amount of cornstarch.)

Mrs. David G. Cummins

CREPES FITZGERALD

Yield: 8 crepes

1 (3 oz.) pkg. cream cheese
½ c. sour cream
8 crepes (see Crepes
  recipe on preceding page)
1½ T. butter
2 c. strawberries, sliced
  (fresh or frozen, thawed)
2 to 4 T. sugar
2 jiggers (6 T.) Kirsch
1 jigger (3 T.) strawberry
  liqueur

Combine cream cheese and sour cream, divide between crepes; roll up. Place on plates. In a chafing dish, melt butter and add strawberries and sugar. Simmer a few minutes; pour in warmed Kirsch and strawberry liqueur and flame. Pour over crepes and serve.

Mrs. H. Alfred Bolton III

BAKED CUSTARD

Serves 6

4 eggs
½ c. sugar
¼ tsp. salt
3 c. milk (scalded)
1 tsp. vanilla
fresh nutmeg, grated

Beat eggs; stir in sugar and salt. Slowly beating with fork, add scalded milk and vanilla and fresh nutmeg. Set custard cups in shallow pan on paper towel. Pour in 1" water. Bake at 350° for 45 minutes or at 400° for 20 minutes. Test with silver knife. If it comes out clean, the custard will be set when cool. Special toppings include:
  fresh fruit and whipped cream
  layer of tart jelly and whipped
    cream
  crumbled macaroons and whipped
    cream
  pour Curacao over custard and add
    whipped cream (omit nutmeg
    from this)

Mrs. Robert Smalley

DATE NUT DESSERT

Serves 8-10   325°
40 min.

2 egg whites
1 c. sugar
1 tsp. baking powder
1 tsp. vanilla
1 c. chopped dates
1 c. chopped pecans
whipped cream

Beat eggs until stiff and slowly add sugar. Add baking powder and vanilla. Flour dates and pecans; add to egg mixture. Bake in buttered casserole for 40 minutes at 325°. Spoon into serving dishes and spoon whipped cream on top.

Mrs. Robert Willis

HEATH BAR DESSERT

Do Ahead   Serves 12

1 c. graham cracker
  crumbs
1 c. crushed saltines
2 (3 oz.) pkgs. vanilla
  instant pudding mix
2 c. milk
1 qt. butter-pecan ice
  cream
3 lge. Heath bars, crushed

Press mixed crackers in bottom of 13 x 9" Pyrex pan. Mix pudding with 2 c. milk. Blend softened ice cream into pudding mix and set aside until firm. Spread over crust. Let set in refrigerator overnight, if possible. At serving time, top each piece with dot of Cool Whip and crushed Heath bars.

Mrs. Waverly H. Branch
Chapel Hill, North Carolina

LEMON FLUFF

Do Ahead   Serves 12

1 envelope unflavored gelatin
¼ c. cold water
1 c. sugar
4 eggs, separated
rind of 2 lemons, grated
juice of 2 lemons
1 pt. whipping cream
18 plain ladyfingers
  (36 halves)

Dissolve gelatin in cold water. When dissolved, fill cup to one cup level with warm water and stir thoroughly. Beat egg yolks and sugar together. Add juice and lemon rind to beaten egg yolks, add gelatin mixture (no longer warm); fold in stiffly beaten whites, and then stiffly beaten whipped cream. Set in refrigerator. While this mixture is stiffening slightly, line a spring-form pan with halves of lady-fingers, the rounded sides turned out. Fill holes with pieces of ladyfingers. When refrigerated mixture has thick-ened enough (about ½ hour), pour into lined pan. Refrigerate. Before serving, remove sides of pan, leaving bottom of pan under cake.

Mrs. Eugene F. Robbins, Jr.

LEMON PUDDINGS

Do Ahead   Serves 8   350°
                                                45 min.

2 T. butter
1 c. sugar
4 T. flour
¼ tsp. salt
5 T. lemon juice
grated rind of 1 lemon
3 eggs, separated
1½ c. milk (sweet or
  evaporated)

Cream butter, add sugar, flour, salt, then lemon juice and rind. Stir in beaten egg yolks which have been mixed with milk. Fold in stiffly beaten egg whites. Pour into custard cups. Set cups in pan of cold water and bake in moderate oven (350°) about 45 minutes. Here is the surprise: when done each cup will contain a layer of custard at the bottom and a layer of sponge cake on the top. May be served hot in custard cups with whipped cream. I serve mine cold, from the refrigerator and when ready to serve, turn them on serving plates upside down so custard is on top. Top with fluff of whipped cream. Do not grease custard cups.

Mrs. William C. Hewitt

MAPLE MOUSSE

Do Ahead†   Serves 8

2 envelopes unflavored
   gelatin
½ c. cold water
1 c. pure maple syrup
4 egg yolks
½ c. brown sugar
4 egg whites
2 c. whipping cream
pecans, toasted and
   chopped

Soften gelatin in cold water. Then heat cup in hot water until gelatin dissolves. Combine with syrup. Beat egg yolks and add to syrup mixture. Cook over moderate heat, stirring constantly until it thickens slightly and coats spoon. Add brown sugar and stir to dissolve. Set aside to cool to room temperature. Beat egg whites. Whip cream. Fold cream into mixture. Then fold in egg whites. Put into large souffle dish and chill until firm. Before serving, sprinkle with chopped, toasted pecans.
Worth the trouble.

Mrs. John J. Flynt, Jr.

GRAPE FILLED MERINGUES

4 c. (2 lbs.) seedless grapes
1 c. sour cream
dark brown sugar
small meringues (see
   Meringue Pie Shell)

Chill grapes. Mix chilled grapes with sour cream and refrigerate overnight. Scoop out meringues. Sprinkle dark brown sugar over sour cream-grape mixture just before serving. Fill meringues and serve immediately.
A pretty dish to assemble and serve at the table.

Mrs. Edward C. Hammond
Atlanta, Georgia

PEACH COBBLER

Easy   Serves 6-8   375°
Do Ahead   35-40 min.

5 c. sliced fresh or canned
   peaches, drained
1 T. lemon juice
1 c. sifted all-purpose flour
1 c. sugar
½ tsp. salt
1 egg, beaten
6 T. butter or margarine,
   melted

Place peaches on bottom of 10x6x2½" baking dish. Sprinkle with lemon juice. Sift together dry ingredients; add egg, tossing with fork until crumbly. Sprinkle over peaches. Drizzle with butter. Bake at 375° for 35 to 40 minutes.

Mrs. John M. Cogburn, Jr.

DURGIN PARK INDIAN PUDDING

Do Ahead   Serves 8-12   250°

1 c. yellow corn meal
½ c. black molasses
¼ c. granulated sugar
¼ c. butter
¼ tsp. salt
¼ tsp. baking soda
2 eggs
1½ qts. hot milk

Mix all ingredients thoroughly with ¾ qt. of hot milk and bake in very hot oven until it boils. Stir in remaining hot milk and cook in slow oven 5 to 7 hours. Bake in stone crock, well greased inside. May be served hot with vanilla ice cream. Can be made day before and reheated. *This I always serve with Thanksgiving dinner either as dessert or as a starch. When my boys studied Indians in the lower grades, I made a crock full for the children in their class to taste food that was eaten long ago.*

Mrs. James S. Murray
Durham, New Hampshire

STRAWBERRIES CAPRI

Do Ahead   Serves 4

4 egg yolks
4 T. sugar
dash salt
½ c. milk
½ c. half and half
1 T. rum flavoring
2 c. strawberries (washed
   and hulled)
confectioners sugar

In top of double boiler beat egg yolks with sugar and salt until light. Stir in milk and cream. Cook over simmering water for 8 minutes or until mixture thickens and coats a metal spoon. Strain at once into bowl. Stir in rum flavoring and cool. To serve, place strawberries in sherbet dishes, pour sauce around berries and sprinkle lightly with powdered sugar.

Mrs. Lutie C. Johnston

STRAWBERRY FORGOTTEN TORTE

Do Ahead Serves 10 450°
Overnight

6 egg whites
¼ tsp. salt
½ tsp. cream of tartar
1½ c. sugar
1 tsp. vanilla
½ pt. whipping cream
1 qt. sliced sweetened fresh
strawberries or 1 (16 oz.)
pkg. frozen strawberries

Preheat oven 450°. Butter the bottom only of a 9" angel cake pan. Have egg whites at room temperature. Add salt and cream of tartar. Beat until almost stiff. Gradually add sugar, 2 T. at a time, and continue to beat. It will be very stiff. Beat vanilla in last. Spread evenly in buttered pan. Put in oven, close the door, and AT ONCE TURN OFF HEAT. Let stand overnight; do not open oven. Just forget about the torte. In the morning remove from oven. Loosen edges, turn out on serving plate. Frost with stiffly beaten cream. Chill until serving time, then slice and serve topped with strawberries.

Mrs. Mark Kapiloff

Editor's note: The Forgotten Torte is also delicious filled with a lemon pudding made with the remaining egg yolks.

STRAWBERRY PARFAIT

Easy Serves 2

1 pt. strawberries
1 T. granulated sugar
½ pt. sour cream
4 T. brown sugar
handful of chopped
nuts

Clean strawberries. Sprinkle with sugar. In parfait glasses or any drinking glass, layer strawberries, sour cream, 1 T. brown sugar. Repeat, using all brown sugar. Top with chopped nuts. Refrigerate until ready to serve.

Mrs. Sid Esary

TIPSY PARSON

Do Ahead†   Serves 12

1 lge. angel food cake
1 pt. cream, whipped
1 qt. boiled custard
  with bourbon to taste
¾ c. chopped pecans
1 (6 oz.) bottle maraschino
  cherries, sliced

Layer cake slices, cherries, nuts, custard and whipped cream in 3 qt. casserole. Repeat layers. Chill overnight.

Boiled Custard:
  4 c. milk
  4 eggs
  ¼ tsp. salt
  8 T. sugar
  1 tsp. vanilla
  bourbon to taste
    (optional)

Scald milk in double boiler. Beat together slightly the eggs, salt and sugar. Add hot milk. Mix thoroughly and return to double boiler. Cook over hot (not boiling) water, stirring constantly until mixture coats spoon. Add vanilla. When cool, add bourbon to taste.

Mrs. Randolph Gilbert

ENGLISH TOFFEE SQUARES

Do Ahead   Serves 9

20 vanilla wafers (1 c.
  crumbs)
1 c. chopped nuts
½ c. butter or margarine
1 c. powdered sugar
3 eggs separated
1½ (1½ oz.) squares
  unsweetened chocolate
  (melted)
2 T. vanilla
½ pt. whipping cream,
  whipped

Roll wafers into crumbs and mix with nuts. Spread half in buttered 9" square pan. Cream butter and sugar. Add beaten egg yolks, melted chocolate and vanilla. Fold in stiffly beaten egg whites. Pour over wafers and spread remaining crumbs on with spoon. Make the day before serving, and let set in refrigerator overnight. Cover with whipped cream. Cut into squares to serve.

Mrs. Lutie C. Johnston

MOCHA TOFFEE PARFAITS

Do Ahead   Serves 4

1 (3 or 3¼ oz.) pkg. regular
  vanilla pudding mix
1 T. instant coffee powder
1¾ c. milk
½ c. semi-sweet chocolate
  pieces
1 (6 oz.) can (²/₃ c.)
  evaporated milk
2 chocolate-covered English
  toffee bars (⅝ oz. each)
  coarsely crushed
whipped cream

In medium saucepan combine pudding mix and coffee powder, gradually stir in milk until mixture is blended. Cook over medium heat, stirring constantly until mixture comes to a boil. Remove from heat and cover surface of pudding with waxed paper or clear plastic wrap; cool and chill. In a small saucepan, combine chocolate pieces and evaporated milk. Cook and stir over low heat until mixture boils and chocolate is melted. Cool and chill. Remove paper from pudding mixture. Spoon half the mixture into 4 parfait glasses. Top with half the chocolate sauce and half the crushed candy. Repeat layering in parfait glasses with remaining pudding mixture and chocolate sauce. Top parfaits with whipped cream and the remaining candy.

Mrs. William Valdon Smith

TOFFEE CAKE DESSERT

Do Ahead   Serves 10-12

1 angel food cake
1 pt. whipping cream
4 T. cocoa
1 c. confectioners sugar
1 c. crushed Heath bars

Let whipping cream stand in beating bowl in refrigerator overnight with cocoa and confectioners sugar added. Next day, whip and add Heath bars which have been crushed (between waxed paper works well). Cut angel food cake twice, making 3 layers. Fill and frost cake. Chill in refrigerator before serving.

Mrs. Eugene F. Robbins, Jr.

WINE JELLY

Serves 6-8

2 envelopes plain gelatin
1 c. cold water
1 c. sugar
juice of 1 lemon
2 c. boiling water
2 c. sherry wine or
   Sauterne

Soak gelatin in cold water. Add sugar, lemon juice and hot water. Stir until sugar dissolves. Add sherry. Chill until set. (This makes a soft jelly - more gelatin may be added if desired.)

An elegant old fashioned Virginia dessert. Easy to make and when served with baked custard, it is food for the gods.

Mrs. H. McCall Freeman
Petersburg, Virginia

GRIFFIN SWIM CLUB SPECIAL

1 lb. dry roasted peanuts
1 lb. raisins
1 lb. M & M's plain
(optional - sprinkling of
   coconut)

Mix together.
A quick - energy snack.

FROZEN DESSERTS

BISCUIT TORTONI

Do Ahead†

Serves 8

¾ c. dry macaroons (¼ lb.)
   crushed fine
¾ c. heavy cream (or melted
   ice cream)
¼ c. sugar
dash salt
½ pt. whipping cream,
   whipped
½ tsp. vanilla
¼ tsp. almond flavoring
¼ c. toasted almonds

Mix ½ c. macaroons with cream. Add sugar and salt. Mix well. Let stand for 1 hour. Fold in whipped cream and flavorings. Turn into 8 paper dessert cups. Sprinkle top with the remaining crumbs and finely chopped almonds. Freeze.

Mrs. Louis C. Thacker

KNICKERBOCKER DESSERT

Do Ahead†   Serves 6-8

1½ c. orange juice, fresh
   or frozen
¼ c. lemon juice
¾ c. sugar
½ pt. heavy cream
½ c. sifted powdered sugar
1 tsp. vanilla
½ c. chopped pecans

Mix well and freeze first 3 ingredients in ice cube tray. Whip cream until stiff and add sugar, vanilla and pecans. Spread over orange mixture and freeze. Cut into squares.

Mrs. Champ Vance

COLD BUTTERED RUM DESSERT

Easy†   Serves 4
Do Ahead

1 qt. butter pecan ice
   cream
4 oz. Myers dark rum

Put ingredients in blender. Pour into small glasses. Can be made in large quantities and put in freezer days in advance. Just stir and serve. Much less rum can be used - and when frozen less rum should be used.

Mrs. James R. Fortune, Jr.

LALLA ROOKH

Easy   Serves 4

4-6 T. Puerto Rican rum
1 pt. vanilla ice cream
   (preferably French
   vanilla), softened

Add rum to ice cream and beat until smooth in a blender. Serve in champagne or sherbet glasses, to be drunk from the glass.

Mrs. H. Alfred Bolton III

SANS RIVAL

Do Ahead†   Serves 12   300°
                                                          10-15 min.

Torte:
  10 egg whites
  2 c. sugar
  3 c. cashew nuts,
    chopped
  1 tsp. vanilla

Rinse cashew nuts and toast to dry; chop. Beat egg whites until firm but not dry. Add sugar and beat. Fold in cashew nuts and vanilla. Grease inverted baking sheet well and flour. Spread mixture leaving a space of about 1" from edge. Bake at 300° for 10-15 minutes. Immediately scrape off. This should make 3 or 4 layers.

Filling:
  ²⁄₃ c. sugar
  5 egg yolks
  ¼ c. water
  1 c. butter

Add sugar to water and boil. Beat egg yolks until lemon colored. Add to sugar syrup, beat and add butter. Spread on top of each layer including top layer. Freeze until ready to serve.

Mrs. Arthur K. Weathers

FROSTY STRAWBERRY SQUARE

Do Ahead†   Serves 15 or 18   350°
                                                          20 min.

1 c. sifted flour
¼ c. brown sugar
½ c. chopped pecans
1 stick margarine
  (melted)
2 tsp. lemon juice
1 c. sugar
2 c. sliced fresh strawberries
  or 10 oz. pkg. frozen berries
2 egg whites
1 pt. heavy cream (whipped)

Stir together first 4 ingredients. Spread evenly in shallow baking pan. Bake 350° for 20 minutes, stirring several times. Sprinkle ²⁄₃ of this mixture in 3 qt. flat Pyrex dish. Reserve the rest for later. Combine lemon juice, sugar, berries and egg whites in large bowl. Beat at high speed to stiff peaks - at least 10 minutes. Fold in whipped cream. Spread in Pyrex dish. Top with remaining crumbs. Freeze at least 6 hours. Cut in squares to serve. May be topped with more fresh berries.

Mrs. Taylor Manley, Jr.
Mrs. Newton Penny

ICE CREAM AND SHERBET

CHOCOLATE-HONEY ICE CREAM

Do Ahead†   Serves 16 - 8 oz. servings

1¼ c. semi-sweet chocolate
  pieces
5 T. all-purpose flour
3¾ c. milk
dash salt
1¼ c. honey
5 beaten eggs
5 c. whipping cream
1¼ tsp. vanilla

In a saucepan, combine semi-sweet chocolate pieces, flour and salt. Stir together milk and honey. Gradually stir into dry ingredients. Cook and stir over medium heat until chocolate melts and mixture thickens and boils. Add a moderate amount of the hot mixture to the eggs and mix well; return slowly to hot mixture. Cook and stir 1 minute more. Chill. Stir in cream and vanilla. Freeze in 4 qt. ice cream freezer. Let ripen. Garnish with additional semi-sweet chocolate pieces, if desired. Makes 4 qt. ice cream.

Mrs. William L. Wages

GRAPE SHERBET ICE CREAM

Easy†   Serves 12
Do Ahead

3 c. sugar
1 sm. can crushed
  pineapple (with juice)
1 pt. grape juice
½ pt. whipping cream
6 c. whole milk

Mix sugar, pineapple and grape juice and chill. Just before freezing add whipping cream and milk. Freeze according to freezer instructions.

Mrs. Wm. F. Early

LEMON ICE

Do Ahead†   Serves 8

1 pt. half and half
1 c. sugar
3-5 T. lemon juice
1 grated lemon rind
8 lemons

Garnish:
  1 c. whipped cream
  1 oz. grated chocolate

Freezer proportions:
  12 lemons
  2 lbs. sugar (4⅓ c.)
  2 qts. half and half

Scoop out large lemons and freeze shells. Mix half and half, sugar, lemon juice and rind. Freeze slightly and put in lemon shell. Freeze until needed. To garnish, add whipped cream and grated chocolate. (Can use mixture alone, without lemon shells for a delicious lemon sherbet.)

Make according to freezer directions. Will keep in refrigerator freezer without getting icy.

Mrs. J. Denny Hall

EASY ORANGE SHERBET

Easy†
Do Ahead

Serves 6-8

5 (12 oz.) cans Fanta orange
or grape
1 (14 oz.) can sweetened
condensed milk
1 sm. can crushed
pineapple

Mix together (in freezer, if you like).
Pour in electric or hand turned
freezer.

Mrs. Paul H. Walker, Jr.

PEACH ICE CREAM

Do Ahead†

Yield: 1 gallon

½ gal. sweet milk (scant)
2½ c. sugar
6 T. flour
8 eggs beaten separately
2 tsp. vanilla (less if
you like)
pinch of salt
1 can evaporated milk
½ pt. whipped cream
(optional)
3-4 c. peaches (optional)

Beat egg yolks well. Sift flour and
sugar together, stir into well beaten
egg yolks. Scald milk, pour slowly
over mixture, cook until it coats
spoon, cool slightly, add beaten
whites. After thoroughly cool, add 1
tall can canned milk, whipped. Add
½ pt. whipped cream, if you want
really rich cream. Add 3-4 c. mashed
peaches (fresh), or whatever fruit you
like.

Mrs. Larry H. Evans

SIX-THREE ICE CREAM

Do Ahead†

Serves 6-8

3 bananas
juice of 3 oranges (or
1⅓ c. orange juice)
juice of 3 lemons
3 c. milk
3 c. coffee cream
3 c. sugar

Mash bananas. Quickly pour orange
juice and lemon juice over bananas.
Set aside. Combine milk, coffee
cream and sugar, stirring thoroughly.
Pour into ice cream freezer and freeze
until mixture begins to thicken. Add
fruit mixture and finish freezing. If
using strawberries or peaches, use
amount of the fruit which equals the
amount of the fruit mixture used
above. Strawberries and peaches
should be sweetened slightly. This is
called 6-3 ice cream because there are
6 ingredients - 3 parts of each. This
ice cream keeps well in the freezer and
does not taste icy when served.

Mrs. F. Ted Wilder, Jr.

"NO COOK" VANILLA ICE CREAM

Easy†
Do Ahead

Yield: 1 gallon

6 eggs
1 pt. whipping cream
2 c. sugar
2 T. vanilla
½ gal. milk or enough
   to fill freezer ¾ full

Beat eggs for two minutes. Add sugar and beat until dissolved. Add cream and beat until all ingredients are thoroughly mixed. Add 1 qt. milk and then vanilla. Beat. Pour in 1 gal. or 5 qt. freezer and add remaining milk up to ¾ full. Freeze according to freezer's directions.

Mrs. J. Henry Walker III

COOKIES

ALMOND COOKIES

†

Yield: 18 dozen   350°
1½" cookies   10-12 min.

2 c. butter or margarine
1½ c. superfine sugar
3 egg yolks
1 T. vanilla
3 T. heavy cream
4 c. sifted all-purpose
   flour
1 c. ground or finely
   chopped blanched
   almonds

Beat butter, sugar, egg yolks, vanilla and heavy cream together in a large bowl with electric mixer until light and fluffy. Stir in flour and blanched almonds. Chill dough for several hours. Roll out ¼ of chilled dough at a time on a lightly floured surface to ⅛" thickness. (Keep remaining dough refrigerated until ready to use.) Cut out dough with decorative small cutters. Place on lightly greased cookie sheets. Repeat with remaining dough. Bake at 350° for 10-12 minutes or until lightly browned. Cool on wire racks. Store cookies in tightly covered containers in a cool place for up to one week or label and freeze for up to two months.

Mrs. W. Everett Beal

ALMOND TARTS

Yield: 4-5 dozen   350°

1 c. butter
1 c. sugar
2 eggs
2¾ c. flour
1 tsp. almond extract

Cream butter, add sugar gradually. Add eggs and flavoring; beat well and add flour. Press small piece of dough into well greased (1") individual tart tins, beginning at the bottom and working upward to top to form a thin hollow shell. Bake at 350° until browned lightly. Invert on rack to cool - cookies should fall out. Delicious served plain or with lemon filling. Will keep several weeks in tight tin.

Mrs. William S. Colvin

APRICOT BALLS

Do Ahead

1½ c. dried apricots,
   chopped very fine
2 c. shredded coconut
⅔ c. condensed milk
powdered sugar

Mix apricots and coconut. Add milk.
Blend well. Shape into small balls.
Roll in powdered sugar.

Mrs. Andrew E. Blake

BENNE SEED COOKIES

Easy   Yield: 7 dozen   325°
                                           30 min.

¾ c. butter
1½ c. light brown sugar
2 eggs
1¼ c. plain flour, sifted
½ c. toasted benne seed
   (sesame seed)
1 tsp. vanilla
¼ tsp. baking powder

Cream butter and sugar and mix with
other ingredients in order given. Drop
with a teaspoon onto waxed paper
lined cookie sheet far enough apart to
allow for spreading. Bake 30 minutes
at 325°. Let cool on waxed paper and
cookies can be "peeled off".
A Charleston tradition!

Mrs. John H. Goddard

SPRITZBAAKEN (BUTTER COOKIES)

†   Yield: 10-11 dozen   350°
                                           15 min.

2 c. butter or margarine
1 c. sugar
1 whole egg plus 2 egg
   yolks
4½ c. flour
1 tsp. vanilla

Cream butter and sugar. Add flour
and eggs alternately. Add vanilla.
Refrigerate for 30 minutes. Use
cookie press. (If you use the star
shaped press, press out 1" and cut.)
Bake at 350° for 12 to 15 minutes.

For variety substitute lemon
or orange flavoring for vanilla.

Mrs. William L. Joiner
First President of The Utility Club

DATE BALLS

Easy   Yield: 7 dozen

¾ c. butter
1 c. sugar
1 (8 oz.) pkg. chopped dates
2 c. Rice Krispies
1 c. pecans, chopped
confectioners sugar

Melt butter in saucepan over medium heat. Add sugar and blend. Add dates and cook for about 5 to 6 minutes or until soft. Cook no more than 10 minutes. Remove from heat and add pecans and Rice Krispies. Drop by teaspoon onto waxed paper. Roll into balls and cover with confectioners sugar in paper bag. Put in cookie tin and refrigerate. Refrigeration makes balls hard so remove from refrigerator about 15 minutes before serving.

Mrs. William C. Hewitt

FRUITCAKE DROPS

Yield: 7 dozen   350°
                       12 min.

1 c. sifted regular flour
¼ tsp. baking soda
¼ tsp. salt
½ tsp. ground cinnamon
¼ c. butter or margarine
½ c. sugar
1 egg
2 T. brandy or milk
1 (8 oz.) pkg. pitted dates
   chopped
1 (4 oz.) container candied
   pineapple, chopped (green)
1 (8 oz.) container candied
   cherries, chopped (red)
1 c. chopped pecans

Sift flour, soda, salt and cinnamon onto waxed paper. Cream butter or margarine with sugar until fluffy-light in a medium-size bowl; beat in egg and brandy (or milk). Stir in flour mixture, half at a time, blending well to make a soft dough. Stir in dates, candied fruits and nuts. Drop batter, a rounded teaspoonful, onto lightly greased cookie sheets. Bake at 350° for 12 minutes. Remove to wire racks; cool completely.

Mrs. Richard L. Mullins

HUNGARIAN COOKIES

Yield: 12 dozen   400°
12-15 min.

Cookies:
1¼ c. shortening
1 c. sugar
3 eggs
½ tsp. almond extract
3¼ c. all-purpose flour

Topping:
4 T. grated fresh orange
    rind
8 T. sugar
    (Mix well)

Cream shortening, add sugar gradually. Add eggs one at a time, beating thoroughly after each. Add almond extract, mix well. Add flour gradually, stir until smooth. Pinch off and roll into walnut sized balls, place on greased cookie sheet. Flatten balls with floured tines of fork. Sprinkle cookies with orange rind mixture. Bake in hot oven 400° for 12 to 15 minutes. Makes 12 dozen.

Mrs. William T. Johnson

LEMON SNOWFLAKES

†

Yield: 4 dozen   350°
15 min.

1 c. margarine
½ c. confectioners sugar
¾ c. cornstarch
1½ c. sifted flour
1 c. finely chopped pecans

Cream margarine, add sugar, cornstarch, and flour. Shape dough into 48 small balls and drop into the finely chopped pecans. Flatten with finger on greased cookie sheet and bake. When cool, put small amount of icing in center of cookie.

Icing:
1 c. confectioners sugar
2 T. melted margarine
1 T. pure lemon juice

Mix until smooth. Tint pale green or yellow and put in center of cookie.

Mrs. David G. Cummins

OATMEAL CRISPIES

†

Yield: 5 dozen   350°
10-13 min.

1 c. shortening
1 c. brown sugar
1 c. granulated sugar
2 beaten eggs
1 tsp. vanilla
1½ c. flour
1 tsp. salt
1 tsp. soda
3 c. quick oats
½ c. chopped nuts

Cream shortening and sugars. Add eggs and vanilla, beat well. Add sifted dry ingredients, then oatmeal and nuts. Mix well. Shape into long rolls. Wrap in waxed paper. Chill. (You can freeze and bake later.) Slice in ¼" slices. Bake 350° for 10-13 minutes.

Mrs. Frank Harris, Jr.

OATMEAL-TOLL HOUSE COOKIES

Yield: 7-8 dozen   350°
10-15 min.

1 c. margarine
¾ c. brown sugar, packed
  (light or dark)
¾ c. white sugar
2 eggs unbeaten
1⅞ c. flour (all-purpose)
1 tsp. salt
1 tsp. soda
1 c. chopped nuts
1 (6 oz.) pkg. Toll House
  chocolates
1 tsp. vanilla
2 c. oatmeal (uncooked)

Cream margarine and sugars. Add eggs. Beat thoroughly. Add sifted flour, soda, and salt. Mix well. Add chocolate drops, nuts and vanilla. Mix in oatmeal. Dough will be very stiff. Drop by spoonfuls on greased cookie sheet. Bake.

Mrs. Walter E. Jones

PEANUT BUTTER COOKIES

Easy

Yield: 8 dozen   325°
12-15 min.

1 c. butter
1 c. peanut butter (plain
  or crunchy)
1 c. sugar
1 c. brown sugar
2 eggs
2 c. flour (plain)
pinch of salt
1 tsp. baking soda
1 (6 oz.) pkg. semi-sweet
  chocolate morsels
1 (6 oz.) pkg. butterscotch
  morsels
*(use either chocolate or
butterscotch or both)*

Cream butter and peanut butter; add sugars and beat, add eggs, beat. Add remaining ingredients in order given. Drop from spoon - flatten on ungreased cookie sheet. Cook at 325° for 12-15 minutes.

Mrs. Tom Barrett

OATMEAL-PEANUT BUTTER COOKIES

Easy†   Yield: 5 dozen

1½ c. sugar
¼ c. butter
¾ c. flour
½ c. milk or ⅔ c.
 evaporated milk
1½ c. quick cooking
 rolled oats
⅔ c. peanut butter
½ c. chopped walnuts
½ c. flaked coconut
1 tsp. vanilla
¼ tsp. salt

Combine sugar, butter, flour and milk in saucepan. Bring to a full boil; boil hard 3 minutes, stirring constantly. Remove from heat; add remaining ingredients. Blend well. Drop by teaspoonfuls onto foil or greased cookie sheet. Cool. Makes 60 cookies.

Mrs. R. Lee Pfrogner

PECAN CRESCENTS (SWEDISH COOKIES)

Yield: 4 dozen   375°
                        15 min.

1 c. butter
6 T. sifted confectioners
 sugar
1 T. vanilla
2 c. sifted flour
pinch of salt
2 c. chopped nuts

Cream butter. Add sugar and mix well. Add vanilla, flour, salt and nuts. Roll mixture between hands and shape like fingers (approx. 2" long). Place on buttered cookie sheet. Bake in 375° oven 15 minutes or until slightly brown. While still hot roll cookies in confectioners sugar.

Mrs. J. Gordon Dixon
Mrs. Lewis T. Murphy

PECAN CRISPS

Easy†   Yield: 8 dozen   350°
                                        12-15 min.

½ c. shortening
½ c. margarine
2½ c. brown sugar
2 well-beaten eggs
2½ c. sifted flour
½ tsp. soda
¼ tsp. salt
1 c. chopped pecans

Cream shortening, margarine and sugar. Add eggs. Beat well. Sift dry ingredients and add to creamed mixture. Fold in nuts. Drop by the teaspoonfuls, 2" apart on greased cookie sheet. Bake 12-15 minutes or until lightly browned.

Mrs. Lester L. Luttrell

PECAN REFRIGERATOR COOKIES

†

Yield: 14 dozen   375°
9 min.

1 lb. butter, softened
1 lb. light brown sugar
2 eggs
2 tsp. vanilla
4 c. sifted all-purpose
   flour
1 tsp. cinnamon
1 tsp. baking powder
1 tsp. salt
1 lb. chopped pecans
   (about 3 c.)

Cream butter and sugar together until light and fluffy. Beat in eggs one at a time. Add vanilla. Sift dry ingredients together and add to butter mixture, mixing thoroughly. Stir in pecans. Chill dough for one or two hours. Divide into 6 portions; shape into rolls about 1¾" in diameter. Wrap the rolls in waxed paper and chill overnight or longer (or freeze until needed). Slice about ¼" thick. Bake on greased cookie sheet in preheated oven (375°) for 9 minutes or until cookies are delicately browned.

Mrs. J. Henry Walker III

ROSETTES

Do Ahead

Yield: 4-5 dozen

2 eggs
1 T. sugar
¼ tsp. salt
1 c. milk
1 c. flour

Beat eggs slightly with sugar and salt; add milk and flour. Beat until smooth. Heat 2" oil in pan or skillet (medium to medium high). Heat timbale iron thoroughly in oil. Dip in batter to just below top of timbale rim - do not submerge. Shake excess batter and dip in oil, holding while batter browns - 30-45 seconds. Remove rosette and drain on paper towels and repeat. Will keep well in air-tight container. Can dust with powdered sugar before serving.

Mrs. William S. Colvin

SAND TARTS

Yield: 12 dozen   350°
                                              8-10 min.

1 c. butter
2 c. sugar
2 eggs (well beaten)
1 T. milk
1 tsp. vanilla
½ tsp. baking powder
½ tsp. salt
4 c. sifted flour

Cream butter and sugar. Add eggs, milk and vanilla. Mix well. Mix dry ingredients and add to the above. Refrigerate until cold. Roll out very thin. (Use extra flour for this.) Cut with cutters and bake on greased cookie sheet until light brown. (Keeps in tin for several weeks.)
These are our favorite "Christmas cookies" - great for little helpers.

Mrs. J. Robb Sautter
Highlands, North Carolina

SNICKERDOODLES

Yield: 5 dozen   400°
                                            8-10 min.

1 c. soft margarine
1½ c. sugar
2 eggs
2¾ c. flour
2 tsp. cream of tartar
1 tsp. soda
½ tsp. salt
2 T. sugar
2 tsp. cinnamon

Cream margarine, sugar and eggs. Sift together flour, cream of tartar, soda and salt and add to above mixture. Form dough into balls about size of walnuts. Roll in mixture of sugar and cinnamon. Place 2" apart on ungreased cookie sheet. Bake 8-10 minutes in 400° oven until lightly brown but still soft.

Mrs. Herman Swint
Orchard Hill, Georgia

SNOWFLAKES

Yield: 5 dozen 350°
12-15 min.

1 c. shortening
1 (3 oz.) pkg. cream cheese
1 c. sugar
1 egg yolk
1 tsp. vanilla
1 tsp. grated orange rind
2½ c. sifted plain flour
½ tsp. salt
¼ tsp. cinnamon
food coloring (optional)

Cream shortening, cream cheese and sugar. Beat in egg yolk, vanilla and grated orange rind. Gradually blend in flour, salt and cinnamon. Fill press form and press on ungreased cookie sheet. Bake 12-15 minutes. Remove at once to cookie racks. *A good holiday cookie!*

Mrs. David Clements

OLD FASHIONED TEA CAKES

Easy Yield: 4 dozen 350°
10 min.

1 c. sugar
½ c. margarine
1 egg, beaten
1 tsp. vanilla
2 c. sifted self-rising
   flour
sugar

Cream sugar and margarine. Add beaten egg and vanilla. Mix. Add flour. Knead until the consistency of biscuit dough. Place small balls of dough on an ungreased cookie sheet and flatten with a fork. Sprinkle top with sugar. Bake at 350° for 10 minutes.

Mrs. Flynt Langford

BARS

AUSTRIAN LINZER COOKIES

Do Ahead†   Yield: 2-3 dozen   375°
                                                25-30 min.

1½ c. sifted all-purpose
    flour
¼ c. granulated sugar
½ tsp. baking powder
½ tsp. salt
½ tsp. cinnamon
½ c. brown sugar
½ c. butter or margarine
1 slightly beaten egg
⅓ c. blanched almonds,
    ground
½ c. red-raspberry or
    strawberry jam
1 slightly beaten egg
    yolk
1 tsp. water

Sift together flour, sugar, baking powder, salt and cinnamon; stir in brown sugar. Cut in butter or margarine until mixture is crumbly. Add egg and ground almonds; mix with fork. Reserve ½ c. mixture for lattice and into it mix 2 T. additional all-purpose flour. Chill 1 hour. Meanwhile, press remaining mixture into 9 x 12 x 2" baking pan. Spread with jam. Roll out reserved mixture on well-floured surface to ¼" thickness. Cut in strips a little less than ¼" wide. For lattice top, line up 11 strips across filling; then lay 11 strips diagonally across. Combine slightly beaten egg yolk and water. Brush over lattice. Bake and cool. Cut into bars or squares.

Mrs. James E. Scharnhorst

BUTTERSCOTCH BROWNIES

Easy   Yield: 16 squares   350°
                                                30 min.

¼ c. margarine
1 c. dark brown sugar,
    packed
1 egg
1 tsp. vanilla
½ c. flour
1 tsp. baking powder
½ tsp. salt
1 c. broken nut meats

Melt margarine. Add sugar, egg and vanilla. Sift together dry ingredients, add to first mixture, then add nuts. Mix well. Spread into 8 x 8" pan. Bake 30 minutes at 350°. Cool slightly and cut into 16 squares. Do not overcook. They should be chewy. These keep well in an air-tight container.

Mrs. E. Herben Turner

CHOCOLATE FUDGE CAKES

†   Serves 16   375°
                                                                35-40 min.

1 c. butter
4 squares unsweetened
    chocolate
2 c. sugar
1½ c. flour
4 eggs
pinch salt
2 tsp. vanilla
1½ c. pecans

Melt butter and chocolate in double boiler. Pour sugar over mixture and add flour and eggs alternately. Add salt, vanilla and nuts. Bake in 9 x 13" pan for 35-40 minutes at 375° until set but not done. Leave in pan until cool.

Mrs. Ray Taylor
Greensboro, North Carolina

FILLED BROWNIES

†   Yield: 54 squares   350°
                                                                30-35 min.

1 c. butter or margarine
2 c. firmly packed dark
    brown sugar
2 eggs
1 tsp. vanilla extract
1½ c. all-purpose flour
1 tsp. soda
¾ tsp. salt
2 c. coarsely crushed
    cornflakes
2 c. oatmeal
1 c. chopped pecans

Cream butter and sugar in large bowl. Add eggs, one at a time, beating well after each addition. Add vanilla and beat thoroughly. Blend in flour, soda, and salt, which have been sifted together. Stir in cornflakes, oatmeal and nuts. Press half this dough into bottom of greased 15 x 10 x 1" jelly roll pan and set aside. This dough is sticky; flour your fingers repeatedly to press down easily.

Filling:
   2 c. semi-sweet chocolate
     bits
   2 T. butter or margarine
   2 tsp. vanilla
   ¾ c. sweetened condensed
     milk
   ½ tsp. salt
   1 c. finely chopped pecans

Melt chocolate and butter over hot water. Remove from heat; stir in flavoring, condensed milk and salt. Add nuts, stir until smooth, then spread evenly over dough in pan. (A small spatula dipped repeatedly in hot water helps.) Spread reserved half of dough over chocolate filling, again using the hot spatula. Bake at 350° for 30 to 35 minutes. The usual test for doneness won't work here as filling remains moist, but cake shrinks slightly from edges of pan when done. Let cool about 5 minutes, then using sharp knife cut into 1½" squares. Cool completely before removing from pan. Yield 54 squares.

Freezes well. Excellent for shipping.

Mrs. Richard Shapard

FRUIT BARS

† Yield: 2-2½ dozen 300°
1 hr.

2 c. chopped pecans
½ c. butter
1¼ c. dark brown sugar
2 eggs
1 tsp. vanilla
1 c. self-rising flour
½ lb. candied cherries, chopped
½ lb. candied green pineapple,
chopped

Grease and flour two 8" or 9" square pans. Cover bottom of pans with nuts. Cream butter and sugar. Add eggs and vanilla. Mix flour and candied fruit; add to creamed mixture. This mixture will be very stiff. Pat by spoonfuls into pans without disturbing nuts. Bake at 300° for 1 hour. Cut while still warm - but not hot.

Mrs. Ashley P. Hurt

LEMON BARS

Yield: 2½ - 3 dozen 350°
45-50 min.

2 c. sifted all-purpose flour
½ c. sifted confectioners sugar
1 c. butter or margarine

4 beaten eggs
2 c. granulated sugar
⅓ c. lemon juice
¼ c. all-purpose flour
½ tsp. baking powder

Sift 2 c. flour and confectioners sugar together. Cut in butter or margarine until mixture clings together. Press in 13 x 9 x 2" baking pan. Bake in 350° oven for 20-25 minutes or until lightly browned. Beat together eggs, granulated sugar and lemon juice. Sift flour and baking powder; stir into egg mixture. Pour over baked crust. Bake in 350° oven for 25 minutes longer. Sprinkle with additional confectioners sugar, if desired. Cool. Chill in refrigerator for several hours or overnight. Cut in bars.

Mrs. H. Ray Simonton

NANAEMO BARS

† Yield: 4 dozen

½ c. butter, softened
¼ c. granulated sugar
5 T. cocoa
1 tsp. vanilla
1 egg
2 c. graham cracker crumbs,
  finely crushed
1 c. coconut
½ c. chopped walnuts

Place softened butter, sugar, cocoa, vanilla and egg in medium size bowl. Set bowl in pan of boiling water, stir well until butter has melted and mixture resembles a thin custard. Combine crumbs, coconut and walnuts, blending well. Add to custard mixture. Pack evenly in a 9 x 9 x 2" pan.

Icing:
  ¼ c. butter
  3 T. milk
  2 T. vanilla pudding mix
    (regular or instant)
  2 c. confectioners sugar
  4 squares (4 oz.) semi-sweet
    chocolate
  2 T. butter

Cream the ¼ c. butter, add milk which has been combined with powdered vanilla pudding mix; blend in powdered sugar. Spread over filling; chill at least 15 minutes in refrigerator. Melt semi-sweet chocolate and butter; spread on the custard icing. Cut into squares and chill. Wrap and store in refrigerator.

Mrs. H. Alfred Bolton III

NUT SQUARES

Do Ahead† Yield: 3 dozen 275°
1 hr.

1 c. soft butter
1 c. sugar
2 c. sifted flour
1 egg yolk
1 tsp. vanilla
1 egg white
1 or more cups chopped
  nuts

Cream butter and sugar. Add flour, egg yolk and vanilla. Spread evenly in bottom of well greased jelly roll pan (or other pan with low sides). Brush top with egg white. Sprinkle with chopped nuts. Bake at 275° for 1 hour or until golden brown. Cut in squares. Store covered for 3 days before serving.

Mrs. William S. McDaniel
Mrs. Thomas W. Fetzer

ICED PEANUT BUTTER BARS

Easy   Yield: 2½-3 dozen   350°
                                                             25-30 min.

½ c. chunky peanut butter   Melt peanut butter and margarine in
½ c. margarine   bowl over hot water. Add remaining
1½ c. sugar   ingredients. Stir until blended. Put
2 eggs   in greased and floured 9 x 13" pan.
1½ tsp. baking powder   Remove from oven when done. Top
½ tsp. salt   with 6 milk-chocolate Hershey bars (no
1 tsp. vanilla   almonds). Let melt, spread, then
1 c. all-purpose flour   remove from pan in bars.

6 Hershey bars   Mrs. John R. Carlisle

ENGLISH TEA COOKIES

†   Yield: About 5 dozen   350°
                                                             15-20 min.

½ box raisins   Have raisins cooked, drained and
1½ c. shortening   cooled. Cream shortening and sugar
3 c. brown sugar   together. Add eggs separately, beating
3 eggs   after each one. Add 1½ c. cake flour,
4½ c. cake flour   cold coffee, soda, vanilla and salt.
⅜ c. cold coffee   Then mix in remaining 3 c. flour. Add
1½ tsp. soda   raisins and nuts. Spread in large
1 tsp. vanilla   greased cake pan (9 x 13") and 2 round
1 tsp. salt   layer cake pans. Bake 15-20 minutes
1 c. chopped nuts   at 350°. Test to be sure they are
  (optional)   done. Cool. Dust top with powdered
                                sugar. Cut in squares and store in
                                cookie tin or will freeze.

                                Mrs. Arthur C. Krepps II

CAKES and PIES

MRS. MANN'S ANGEL FOOD CAKE

225-450°
45 min.

12 egg whites
¼ tsp. salt
2 tsp. cream of tartar
1⅓ c. fine granulated sugar
1 c. cake flour
¼ tsp. almond extract
1 T. orange juice
1 tsp. vanilla

Add salt to whites and begin to beat (a wire whisk and copper bowl are best for this). As soon as the whites begin to foam, add cream of tartar and beat until stiff enough to invert bowl. Fold in sugar gradually and sift in flour the same way. Fold in flavoring and bake in ungreased tube pan at 225° for 30 minutes. Increase heat gradually to 450° to brown. Total baking time is 45 minutes. Invert pan and cool cake before removing by running thin knife around the edge and tube.

Mrs. H. W. Barnes

FRESH APPLE CAKE

350°
1 hr. 10 min.

1 c. oil
3 eggs
2 c. sugar
1 tsp. vanilla
3 c. flour
1 tsp. salt
1 tsp. soda
1 tsp. cinnamon
1 tsp. nutmeg
1 tsp. ground cloves
3 c. mellow apples,
    diced and peeled
1 c. pecans, chopped

Mix oil, eggs, sugar and vanilla well. Sift dry ingredients; blend with first mixture. Mixture will be thick. Add apples and pecans. Coat well. Grease and flour Bundt pan. Put in cold oven. Let cake cool somewhat before removing from pan. While still warm, glaze.

Glaze:
    ¼ c. margarine
    ½ tsp. vanilla
    ½ c. light brown sugar
    2 T. milk

Mix and boil 1 minute.

Mrs. Walter E. Jones

BANANA CAKE

Easy†
Do Ahead

350°
25 min.

¾ c. shortening (Crisco
  or margarine)
1½ c. sugar
2 eggs
1 tsp. salt
1 c. mashed bananas
½ c. buttermilk (or ½ c. sweet
  milk with 1 tsp. vinegar)
1 tsp. baking powder
1 tsp. soda
2 c. flour

Cream shortening and sugar. Add eggs. Beat. Mix in bananas, milk, salt, baking powder, soda and flour. Bake about 25 minutes at 350° in greased tube pan.

Icing:
  ¼ c. margarine, softened
  1 box 10X confectioners
    sugar
  ⅛ - ¼ c. milk
  1 tsp. lemon flavoring

Cream margarine, adding sugar slowly. Use just enough milk to get the right consistency. Add lemon flavoring. Spread on cake.

Mrs. Lewis T. Murphy

BLUEBERRY TEA CAKE

Do Ahead

375°
40-45 min.

2 c. sifted flour
2 tsp. baking powder
½ tsp. salt
¼ c. butter
¾ c. sugar
1 egg beaten
½ c. milk
2 c. washed and drained
  blueberries

Sift together flour, baking powder and salt. Cream butter. Gradually beat in sugar and add egg and milk. Beat until smooth. Add dry ingredients. Fold in blueberries. Spread batter in an 8 or 9" greased square pan. Sprinkle topping over cake. Bake at 375° for 40 to 45 minutes.

Topping:
  ½ c. sugar
  ¼ c. flour
  ½ tsp. cinnamon
  ½ c. butter

To mix topping - combine sugar, flour and cinnamon. Cut in butter to form coarse crumbs. Spread on top of cake mixture.

Mrs. James R. Fortune, Jr.

BOURBON CAKE

Do Ahead

275°
3½ hrs.

2 c. red candied cherries
1½ c. seedless raisins
2 c. bourbon
1½ c. butter or margarine
2⅓ c. granulated sugar
2⅓ c. brown sugar
6 eggs, separated
5 c. sifted cake flour
4 c. pecan meats (about
   1 lb.)
2 tsp. nutmeg
1 tsp. baking powder

Combine cherries, raisins and bourbon. Cover and let stand overnight. Drain fruits; reserve bourbon. Cream butter and sugars together until light. Add egg yolks and beat well. Combine ½ c. flour, nutmeg, baking powder and pecans together. Add remaining flour and bourbon alternately to butter mixture, beating well after each addition. Beat egg whites until stiff, but not dry. Fold egg whites into flour mixture. Fold soaked fruits and pecan-flour mixture into batter. Turn into greased 10-inch tube pan lined with greased waxed paper. Bake in slow oven, 275°, for 3½ hours. Cool. Remove from pan. Fill center of cake with cheesecloth which is saturated with bourbon. Wrap in heavy waxed paper or aluminum foil. Store in tightly covered container. Keep in cool place (in refrigerator, if necessary).

Mrs. Allen J. Brock
Atlanta, Georgia

BUTTERCUP CAKE

Easy†

350°
25 min.

¾ c. butter
1½ c. sugar
8 egg yolks
1 whole egg
½ c. milk
2 c. cake flour
½ tsp. soda
1½ tsp. cream of tartar
1 tsp. mace oil
1 tsp. lemon

Gently mix all ingredients. Bake in two greased 9" pans at 350° for about 25 minutes or until springy.

Mrs. John H. Goddard

CARROT CAKE

Do Ahead

350°
1 hr.

3 c. flour
2 tsp. baking powder
2 tsp. baking soda
½ tsp. salt
2¼ c. sugar
2 tsp. cinnamon
1 tsp. nutmeg
½ tsp. allspice
1½ c. salad oil
2 c. grated carrots
4 eggs
1 tsp. vanilla
1 c. chopped nuts

Sift flour, baking powder, soda and salt. Mix together sugar and spices and add to dry ingredients. Mix together oil, carrots, eggs, vanilla and nuts. Add to mixture of dry ingredients. Pour into ungreased 10" tube cake pan. Bake in pre-heated oven at 350° for 1 hour.

Icing:
    2 (3 oz.) pkgs. cream
      cheese
    3 c. powdered sugar
    1 tsp. butter
    1 tsp. vanilla
    chopped nuts

Soften cream cheese and mix with sugar, butter and vanilla. Spread on cake and sprinkle with nuts.

Mrs. Fred R. Smith

CHINESE WEDDING CAKE

350°
25 min.

6 eggs, separated
1 c. sugar
1 c. flour
1 tsp. salt

Beat egg whites. When foamy add sugar and continue beating until very stiff. (This may take a while, but be sure they are stiff.) Add 1 egg yolk at a time. Beat well after each. Fold in flour and salt. Line two 8" pans with waxed paper. Pour in cake batter and bake for 25 minutes. Cool for 10 minutes and remove from pan.

Topping:
    1 pt. whipping cream
    ½ c. sugar
    1 tsp. vanilla
    1 sm. can crushed pineapple,
      drained

Whip cream, then add sugar. Fold in vanilla and pineapple.

Mrs. Gerald I. Lawhorn

CHOCOLATE SHEATH CAKE

Easy†   400°
Do Ahead   20 min.

2 c. sugar
2 c. flour
½ tsp. salt
½ c. Crisco
½ c. margarine
4 T. cocoa
1 c. water
½ c. buttermilk
2 eggs, slightly beaten
1 tsp. soda
1 tsp. vanilla
1 tsp. cinnamon

Sift into large mixing bowl sugar, flour and salt. Into saucepan put Crisco, margarine, cocoa and water; bring to a rapid boil. Pour this hot mixture over flour mixture and stir well. Add buttermilk, eggs, soda, vanilla and cinnamon. Mix well and pour into a greased pan 16 x 11". Bake 20 minutes at 400°.

Icing:
   ½ c. margarine
   4 T. cocoa
   6 T. milk
   1 box powdered sugar,
      sifted
   1 tsp. vanilla
   1 c. chopped nuts

Start making icing before cake is done. Put margarine, cocoa and milk in pan. Melt and bring to a boil, stirring constantly. Remove from heat and add powdered sugar, vanilla and nuts. Beat well and spread on cake while still hot. When cake is cold, cut in squares and remove from pan.

Mrs. Joe G. Hunter, Jr.
Opelika, Alabama

CHOCOLATE UPSIDE DOWN CAKE

Easy   350°
                                                  45 min.

1 T. shortening
¾ c. sugar
1 c. flour
2 tsp. baking powder
½ tsp. salt
2 T. cocoa
½ c. milk
1 tsp. vanilla
1 T. shortening (grease
   pans)
2½ T. cocoa
½ c. white sugar
½ c. brown sugar
1 c. boiling water

Cream shortening and sugar. Add flour, baking powder, salt and cocoa which have been sifted together, alternately with milk. Add vanilla. Put in greased 8 x 8" cake pan. Mix cocoa, white and brown sugar in boiling water and pour on top of cake mixture. Bake. Best served hot.

Mrs. Charles L. Smith

Editor's note: This is an old-fashioned "pudding cake."

GERMAN CHOCOLATE CAKE

Do Ahead†

350°
30-40 min.

1 (4 oz.) pkg. German chocolate
½ c. boiling water
1 c. butter or margarine
2 c. sugar
4 egg yolks
1 tsp. vanilla
2½ c. sifted cake flour
1 tsp. baking soda
½ tsp. salt
1 c. buttermilk
4 egg whites, stiffly beaten

Melt chocolate in boiling water. Cool. Cream butter and sugar until fluffy. Add egg yolks, one at a time. Blend in vanilla and chocolate. Sift flour with soda and salt; add alternately with buttermilk to chocolate mixture beating after each addition until smooth. Fold in beaten egg whites. Pour into three 8 or 9 inch pans, well greased. Bake 350° 30-40 minutes. Cool. Frost tops only with Coconut Pecan Frosting.

Variation: To make a white chocolate cake, substitute ¼ lb. white chocolate for German chocolate and add 1 c. coconut and 2 tsp. vanilla. Frost with Coconut Pecan Frosting.

Coconut Pecan Frosting:

1 c. evaporated milk
1 c. sugar
3 egg yolks, slightly beaten
½ c. butter or margarine
1 tsp. vanilla
1⅓ c. coconut
1 c. chopped pecans

Combine milk, sugar, egg yolks, butter and vanilla. Cook and stir over medium heat until thickened - about 12 minutes. Add coconut and pecans. Cool until thick enough to spread; beat occasionally. Spread on cake. Makes about 2½ c.

Mrs. William A. Harris

"TIP"

To prevent cake from sticking to plate, sift powdered sugar on plate before placing fresh cake on it.

COCA-COLA CAKE

Easy   Serves 16   350°
                                                        35 min.

2 c. unsifted all-purpose
  flour
2 c. granulated sugar
3 T. cocoa
1 c. Coca-Cola
1 c. margarine
1½ c. miniature marshmallows
2 eggs
½ c. buttermilk
1 tsp. baking soda
1 tsp. vanilla

Mix flour and sugar. Bring to boil cocoa, Coke, margarine and marsh-mallows. Mix boiled mixture with flour mixture. Mix remaining ingredients and add to first mixture. Bake in greased and floured 13 x 9 x 2" pan for 35 minutes.
Very moist chocolate cake.

Frosting:
  ½ c. margarine
  1 T. cocoa
  6 T. Coca-Cola
  1 box 4X powdered sugar
  ½ c. chopped nuts

Bring all but sugar and nuts to boil over medium-high heat. Stir sugar in and mix well. Add nuts. Spread over cake while both icing and cake are still warm.

Mrs. Jack Keene
Williamson, Georgia

MILLION DOLLAR CHOCOLATE CAKE

350°
25-30 min.

1 c. sugar
2 T. cocoa
½ tsp. salt
1 egg
½ c. shortening
1 tsp. soda in ½ c. sour
   Milk
1½ c. cake flour
¼ c. boiling water

Combine ingredients in order given and bake in 2 greased and floured 8" or 9" layer pans at 350° for 25-30 minutes. Cool and fill with following filling and frost with Seven Minute Brown Sugar Frosting.

Filling:
   1 c. sugar
   1¾ c. water
   2 T. cocoa
   3 T. cornstarch
   4-6 T. butter
   ½ c. nutmeats
   1 tsp. vanilla extract

Combine all ingredients in top of double boiler. Cook over hot water until quite thick. While still warm, spread between layers and on top of cake.

7 Minute Brown Sugar Frosting:

   ½ c. light brown sugar
   ½ c. granulated sugar
   3 T. cold water
   ½ tsp. cream of tartar
   2 egg whites
   ½ tsp. vanilla extract (or
      1 tsp. lemon juice)

Mix all ingredients in top of a double boiler. Water in lower part should be boiling gently. Beat exactly 7 minutes as it cooks. Remove from heat and cool. Spread over top and sides of cake.

   3 (1 oz.) squares unsweetened
      chocolate

Seal chocolate in aluminum foil (for homemade icing tube). Place in warm oven until melted. Snip one corner and squeeze chocolate over top and sides.
Do not make Million Dollar Chocolate Cake, Filling or 7 Minute Brown Sugar Frosting when excessive moisture is in the air.

Mrs. Charlie T. Phillips

Not a "high" chocolate cake but small, rich and delicious.

MISSISSIPPI MUD CAKE

Serves 16   325°
40 min.

1 c. butter or margarine
2 c. sugar
½ c. cocoa
4 eggs
1½ c. cake flour
dash salt
1½ c. pecans, chopped
1 tsp. vanilla
1 (6 oz.) pkg. miniature
  marshmallows

Cream butter, sugar and cocoa. Add eggs, one at a time, and beat well after each addition. Add flour, salt, nuts and vanilla; mix well. Put batter in greased and floured 13x9x2" pan. Bake at 325° for 40 minutes or less. Remove and spread with marshmallows until melted. Ice with chocolate frosting while warm.

Mississippi Mud Icing:

6 T. butter or margarine
1½ boxes powdered sugar
6 T. cocoa
1½ tsp. vanilla
canned milk

Cream butter thoroughly; add sugar and cocoa and beat well. Add vanilla and milk until it reaches spreading consistency. Spread on warm cake.

Mrs. Richard P. Gaston

MRS. MANN'S DEVIL'S FOOD CAKE

350°

1 c. grated unsweetened
  chocolate
1 c. brown sugar
½ c. milk
1 egg yolk
1 tsp. vanilla
½ c. butter
1 c. sugar
2 c. flour
½ c. milk
2 egg yolks, beaten
1 tsp. soda
1 T. boiling water
3 egg whites, stiffly
  beaten

Make a custard in double boiler of chocolate, brown sugar, milk and egg yolk. Cool and add vanilla. In another bowl cream butter and sugar. Add flour, milk and egg yolks alternately. Add soda dissolved in boiling water. Fold custard into batter, then add stiffly beaten egg whites. Bake in 2 layer cake pans at 350° until done.

Mrs. H. W. Barnes

GINGERBREAD

Easy†
Do Ahead

350°
30 min.

1 c. sifted all-purpose flour
½ tsp. soda
¼ tsp. salt
1 tsp. cinnamon
1½ tsp. ginger
pinch of cloves
1 egg
6 T. packed brown sugar
¼ c. molasses
½ c. sour skim milk*
2 T. margarine softened

Sift all dry ingredients onto waxed paper. Beat egg with sugar and molasses until light. Add soured milk, butter and dry ingredients. Beat until smooth. Put in 8" square non-stick baking pan (or can lightly grease pan, but adds calories.) The cake is done when center springs back when lightly pressed.
*To sour milk: Put 2 tsp. lemon juice or vinegar in a 1 c. measure; add skim milk to ½ c. mark.

Mrs. Donald L. Hutcheson

SUMMER FRUIT CAKE

Do Ahead

1 (4½ oz.) can blanched whole almonds
2 (3 oz.) pkgs. cream cheese
1 (8 oz.) pkg. cream cheese
⅓ c. milk
½ c. confectioners sugar
1 c. seedless green grapes
½ c. pecans
⅓ c. slivered almonds
1 c. soft bread crumbs
1 T. grated lemon peel
10 lge. strawberries
1 lge. peach, peeled and quartered

Day before serving: In blender at low speed, finely grind almonds; set aside. In small bowl with beater at high speed, blend cream cheese and 5 T. milk until smooth and fluffy. Beat in ½ c. ground almonds and sugar. With wooden spoon, stir in grapes, pecans and almonds. In small bowl with fork, mix together bread crumbs, remaining ground almonds and lemon peel. Add 1 T. milk and toss with two forks until mixture begins to stick together. Line bottom and sides of 8 x 5" pan with waxed paper. Press ½ of crumb mixture into bottom. Spread ⅓ cheese mixture over crumbs and arrange ¾ of fruit on top. Gently press fruit halfway into mixture. Add about 1⅓ c. of cheese and press remaining fruit into it. Smooth rest of cheese over fruit and sprinkle remaining crumbs evenly over top. Fold waxed paper extensions over cake; press down firmly. Refrigerate overnight.

Mrs. Harvey Andress
Galax, Virginia

HARVEST LOAF CAKE

Do Ahead†

350°
65-75 min.

1¾ c. flour
1 tsp. soda
½ tsp. salt
1 tsp. cinnamon
½ tsp. nutmeg
¼ tsp. ginger
¼ tsp. ground cloves
½ c. butter
1 c. sugar
2 eggs
¾ c. canned or cooked
   pumpkin
¾ c. chocolate morsels
¾ c. chopped walnuts

Grease bottom of 9x5x3" pan. Combine flour with soda, salt and spices and sift together. Cream butter in large mixing bowl. Gradually add sugar and cream at high speed of mixer until light and fluffy. Blend in eggs; beat well. At low speed add dry ingredients alternately with pumpkin; begin and end with dry ingredients. Blend well after each addition. Stir in chocolate morsels and ½ c. walnuts. Pour into pan. Sprinkle with ¼ c. walnuts and bake at 350° for 65 to 75 minutes until cake springs back when touched lightly in center. Cool. Drizzle with glaze. Let stand 6 hours before slicing.
Tip: I always make 2 cakes at the same time and freeze one. Better fresh but does freeze okay.

Spice Glaze:
   ½ c. confectioners sugar,
     sifted
   ⅛ tsp. nutmeg
   ⅛ tsp. cinnamon
   1-2 T. cream

Combine confectioners sugar, nutmeg and cinnamon. Blend in cream until the consistency of a glaze. Drizzle on cake.

Mrs. William C. Hewitt

ITALIAN CREAM CAKE

350°
25 min.

½ c. shortening
½ c. margarine
2 c. sugar
5 egg yolks
2 c. flour
1 tsp. soda
1 c. buttermilk
1 tsp. vanilla
1 sm. can or pkg. coconut
1 c. chopped nuts
5 egg whites, stiffly beaten

Cream shortening, margarine and sugar. Add egg yolks one at a time. Combine flour and soda. Add to mixture alternately with buttermilk. Stir in vanilla. Add coconut and nuts. Fold in egg whites. Pour in 9" cake pans (3). Bake at 350° oven for 25 minutes or until cake is done.

(Continued on next page)

Cream Cheese Frosting:

1 (8 oz.) pkg. cream cheese
¼ c. margarine
1 tsp. vanilla
1 box powdered sugar
½ c. chopped nuts

Beat cream cheese and margarine until smooth. Add vanilla and sugar. Spread on cool cake. Sprinkle top and sides with nuts.

Mrs. Alyn R. Jones, Jr.
Zebulon, Georgia

MRS. MULLINS' LANE CAKE

Do Ahead

375°
20 min.

1 c. butter or margarine
2 c. sugar
3 c. flour (plain)
2 tsp. baking powder
¾ tsp. salt
1 c. milk
1 tsp. vanilla
8 egg whites

Cream butter and sugar. Sift flour, baking powder and salt. Beat in small amount of flour mixture into the creamed butter and sugar. Beat in small amount of milk. Alternate flour mixture and milk, beginning and ending with flour. Add vanilla. Beat egg whites stiff. Fold egg whites into cake batter. Pour into three, 9" cake pans which have been greased and floured. Bake at 375° for 20 minutes.

Filling for Lane Cake:
  ½ c. butter
  1 c. sugar
  8 egg yolks, beaten
  1½ c. nuts
  1½ c. seedless raisins
  1½ c. coconut
  1 tsp. vanilla
  ¼ c. orange juice

Cream butter and sugar. Add beaten egg yolks. Cook in double boiler until thick but not sugar-like. Pour over nuts, raisins and coconut. Add vanilla and juice. Mix well. Spread between layers and on top of the cooled cake.

Mrs. Richard L. Mullins

OLD FASHIONED LEMON CHEESE CAKE

Do Ahead

350°
30 min.

¾ c. margarine
1½ c. sugar
5 egg whites
3 c. flour (all-purpose)
3 tsp. baking powder
1 c. milk
1 tsp. lemon flavoring

Cream margarine and sugar. Add egg whites one at a time and beat well after each. Sift together flour and baking powder. Add flavoring to milk. Add flour and milk alternately. Pour into two greased 10" pans and bake 30 minutes at 350°.

Filling:
  1 c. sugar
  ½ c. margarine
  juice and rind of
    1 lemon
  7 egg yolks

Mix all ingredients in double boiler. Cook until thick, stirring occasionally. Spread between layers and on top.

Frosting:
  ⅛ tsp. cream of tartar
  1 c. sugar
  ⅓ c. water
  2 egg whites, beaten
    stiff
  ½ tsp. vanilla

Boil cream of tartar, sugar and water until it spins a thread. Pour into stiffly beaten egg whites; mix well and add vanilla. Spread on cake.

Mrs. Walter E. Jones

1 - 2 - 3 - 4 CAKE

350°
25-60 min.

2 c. sugar
1 c. shortening
4 egg yolks
1 tsp. vanilla
3 c. flour, sifted
3 tsp. baking powder
¼ tsp. salt
1 c. milk
4 egg whites, stiffly
  beaten

Cream together sugar and shortening, add egg yolks and vanilla. Add dry ingredients alternately with milk. Beat 4 minutes. Fold in egg whites. Put into two greased 8" square pans or a tube pan may be used. Bake 350° for about 1 hour if a tube pan is used, or 25 minutes for square pans. Ice with any type of icing or serve plain.

Mrs. James S. Murray
Durham, New Hampshire

PORK SPICE CAKE

250°
2½-3 hrs.

1 pt. boiling water
1¼ lbs. fresh fat from pork,
  ground
6 eggs, beaten
2 lbs. light brown sugar
5 c. flour
1 T. soda
½ tsp. salt
2 tsp. nutmeg
1 tsp. allspice
1 tsp. cloves
2 tsp. cinnamon
1 lb. (4½ c.) chopped nut
  meats (pecans, walnuts)
2 lbs. white raisins

Pour boiling water over fat. Add beaten eggs to brown sugar; combine fat and egg mixture. Sift flour, soda, salt and spices together and add to the above mixture. Lightly coat nuts and raisins with flour and add to cake mix. Line bottoms of two tube or loaf pans with brown paper, grease and flour. Bake at 250° for 2½ to 3 hours until browned.

Mrs. William T. Johnson

OLD FASHIONED POUND CAKE

Do Ahead†

325°
1 hr. 30 min.

8 eggs
2²⁄₃ c. sugar, sifted
2 c. butter
3½ c. Swans Down Cake
  Flour
8 T. whipping cream
2 tsp. vanilla
pinch salt

Separate eggs. Beat egg whites with 6 T. of the sugar, place in refrigerator until rest of cake is mixed. Cream butter, add rest of sugar gradually - beat until light (10 minutes with electric beater). Add egg yolks 2 at a time, beating well. Add flour and cream alternately. Add vanilla. Fold in egg whites. Bake in greased and floured tube pan 1½ hours at 325°. Cool 5 minutes, loosen around sides and tube carefully before removing. Preheat oven and do not open oven during baking. Makes a large cake.

Mrs. Carl H. Cartledge

Editor's note: Well worth the effort.

BUTTERNUT POUND CAKE

Do Ahead

325°
1 hr.
10-20 min.

1 c. Crisco shortening
2 c. sugar
5 eggs, at room
temperature
2½ c. cake flour
½ c. self-rising flour
1 c. milk
3 tsp. butternut flavoring

Cream shortening and sugar for 10 minutes. Add eggs one at a time. Beat slowly 1 minute. Add 1 c. flour; beat 1 minute. Alternately add remaining flour and milk a little at a time, mixing until creamy. Add flavoring. Turn into well greased and floured Bundt pan. Bake 1 hour at 325°, increase temperature to 350° and bake 10-20 minutes.

Frosting:
  ½ c. margarine
  1 (8 oz.) pkg. cream
    cheese
  1 box 4X sugar
  1 tsp. butternut flavoring
  1 c. pecans, chopped

Have ingredients at room temperature. Cream the margarine with cream cheese, then add sugar. When well blended, add flavoring and nuts. Keep in the refrigerator as the frosting tends to be too soft if left at room temperature.

Mrs. Enrique Montero

CREAM CHEESE POUND CAKE

Easy†
Do Ahead

300°
1 hr. 45 min.

3 c. sugar
1½ c. margarine
8 oz. cream cheese, softened
6 eggs
2 tsp. vanilla
3 c. cake flour

Cream sugar and margarine. Cut cream cheese into three parts and add, alternately, with eggs one at a time. Add vanilla. Sift flour and add to mixture 1 c. at a time. Bake in greased and floured tube pan.

Mrs. C. Ray Barron
Mrs. Joe G. Hunter, Jr.
Opelika, Alabama

CHOCOLATE POUND CAKE

Do Ahead†

350°
1 hr. 15 min.

8 (1.2 oz.) Hershey Bars
1 (5½ oz.) can Hershey syrup
½ tsp. soda
1 c. buttermilk
1 c. margarine
2 c. sugar
4 whole eggs
2½ c. sifted flour
1 tsp. vanilla

Melt candy bars in syrup. Add soda to buttermilk. Cream margarine and sugar in mixer. Add eggs one at a time, then buttermilk and flour alternately. Add chocolate mixture and vanilla. Cook at 350° about 1 hour and 15 minutes in greased and floured large tube pan. Cool in pan for about 10 to 15 minutes on rack before turning out onto plate.

Mrs. Fred R. Smith

"TIP"

To keep cakes fresh; put half of an apple in the container.

COCONUT POUND CAKE

Do Ahead†

325°
1 hr. 20 min.

1½ c. butter
3 c. sugar
6 eggs
3 c. sifted flour
¼ tsp. salt
¼ tsp. soda
1 c. sour cream
1 tsp. vanilla
1 (6 oz.) pkg. frozen
    coconut (thawed)

Cream butter; add sugar slowly until mixture is light and fluffy. Add eggs one at a time, beating well after each addition. Sift flour and measure. Resift three times with salt and soda. Add flour mixture alternately with sour cream, beginning and ending with flour mixture. Add flavoring. Remove from electric mixer at this point. Fold in package of coconut. Bake in 10" tube pan that has been well greased and bottom lined with waxed paper (grease over liner, too). Bake at 325° for 1 hour and 20 minutes until done. When baking, use rack about 5" from bottom of oven.

Mrs. Tom Lockhart

SOUR CREAM POUND CAKE

Easy†   350°
Do Ahead   1½ hr.

1 c. butter
3 c. sugar
6 eggs
3 c. flour
¼ tsp. baking soda
1 c. sour cream
1 tsp. water
1 jigger bourbon (1½ oz.)

Cream butter and sugar. Add eggs, one at a time, beating well. Sift flour with baking soda and add alternately with sour cream. Add water and bourbon. Bake in oven in greased and floured tube pan for 1½ hours at 350°.
Note: For variation, add 1 tsp. each of orange flavoring, lemon flavoring and vanilla.

Mrs. Eugene F. Robbins, Jr.

PRUNE CAKE I

Easy   325°
Do Ahead   45-50 min.

3 eggs
1 c. Wesson oil
1½ c. sugar
1 c. buttermilk
1 tsp. each cinnamon, nutmeg,
   allspice, vanilla
2 c. plain flour
1 tsp. soda
1 tsp. baking powder
1 c. chopped cooked
   prunes
1 c. chopped nuts

Put all ingredients in a mixing bowl and mix until well blended. Cook in greased 9 x 13" cake pan.

Sauce:
   1 c. sugar
   ½ c. buttermilk with
      ½ tsp. soda
   1 T. white syrup
   ¼ c. butter
   ½ tsp. vanilla

Mix together and boil about 5 minutes. Pour sauce over cake while warm (not hot).

Mrs. Paul McCubbin
Campbellsville, Kentucky

PRUNE CAKE II

Easy†
Do Ahead

350°
1 hr.

2 c. self-rising flour
2 c. sugar
1 tsp. cinnamon
1 tsp. nutmeg
1 tsp. allspice
1 c. chopped nuts
1 c. vegetable oil
3 eggs, slightly beaten
1 (7¾ oz.) junior size jar
of prunes with tapioca
baby food

Sift first five ingredients together. Add nuts. Combine oil, eggs and prunes. Add to dry ingredients and mix until well blended. Turn into a greased and floured tube or Bundt pan and bake.

Mrs. Louis Arnett

Variation: For Plum Nutty Cake substitute 2 (4¾ oz.) jars baby food plums for prunes.
Frosting: ½ c. powdered sugar and enough lemon juice to make spreading consistency.

Mrs. Alyn R. Jones, Jr.
Zebulon, Georgia

VANILLA WAFER CAKE

Do Ahead†

325°
1½-1¾ hr.

2 c. sugar
1 c. margarine
6 eggs
1 (12 oz.) box vanilla
wafers, rolled fine
½ c. milk
1 c. pecans, chopped
1 (7 oz.) bag flaked
coconut

Cream sugar and margarine. Add eggs one at a time beating well after each. Add vanilla wafers and mix well. Add milk; mix. Add nuts and coconut. Pour into a greased and floured tube pan.
Can top with whipped cream or vanilla ice cream.

Mrs. John R. Carlisle

START WITH A MIX

CHERRY DEVILICIOUS CAKE

Do Ahead   350°

1 (2 layer size) pkg. devil's
   food cake mix
1 (8 oz.) pkg. cream cheese,
   softened
2 T. sugar
2 T. milk
1 pkg. whipped topping mix
1 (16 oz.) can dark sweet
   cherries (pitted)
2 T. cornstarch
2 T. sugar
¼ c. water
¼ c. burgundy

Prepare devil's food cake mix by package directions. Bake in Bundt pan. Cool and remove to serving plate. In mixing bowl, beat together cream cheese, 2 T. sugar and milk until fluffy. Prepare topping mix according to package directions; fold into cream cheese mixture. Chill. Drain cherries, reserve syrup. In small saucepan, combine cornstarch, and the remaining sugar, mixing well. Gradually stir in cherry syrup and water. Cook and stir over medium heat until thickened and bubbly. Stir in cherries; heat through. Remove from heat; stir in burgundy. Spoon cheese mixture into center of cake, top with some cherry sauce. Pass additional cherry sauce. Bake the cake a day ahead, also prepare the whipped topping, cream cheese mixture if you wish. The cherry sauce is last minute - can be reheated over low heat.

Mrs. Jerry Hollberg

COCONUT CAKE

Easy†   350°
Do Ahead

1 yellow or white Duncan
   Hines cake mix
2 T. Wesson oil

Coconut Frosting:
   3 (6 oz.) pkgs. frozen
      coconut
   1 c. sour cream
   1½ c. sugar

Follow directions on cake mix box, but add 2 T. Wesson oil. When cake is done and cooled, mix all ingredients for icing and spread. To stay fresh, should be kept in the refrigerator.

Mrs. T. M. Furlow, Jr.

RUM CAKE

Do Ahead

325°
1 hr.

1 c. pecans, chopped
1 pkg. Duncan Hines yellow
  cake mix
1 (3¾ oz.) pkg. instant vanilla
  pudding mix
½ c. water
½ c. Wesson oil
½ c. white rum
4 eggs

1 c. sugar
¼ c. water
½ c. butter
3 oz. white rum

Preheat oven to 325°. Grease and flour 10" tube or Bundt pan. Sprinkle nuts over the bottom of the pan. Mix all cake ingredients except eggs together and beat well. Beat in eggs, one at a time, beating well after each addition. Pour batter over nuts. Bake 1 hour. Ten minutes before the cake is done, mix sugar, water and butter in a saucepan. Boil 1 minute, remove from heat, stir in rum. Pour over cake as soon as it is removed from the oven. Allow cake to absorb glaze and repeat until all glaze is used up. Remove from pan while still warm.

Mrs. Frank Harris
Mrs. Donald E. Hutcheson

SOUR CREAM PECAN CAKE

Easy†
Do Ahead

300°
1 hr.

1 pkg. Duncan Hines Butter
  Recipe Golden cake mix
½ c. sugar
1 pt. sour cream
pinch of salt
4 eggs
4 T. dark brown sugar
1 c. pecan pieces
2 tsp. cinnamon

Combine cake mix with sugar, sour cream, salt and eggs beating after the addition of each egg. In a separate bowl mix brown sugar, pecans and cinnamon. Grease well and flour a Bundt cake pan. Pour into pan a thin layer of batter and then a layer of brown sugar mixture. Repeat until you have 3 layers of batter and 2 layers of the brown sugar mixture. Bake in 300° oven for 1 hour or until done.

Mrs. James R. Fortune, Jr.

CUPCAKES

APPLESAUCE CUPCAKES

Easy†
Do Ahead

375°
20 min.

½ c. butter
1 c. sugar
1 c. applesauce
1 tsp. baking soda, stirred
   in ½ of the applesauce
2 c. flour
1 tsp. cinnamon
½ tsp. cloves (ground)
1 tsp. lemon flavoring
1 c. raisins
1 c. nuts

Cream butter and sugar. Add ½ of the applesauce and beat well. Sift flour, cinnamon and cloves together. Add to butter-sugar mixture alternately with the other ½ of applesauce and soda. Add lemon flavoring, nuts and raisins. Bake in paper shells in muffin tins at 375° for about 20 minutes.

Mrs. Sid Esary

CHOCOLATE CHIP CUPCAKES

Easy†
Do Ahead

375°
20 min.

1 tsp. vanilla
½ c. shortening
1 c. sugar
1 egg
2 c. sifted flour
½ tsp. salt
2½ tsp. baking powder
¾ c. milk
1 (6 oz.) pkg. semi-sweet
   chocolate chips

Add vanilla to shortening, cream in sugar until light and fluffy. Add egg and beat well. Sift flour, then measure and sift together with salt and baking powder. Add flour mixture to creamed mixture alternately with the milk. Stir in chocolate chips. Grease muffin tin or use paper liners, fill ⅔ full. Bake at 375° about 20 minutes. Cool on wire rack.

Mrs. Howell A. Fowler, Jr.

FRUIT CAKE CUPS

300°
30 min.

15 oz. golden raisins
1 c. frozen orange juice
½ c. margarine
1 c. orange marmalade
¼ c. brandy or bourbon
1 lge. egg, beaten
1 c. nuts
2 c. candied chopped fruit
2 c. sifted flour
1 tsp. salt
½ tsp. soda
1 tsp. cinnamon
½ tsp. nutmeg
cherries or nuts

Mix together raisins, margarine and orange juice and simmer 10 minutes. Cool and add marmalade. Mix in brandy, egg, nuts and fruit. Sift together dry ingredients and fold in last. Add cherries or nuts for garnish. Cook in small muffin tins at 300° for 30 minutes.

Mrs. James C. Owen

SELF-FILLED CUPCAKES

Easy†
Do Ahead

350°
15-20 min.

1 (2 layer) pkg. chocolate
    cake mix
1 (8 oz.) pkg. cream cheese,
    softened
⅓ c. sugar
1 egg
dash salt
1 (6 oz.) pkg. semi-sweet
    chocolate chips

Mix cake by cake directions. Fill paper lined muffin tins ⅔ full. Cream cheese with sugar. Beat in salt and egg. Stir in chocolate chips. Drop 1 rounded tsp. cheese mixture into each cupcake. Bake by package directions for cupcakes - usually 350°, 15-20 minutes.

Mrs. Lutie C. Johnston

ICINGS AND SAUCES

CARAMEL CAKE FILLING

Easy†
Do Ahead

2 c. sugar ½ c. brown sugar ½ tsp. baking soda ½ c. butter 1 c. buttermilk 1 T. vanilla	Mix sugars, soda, butter and buttermilk. Cook until it forms soft ball when tested in cold water. Use heavy saucepan. Cool. Add flavoring. Beat until creamy. Nuts may be added if desired. Could be used as base for pralines.

Mrs. Lee Roy Claxton

CHOCOLATE ICING

1 c. brown sugar (light brown) 3 squares Baker's chocolate 3 T. butter ½ c. water 1 tsp. vanilla pinch salt 1 box 4X sugar	Combine first four ingredients in a saucepan and let come to a boil. Boil 3 minutes. Add vanilla and a pinch of salt. Take from stove and beat in 1 box of 4X sugar. Covers an 8" layer cake. *Never gets too hard.*

Mrs. Newton Penny

COCOA FUDGE FROSTING

Easy

½ c. butter ½ c. Hershey's Cocoa 3²/₃c. (1 lb. box) confectioners sugar 7 T. milk 1 tsp. vanilla	Melt butter in saucepan. Add cocoa, heat 1 minute, stirring constantly. Pour in small mixer bowl. Alternately add sugar and milk. Beat to spreading consistency. Add vanilla. Fills and frosts two 8" or 9" layers.

Mrs. Troy Smith, Jr.

MRS. DREWERY'S LEMON CHEESE

Easy
Do Ahead

1½ c. sugar
6 heaping T. plain flour
¼ tsp. salt
juice of 3 lemons
grated rind of 2 lemons
1 c. hot water
¼ c. butter
3 egg yolks

Put all except egg yolks in boiler and cook until thickened - about 15 minutes, stirring all the time. (Cook in heavy saucepan and stir with a wire whisk for quicker, smoother filling.) Gradually add 2 or 3 T. hot mixture to beaten egg yolks to keep them from lumping, then add yolk mixture to other hot ingredients. Cool before spreading on cake.
Cooks in less time than many other recipes. This isn't "tricky", runny or brittle.

Mrs. Lee Roy Claxton

LEMON SAUCE

Easy

2 eggs
1 c. sugar
½ c. margarine
⅓ c. lemon juice
grated rind of 2 lemons

Beat eggs well - add sugar and beat. (I use a blender.) Melt margarine with lemon juice. Very slowly add eggs and sugar to hot mixture. Stir in rind. Cook over low heat until it thickens. If it gets too thick, add ¼ c. water.
Very good served on Angel Food Cake or on gingerbread. Can be refrigerated for several days.

Mrs. Lewis T. Murphy

HOT FUDGE SAUCE

Easy
Do Ahead

½ c. butter
2¼ c. confectioners sugar
   (lightly pack sugar when
   measured)
⅔ c. evaporated milk
3 squares bitter chocolate
   (3 oz. total)

Mix butter and sugar in top of double boiler. (Mix after butter is almost melted.) Add evaporated milk and stir until mixture is free of lumps. Drop chocolate squares into mixture. Do not stir. Cover and cook over hot water for 30 minutes. Remove from heat and beat. This sauce may be stored in the refrigerator and reheated.

Mrs. Warren K. Scoville

PIES

AMBER PIE

Easy
Do Ahead

350°
12-15 min.

½ c. butter
¼ c. flour plus 1 T.
1 c. sugar
3 egg yolks, well beaten
½ c. cream
3 T. blackberry (or
favorite) jam
3 egg whites
6 T. sugar

Melt butter in skillet, blend in flour. Add sugar. Add 2 T. hot mixture to egg mix; blend in eggs. Cook 3 minutes. Add cream and jam. Pour into baked 9" pie shell, cover with meringue made from stiffly beaten egg whites and sugar. Bake.

Mrs. Paul McCubbin
Campbellsville, Kentucky

SOUR CREAM APPLE PIE

Easy
Do Ahead

350°
1 hr.

1 c. sour cream
¾ c. sugar
2 T. flour
¼ tsp. salt
1 tsp. vanilla
1 egg
2 c. diced, peeled apples
⅓ c. light brown sugar
2 T. flour
2 T. soft butter
1 - 9" unbaked pie shell

Beat well first 6 ingredients. Add apples. Pour into 9" unbaked pie shell. Bake 35-45 minutes at 350°. Take from oven and add last 3 ingredients which have been blended together. Return to oven for another 15-20 minutes.

Mrs. Jerry Hollberg

APPLE TART PENNSYLVANIA

Do Ahead†

375°-350°
40 min.

2 c. sliced apples
1 c. sugar
1 tsp. cloves
2 T. flour
1 T. lemon juice
⅓ tsp. salt
3 T. butter
4 T. cream

Mix apples, sugar and spices. Add flour. Pour into uncooked pie shell; add juice and salt. Spread with butter and cream. Bake 10 minutes in hot oven 375°. Put pie pan over pie, reduce heat to 350° and bake 30 minutes.

Mrs. Robert S. Ogletree, Jr.

BLACK BOTTOM PIE

Do Ahead

300°
10 min.

Crust:
30 gingersnaps, ground
5 level T. melted butter

Filling:
1 T. gelatin
¼ c. cold water
2 c. milk
¾ c. sugar
1¼ T. cornstarch
4 egg yolks

Chocolate Layer:
1½ oz. melted sweet
   chocolate
1 tsp. vanilla

Rum Layer:
4 egg whites, beaten
   stiff with ½ c. sugar
¼ tsp. cream of tartar
5 tsp. bourbon or rum

Topping:
1 c. cream, whipped stiff
   with 2 T. powdered
   sugar
½ oz. shredded chocolate

Grind gingersnaps and mix with melted butter. Place in bottom of 9" pie pan. Bake 10 minutes in 300° oven. (Grease bottom of pan with butter.

Dissolve gelatin in cold water. Set aside. Blend sugar and cornstarch well. Mix with milk and well beaten egg yolks. Cook until thick. Add chocolate and vanilla to 1 c. of custard. Mix well and cool. Add gelatin mixture to remaining hot custard. Mix well and cool. Spread cool chocolate custard in pie pan. Let stand until set. Make meringue from egg whites and cream of tartar, beaten until frothy, slowly adding sugar and bourbon. Fold into custard and pour over chocolate layer. Place in refrigerator to set. Whip cream with sugar and smooth over top. Add grated chocolate garnish.

Mrs. Newton Penny

BLUEBERRY PIE

Easy

1 baked pie shell, cooled
1 qt. blueberries
5 oz. currant jelly
5 oz. blackberry-apple jelly
1 c. sour cream

Put blueberries in cooled shell. Melt jelly and pour over. Just before serving, spread sour cream over pie.

Mrs. Robert Smalley

ICE BOX BLUEBERRY PIE

Do Ahead   2 pies

2 cooked pie shells (cooled)
chopped pecans (optional)
8 oz. pkg. cream cheese
1 (1 lb.) box powdered sugar
1 lge. box Dream Whip
  (2 envelopes)
1 (15 oz.) can blueberries with
  juice
3 T. cornstarch
½ c. sugar

Prick pie shells with fork, cover bottom with pecans and bake. Cream the cheese and powdered sugar and fold in both envelopes of Dream Whip, whipped as per directions on the box. Pour into pie shells and top with blueberry topping: drain blueberry juice into boiler and add cornstarch and sugar, stirring constantly. When mixture thickens remove from heat and let cool. Pour topping on both pies. CHILL WELL, but not in freezer.
Delicious served with light meal. This pie is very rich and filling.

Mrs. Ken Fletcher

LEMON CHESS PIE

Easy   375°-325°
Do Ahead   50 min.

½ c. butter
1½ c. sugar
4 eggs
2 T. milk
2 T. cornmeal
1 T. vinegar
1¼ T. lemon juice
⅛ tsp. salt
1 unbaked 9" pie shell

Cream sugar and butter. Add eggs one at a time; add milk, cornmeal, vinegar, lemon juice and salt. Pour into unbaked pie shell and bake at 375° for 10 minutes. Reduce heat to 325° and bake until set, about 40 minutes more.

Mrs. Eugene F. Robbins, Jr.

CHOCOLATE PIE

Do Ahead

325°
15 min.

1 c. sugar
5 T. cornstarch
pinch salt
5 T. cocoa
2 c. milk
4 egg yolks
1 tsp. vanilla
2 T. butter
baked pie shell

Meringue:
¼ tsp. cream of tartar
4 egg whites
½ c. sugar

Mix dry ingredients. Scald milk and add egg yolks to ½ c. milk. Add remaining ingredients to milk mixture and mix. Cook until very thick. Strain mixture and cool. Pour into baked pie shell to set. Meringue: Beat egg whites with cream of tartar and sugar until stiff. Spread on pie and bake 15 minutes at 325°.

Mrs. James B. Dunaway

CHOCOLATE CHIFFON PIE

Easy
Do Ahead

1 T. plain gelatin
¼ c. cold water
1½ oz. cocoa (6 T.)
   (see calculation)
4 egg yolks
¾ c. sugar
¼ tsp. salt
1 tsp. vanilla
4 egg whites
¼ c. sugar

Dissolve gelatin in ¼ c. cold water. Add 1½ oz. cocoa to gelatin. Hold over boiling water in mixing bowl. Add beaten egg yolks, sugar, salt, and vanilla. Stir well. Beat egg whites with sugar and fold chocolate mixture into egg white mixture. Pour into baked pie crust. Place in refrigerator for at least 2 hours before serving. May be served with whipped cream on top.
This is a recipe from the Frances Virginia Tea Room formerly in Atlanta and noted for its delicious food.

Mrs. Newton Penny

COCOA:
4 c.	=	1 lb.	=	16 oz.
1 c.	=	4 oz.		
¼ c.	=	4 T.	=	1 oz.
6 T.	=	1½ oz.		

CHOCOLATE VELVET PIE

Easy
Do Ahead

350°
10 min.

Crust:
   30 vanilla wafers,
      crushed
   2 T. margarine, melted
   ¼ c. Angel Flake coconut

Filling:
   ½ c. butter
   ¾ c. sugar
   1 oz. square unsweetened
      chocolate
   1 tsp. vanilla
   2 chilled eggs
   ½ pt. whipping cream
   black walnuts

Mix wafers, margarine and coconut. Press into a greased 9" pie pan. Bake in moderate oven (350°) for 10 minutes. Cool. Cream butter and sugar. Add melted chocolate and vanilla. Beat. Add chilled eggs, one at a time, beating 2 minutes after each addition. Pour into chilled pie pan. Top with unsweetened whipped cream. Sprinkle with walnuts. Chill 1 hour or longer in refrigerator.
Rich, creamy and delicious!

Mrs. Lee Roy Claxton

COCONUT PIE

Easy
Do Ahead

Yield: 2 pies

350°
30-45 min.

¾ c. butter
2 c. sugar
½ c. buttermilk
6 eggs
7 oz. Angel Flake coconut
1½ tsp. vanilla
2 unbaked pie shells

Combine all ingredients and pour into unbaked pie shells. Cook 350° 30 to 45 minutes or until middle is firm.

Mrs. Thomas V. Pollard

CRUSTLESS COCONUT PIE

Easy†
Do Ahead

350°
50 min.

¼ c. margarine
1 c. sugar
2 eggs
1 c. milk
¼ c. self-rising flour
½ tsp. vanilla
1 (3½ oz.) can flaked coconut

Cream butter and sugar. Add eggs one at a time and beat. Add milk and flour. Mix well. Add other ingredients. Mix. Pour into lightly greased 9" pie pan and bake at 350° for 50 minutes or until firm.

Mrs. William Paul Kurtz

Editor's note: A superb pie - thick firm custard, but light!

COCONUT CREAM PIE

325°
15 min.

²/₃ c. sugar
¹/₃ c. plain flour
¹/₈ tsp. salt
3 egg yolks
2 c. milk
1 tsp. vanilla
1 (7½ oz.) can coconut
3 egg whites
¼ tsp. cream of tartar
4-6 T. sugar

9" baked pie shell

Mix sugar, flour and salt. Beat egg yolks slightly and add to milk. Add dry mixture to milk and eggs, stirring well. Cook in double boiler or heavy pan until mixture thickens, stirring constantly. Cool slightly. Add flavoring and coconut, reserving small amount of coconut to sprinkle on meringue. Pour filling into pie shell. Cover with meringue made from stiffly beaten egg whites, cream of tartar and sugar. Bake at 325° for 15 minutes or until lightly browned.

Mrs. Grady E. Black

FRENCH SILK PIE

350°
5-8 minutes

Crust:
1 c. graham cracker crumbs
3 T. sugar
¹/₃ c. margarine, melted
¹/₈ tsp. mace
¼ c. chopped pecans
(optional)

Blend ingredients and pack in 9" pie plate. Bake at 350° 5-8 minutes. Cool. Chopped pecans patted in bottom before baking is a delicious addition.

Filling:
1 c. butter (room
temperature)
1 c. sugar
2 eggs
2 squares unsweetened
chocolate (melted)
1 tsp. vanilla
1 c. whipping cream
plus 2 T. sugar

Beat together butter and sugar for 30 minutes. Add eggs and beat until well blended. Add chocolate and vanilla and beat again. (The secret is to have this mixture silky smooth.) Pile in cold crust. Top with whipped cream and grated chocolate. If made day before, add whipped cream only a few hours before serving. This is so rich, cut 8 small pieces to serve.

Mrs. Taylor B. Manley, Jr.

GERMAN CHOCOLATE ANGEL PIE

Easy   Yield: 2 pies   350°
                                                              25-30 min.

Pie Shell:
16 saltines or 20 Ritz
   crackers, crumbled
1 c. chopped pecans
1 tsp. baking powder
3 egg whites
1 c. sugar
1 tsp. vanilla

In large bowl mix crackers, 1 c. nuts and baking powder. In another bowl, beat egg whites very stiffly and gradually add sugar and vanilla. Mix two bowls together and pour into two 8" pie plates. Smooth with spatula and build up sides. Bake 350° for 25-30 minutes.

Filling:
2 bars German Chocolate
6 T. water
4 egg yolks
2 qts. Cool Whip
1 c. chopped pecans

Melt chocolate and water in double boiler. Add yolks and stir. Let cool. Fold in Cool Whip. Divide and put in meringue shells. Garnish with pecans. Refrigerate 3-4 hours.

Mrs. Frank Umstead
Chapel Hill, North Carolina

ICE CREAM PIE

Do Ahead†

¾ box chocolate wafers
⅓ c. melted butter
1½ squares unsweetened
   chocolate
1 T. butter
½ c. sugar
1 sm. can evaporated milk
1 qt. coffee ice cream
1 c. whipped cream
nuts

Make crumb crust with wafers and ⅓ c. butter and chill. In boiler, melt chocolate in butter; add sugar and milk. Cook until thickened. When fairly cool, pour into crust and add slightly softened ice cream. Cover and keep in freezer. Take out about 20 minutes before serving time. Slice and put on dessert plates with whipped cream and nuts on top.

Mrs. William R. King

IMPROVED "BOUGHT" PIE CRUST

Brush frozen pie crust with milk and sprinkle lightly with sugar. Bake as directed.

LEMON MERINGUE PIE

Do Ahead

350°
12-20 min.

Filling:
  1 c. sugar
  ¼ c. cornstarch
  ¼ tsp. salt
  1½ c. boiling water
  2 egg yolks
  ⅓ c. lemon juice
  1 T. grated lemon
    rind
  1 T. margarine
  1 baked pie shell

Combine sugar, cornstarch, and salt. Add water gradually and cook over medium heat until smooth and very thick, stirring constantly. Beat egg yolks and pour hot mixture over them gradually. Continue to stir. Return to heat and cook 3 minutes longer. Add lemon juice, rind, and butter. Mix well. Cool. Pour into pie shell.

Meringue:
  2 egg whites
  ¼ c. sugar
  ½ tsp. vanilla
  few grains salt

Beat whites with salt until frothy. Add sugar gradually, beating constantly until stiff. Spoon over outer edge of pie to seal, then on top. Bake 12-20 minutes at 350°.

Mrs. Ivey Burson

Editor's note: Delicious pie! For higher meringue use 3 or 4 egg whites.

FROZEN LEMON PIE

Easy†
Do Ahead

3 egg yolks, well beaten
¼ c. lemon juice
½ c. plus 1 T. sugar
1 c. heavy cream, whipped
3 egg whites, stiffly beaten
¾ c. crushed vanilla wafers

Combine first 3 ingredients and cook until a custard forms in double boiler. Cool slightly. Fold in whipped cream and stiffly beaten egg whites. Sprinkle ½ of the finely crushed wafers into freezing tray. Pour mixture over this. Cover with remaining crumbs. Freeze, slice and serve.

Mrs. John H. Goddard

LEMONADE PIE

Easy
Do Ahead

Yield: 2 pies

1 lge. Cool Whip
1 (14 oz.) can condensed milk
1 sm. can lemonade (thawed)
2 - 9" graham cracker crusts

Mix together all ingredients. Beat thoroughly. Pour into graham cracker crusts. Refrigerate one hour. May garnish with graham cracker crumbs.

Mrs. Thomas G. Gilchrist

KEY LIME PIE

8 double graham crackers, crushed
3 T. sugar
3 T. soft butter
4 egg yolks
1 can sweetened condensed milk
juice of 4-5 limes, enough to make you pucker
4 egg whites
½ c. sugar

Combine crackers, sugar and butter; press firmly into bottom and sides of 9" pie plate. Bake at 375° for 8-10 minutes. Mix egg yolks, milk and lime juice together. Spoon into crust. Beat egg whites until stiff. Add sugar. Cover pie with meringue. Bake at 400° 8-10 minutes until meringue is brown. Chill.

Mary J. Hazleton
Vienna, Virginia

LUSCIOUS LIME PIE

Do Ahead

2 T. plain gelatin
½ c. sugar
¼ tsp. salt
4 eggs, separated
½ c. lime juice
¼ c. water
1 tsp. grated lime rind
few drops green coloring
½ c. sugar
1 c. cream, whipped
1 - 9" pie shell - baked

Mix gelatin, ½ c. sugar and salt in saucepan. Beat egg yolks well. Add lime juice and water. Stir into gelatin mixture. Cook over low heat, stirring constantly just until mixture comes to a boil. Remove from heat, stir in grated rind and coloring. Chill, stirring occasionally until mixture mounds slightly when dropped from spoon. Beat egg whites until soft peaks form. Gradually add ½ c. sugar, beating until stiff. Fold into chilled gelatin mixture. Fold in whipping cream. Pour into prepared crust. Chill until firm.

Mrs. William L. Wages

"HIGH" MERINGUES
Do not use a stationary beater. Use hand beater or wire whisk and lift egg whites for air as you beat.

MACAROON PIE

Easy†

300°
45 min.

14 saltine crackers, rolled
  fine
12 dates, finely chopped
½ c. pecans, finely chopped
1 c. sugar
¼ tsp. salt
½ tsp. baking powder
3 stiffly beaten egg whites
2 tsp. almond extract

Mix together all ingredients except the egg whites. Fold egg whites into the mixture. Spread into an 8" pie plate. Cook 45 minutes at 300°. Cool and garnish with whipped cream.

Mrs. John H. Goddard

PECAN PIE

Easy
Do Ahead

350°
50 min.

3 eggs
⅔ c. sugar
¼ tsp. salt
⅓ c. margarine
1 c. syrup (¼ cane and
  ¾ dark Karo)
1½ to 2 c. pecan halves
9" (deep-dish) pie crust,
  unbaked

Beat eggs slightly. Add sugar, salt, melted margarine, syrup and pecans. Bake until custard sets, approximately 50 minutes.
This is a real Southern pecan pie. Using some cane syrup gives it its special flavor.

Mrs. E. Herben Turner

BLENDER PECAN PIE

Easy†
Do Ahead

425°-350°
45 min.

2 eggs
⅔ c. sugar
½ tsp. salt
½ c. white corn syrup
2 T. melted butter
1 tsp. vanilla extract
1 c. pecans
1 unbaked 9" pie shell
8-10 pecan halves

Put eggs, sugar, salt, corn syrup, butter and vanilla extract in blender and blend well. Add 1 c. pecans and blend just enough to chop nuts coarsely. Pour into pie shell and arrange pecan halves on top. Bake at 425° for 15 minutes. Reduce heat to 350° and bake an additional 30 minutes.
This is easy to slice and easy to eat because most of the pecans are chopped.

Mrs. Will Hill Newton II

PECAN TARTS *

Easy
Do Ahead

325°
25 min.

Pastry:
1 c. butter
8 oz. cream cheese
2 c. flour

Mix pastry ingredients and roll thin. Put in 1" muffin tins. Add mixture below.

Filling:
½ c. butter
1 c. sugar
2 egg yolks
1 c. chopped pecans
1 c. chopped dates
1 tsp. vanilla
2 egg whites, beaten stiff

Mix all filling ingredients, saving egg whites until last. Put in pastry and bake at 325° for 25 minutes.
Make these at Thanksgiving, store tightly covered in a cool place and they will keep beautifully through Christmas.

PECAN TORTE

Easy†
Do Ahead

350°
30 min.

20 Ritz crackers (crumbled)
1 c. sugar (less 2 T.)
1 c. pecans, broken
pinch salt
1 tsp. vanilla
3 egg whites, beaten stiff

Mix all dry ingredients together. Add vanilla. Then add egg whites gently. Do not beat. Pour into well greased 9" pie pan. Cook 30 minutes at 350°. Cool. Top with whipped cream. (To freeze, do not top with whipped cream until thawed.)

Mrs. John M. Garrison

PRALINE PUMPKIN PIE

Easy
Do Ahead

325°
10-30 min.

1 - 9" unbaked pastry shell
⅓ c. finely chopped pecans
⅓ c. firmly packed brown
  sugar
2 T. melted butter
1 c. pumpkin
⅔ c. brown sugar
1 tsp. flour
¼ tsp. nutmeg
½ tsp. cinnamon
½ tsp. ginger
½ tsp. salt
2 well beaten eggs
½ c. evaporated milk

Line bottom of pastry with nuts and brown sugar mixed with butter. Press firmly down on pastry. Bake 10 minutes at 325°.

Combine pumpkin and brown sugar. Mix together flour and spices and add to pumpkin mixture. Add eggs, blend in milk. Pour into partially baked pie shell and bake at 325° for 30 minutes.

Mrs. Warren K. Wells

RUM PIE

Do Ahead†

1 graham cracker pie shell:
  1 c. graham cracker crumbs
  ⅓ c. sugar
  ¼ c. butter
  dash powdered cinnamon

First Filling:
  2 eggs, beaten well
  4 sm. pkgs. cream cheese,
    softened
  ½ c. sugar
  3 T. rum

Second Filling:
  1 c. sour cream
  3 T. sugar
  1 tsp. dry sherry wine

To make pie crust, melt butter and mix with crumbs, sugar and cinnamon. Press this mixture into pie pan.

Cream the ingredients for each of the fillings.

Fill pie shell with first and then second fillings. Refrigerate.

Mrs. Charlie T. Phillips

Editor's note: This is delicious frozen!

"TIP"

Set pies and cobblers on a rack to cool to prevent the bottom crust from being soggy.

RUM CREAM PIE

Do Ahead

graham cracker or chocolate
  wafer crust
6 egg yolks
1 c. sugar
1 T. gelatin
½ c. water
1 pt. heavy cream
½ c. Myers dark rum
unsweetened chocolate

Beat egg yolks and sugar until light. Dissolve gelatin in water and bring to a boil. Pour into egg mixture beating briskly. Let cool. Whip cream until stiff. Fold cream into egg mixture and add ½ c. rum. Pour into crust. Place in refrigerator to set. Shave unsweetened chocolate on top before serving.

Mrs. James R. Fortune, Jr.

SHERRY CHIFFON PIE

Do Ahead

1 - 11" graham cracker crust

1 level T. plain gelatin 1½ T. cold water	Dissolve together.

1½ c. Pet milk ¼ c. water 2 egg yolks (use extra large eggs) 7 T. sugar pinch salt	Mix together, cook in double boiler until custard consistency. Remove from fire, add gelatin, stir until gelatin is dissolved. Cool.

4 egg whites 8 T. sugar 8 T. sherry ½ pt. whipping cream, sweetened to taste toasted pecans or almonds	Beat egg whites until stiff, gradually add sugar. Fold sherry into egg whites. Fold custard into egg whites. Pour into graham cracker crust. Cool in refrigerator 4 to 6 hours before serving. Top with whipped cream and chopped toasted nuts. *Pretty - light dessert.*

Mrs. Carl H. Cartledge

SMOKY MOUNTAIN NUT PIE

Easy Do Ahead	325° 40 min.

1 c. sugar ½ c. margarine, melted 1 c. raisins 1 c. chopped pecans ½ tsp. nutmeg ½ tsp. cinnamon 1 T. vinegar 2 eggs, beaten 1 pie shell (unbaked)	Combine all ingredients and pour into shell. Cook in 325° oven for 40 minutes. Cool on wire rack. Mrs. Grady Norton

STRAWBERRY SATIN PIE

Do Ahead

Creamy Satin Filling:
    ½ c. sugar
    3 T. cornstarch
    3 T. flour
    ½ tsp. salt
    2 c. milk
    1 slightly beaten egg
    ½ c. whipping cream
    1 tsp. vanilla

Glaze:
    ½ c. crushed strawberries
    ½ c. water
    ½ c. sugar
    2 tsp. cornstarch
    few drops red food
        coloring

1 baked 9" pastry shell
½ c. sliced toasted almonds

Garnish:
    2 c. strawberries (a few perfect
        whole ones, halve the rest)
    whipped cream

Combine sugar, cornstarch, flour and salt. Gradually stir in milk; bring to boil, stirring constantly. Lower heat, cook until thick and bubbly. Pour little of the hot liquid into beaten egg and add to hot mixture. Bring just to a boil, stirring continually. Cool and chill thoroughly. Beat mixture well; whip cream and fold cream into egg mixture with vanilla. Chill. Combine crushed berries and water, cook 2 minutes and push through sieve. Mix sugar and cornstarch; gradually add berry juice. Cook until thick and clear; tint with coloring. Cool slightly. To assemble: Cover bottom of cooled pastry shell with almonds. Fill with Creamy Satin Filling; top with berry glaze and garnish with berries and whipped cream.

Mrs. Dan Baker

SWEET POTATO PIE

Easy   325°
Do Ahead   1 hr.

2½ c. cooked mashed sweet
    potatoes
¼ c. margarine or butter,
    softened
½ c. sugar
¼ c. brown sugar, packed
¼ c. milk
¼ tsp. salt
½ tsp. cinnamon
1 - 9" unbaked pastry shell

Combine all ingredients and mix until smooth. Pour into unbaked pie shell and bake for about 1 hour or until knife thrust into center comes out clean.

Mrs. Arthur Lesser III

ZWIEBACK PIE

325°

Crust:
  2 c. crushed Zwieback
  ½ c. melted butter
  ½ c. sugar
  1 tsp. cinnamon

Mix crust ingredients together, press in a 9" pie pan and bake at 325° for 10 minutes.

Filling:
  2 c. milk
  ¾ c. sugar
  3 T. cornstarch
  ¼ tsp. salt
  3 egg yolks
  1 T. vanilla

Scald milk and pour over dry ingredients. Cook in double boiler 5 or more minutes. Add beaten egg yolks, and cook until thick (about 5 minutes). Cool; add vanilla and pour into crust.

Meringue:
  3 egg whites
  ¼ tsp. cream of tartar
  ¼ c. sugar

Top with stiffly beaten meringue and bake at 325° until light brown.

Mrs. James B. Dunaway

PIE SHELLS

MIRACLE PIE CRUST

Do Ahead†

Yield: 2 double pastry shells
         and 1 single shell

4 c. flour
1¾ c. shortening
1 tsp. salt
1 T. sugar
1 egg
1 T. vinegar
½ c. cold water

Cut first four ingredients together until of coarse consistency. Beat next three ingredients together. Mix together. Roll into ball. Divide into 5 parts. Refrigerate at least 15 minutes before using. Form patties and wrap individually for freezer. They keep for several months. Thaw for about 2 hours. Vinegar will smell strong after freezing, but taste isn't impaired.

Mrs. Thomas W. Fetzer
Mrs. Jerry Hollberg

CHOCOLATE CRUMB PIE SHELL

1 box Famous Chocolate
  Wafers
⅓ c. melted butter

Mix ingredients and press into 9" pie plate. Chill before serving.

GINGERSNAP PIE SHELL

1½ c. gingersnap crumbs
6 T. melted butter
1 tsp. confectioners sugar

Mix ingredients and press into 9" pie plate. Chill 1 hour before serving.

GRAHAM CRACKER PIE SHELL

1½ c. graham cracker crumbs
  (approximately 15 crackers)
½ c. melted margarine
3 T. sugar
dash cinnamon

Mix ingredients and press into 9" pie plate.

MERINGUE PIE SHELL

350°
50 min.

4 egg whites, beaten stiff
¾ c. sugar (4X)
½ c. sugar (granulated)

Add sifted sugars to beaten egg whites gradually. Grease pie plate with butter and flour. Pour into plate and bake at 350° for 50 minutes. (Do not make on a humid day.)

VANILLA WAFER OR ZWIEBACK PIE SHELL

2 c. vanilla wafer or Zwieback
  crumbs
2 T. sugar
¼ c. melted margarine

Mix together and press into 9 or 10" pie plate.

Notes

CANDY

CHINESE CHEWIES

Easy†
Do Ahead

2 pkgs. (6 oz.) butterscotch bits
1 pkg. (6 oz.) chocolate bits
1 can Chinese noodles (sm. size)
½ c. cashew nuts

Melt bits over hot water. Stir in Chinese noodles and cashew nuts. Drop by small spoonfuls on waxed paper. Cool.

Mrs. Fred L. Omundson

BOURBON BALLS

Do Ahead   Yield: 2 dozen

2½ c. sugar
½ c. bourbon
½ c. water
⅛ tsp. cream of tartar

½ c. pecans
1 jigger bourbon

1 (12 oz.) pkg. semisweet
   chocolate bits
1 block paraffin

Combine first 4 ingredients in a pan, stirring over medium heat until boils. Cook slowly to 238°. Turn out on a buttered marble slab and work with hands, gradually adding next two ingredients until the mixture creams. Form into balls. Chill. Dip in melted chocolate and paraffin.

Mrs. Paul McCubbin
Campbellsville, Kentucky

CONCORD BUTTER MINTS

Do Ahead   Yield: 1 pound

2 c. sugar
1 c. boiling water
¼ c. butter
4 drops oil of
    peppermint
4 drops of food
    coloring

Let water and butter come to a boil then add sugar. Stir until dissolved. Cook until candy forms a firm ball when dropped in water, 260°. Do not stir. Pour on buttered marble slab. When cool enough to handle, pull and add flavor and color. Pull until candy will draw up in length when dropped on slab. Pull into rope 1½ inches in thickness. With shears cut into ½ inch pieces. When cold, place in tin containers until it creams. You may use any mint flavor.

Mrs. Mark Kapiloff

CHOCOLATE COVERED CARAMELS

Do Ahead   Yield: 5 pounds

1 c. white sugar
1 c. brown sugar
1 c. dark Karo syrup
1 c. butter
2 c. thick cream
1 lb. chopped pecans
1 tsp. vanilla
1 lb. plain Hershey bars
⅛ lb. paraffin

Combine first 4 ingredients and 1 c. cream. Bring to a boil, add second cup of cream, cook to "soft ball". Remove from heat and add pecans and vanilla. Pour into buttered 9 x 13" pan. Cool - cut into 1" squares (or smaller) and dip in chocolate melted with paraffin.

Mrs. Paul McCubbin
Campbellsville, Kentucky

CHOCOLATE COVERED CHERRY CANDY

Do Ahead   Yield: 4 dozen

1 can condensed milk
4 T. margarine
1 T. vanilla
2 (1 lb.) boxes powdered
  sugar
1 qt. chopped pecans
¾ box paraffin
8 ozs. dark or creamy
  chocolate
1 (16 oz.) bottle cherries

Drain cherries. Mix milk, margarine and vanilla. Add sugar, a small amount at a time blending well until all sugar is used. Add nuts to mixture. (I use my hands to blend nuts mixture becomes stiff dough.) Pinch off enough mixture to make small ball around one cherry. Continue until mixture is used. Place on waxed paper. Let stand 1 hour.

In double boiler melt chocolate and paraffin. Dip each piece of candy in the chocolate mixture until covered. Place on waxed paper to set. DO NOT HAVE CHOCOLATE MIXTURE TOO HOT. Makes 40 to 50 pieces. Keeps well.

Mrs. Ronald D. Peaden

CHOCOLATE FONDUE DROPS

†   Yield: 10-12 dozen

2 boxes confectioners sugar
½ c. margarine, melted
1 can condensed milk
2 cans Angel Flake coconut
2 c. pecans, finely
  chopped

½ block paraffin wax
8 ozs. Nestle chocolate
  chips (or semi-sweet
  chocolate blocks)

Mix all together. Roll in balls, freeze for 2 hours or leave in refrigerator overnight. In a double boiler melt ½ block of paraffin wax and Nestle chocolate chips. While still warm dip balls and drop on waxed paper.

Mrs. Barbara J. Searcy
St. Simons, Georgia

Editor's Note: Coconut can be omitted and more nuts added or add chopped cherries to mixture for a different taste.

HOW TO PREPARE COCONUT

Pierce the 3 eyes and pour out milk. Put coconut into 350° oven for 30 minutes. Let cool and break. Meat will come out much more easily when prepared this way.

"TIP"

Coconut grates easily if you freeze it first.

CHINESE CANDIED COCONUT STRIPS

Do Ahead   Yield: 1½ pounds

1 coconut
¾ c. water
1½ c. sugar
  (superfine sugar)

Remove coconut meat from shell in large pieces. Remove brown skin. Slice coconut into very thin strips, using vegetable peeler. Combine with water and 1½ c. sugar. Broil for 20 - 30 minutes, stirring frequently, until all water evaporates. Pour out onto a cake rack, placed on cookie sheet, and separate strips with a fork. Roll in superfine sugar and store in air tight containers when thoroughly dried. Makes 1½ pounds.

Mrs. William Kagey
Roanoke, Virginia

CREAM PULL

Yield: 4 dozen

4 c. white sugar
1⅓ c. boiling water
1 c. whipping cream
2 T. butter

Add sugar to boiling water. Cook to soft ball. Gradually add cream. Cook to hard ball. Just before reaching hard ball add butter. Pour on buttered marble slab. As quickly as you are able to handle, pull until it sets. Twist into "ropes" and cut individual pieces with scissors.

Mrs. Paul McCubbin
Campbellsville, Kentucky

GRANDMA'S CHOCOLATE FUDGE

Do Ahead

2 c. sugar
2 T. light corn syrup
2 squares unsweetened
  chocolate
¾ c. milk
2 T. butter
1 tsp. vanilla
1 c. chopped nuts

Combine all ingredients except butter, vanilla and nuts. Put in heavy 2 qt. saucepan. Cook over medium heat, stirring constantly until mixture boils. Continue cooking until mixture forms a soft ball when dropped into very cold water. Remove from heat and add vanilla and butter. Cool to luke warm. Beat by hand until mixture begins to thicken and lose its gloss. Stir in nuts. Drop by teaspoonfuls onto waxed paper or pour into buttered dish and cut into squares when cool. If fudge should become too hard while dropping by teaspoonfuls, return mixture to low heat and add a few tablespoonfuls of evaporated milk straight from can and beat slightly until creamy.

Mrs. Frank Jolly

MARSHMALLOW FUDGE

Do Ahead   Yield: 3 pounds

4 c. sugar
14½ oz. evaporated milk
1 c. butter
12 oz. chocolate chips
1 pt. marshmallow cream
1 tsp. vanilla
1 c. chopped nuts

Bring sugar, milk, and butter to a boil. Cook to med. soft stage (236°), stirring. Remove from heat. Add marshmallow cream, chips, vanilla and nuts. Stir. Pour into pan, at least 9 x 9". Cut into squares when cool. Makes 3 lbs.

Mrs. M. D. Hollberg, Jr.

"TIP"

Grease or oil the pot in which you intend to melt chocolate to prevent the chocolate from sticking.

DIVINITY FUDGE

Do Ahead

2½ c. sugar
½ c. light corn syrup
½ c. water
2 egg whites
2 tsp. vanilla
1 c. nuts coarsely chopped
¼ tsp. salt

In heavy saucepan combine sugar, corn syrup and water. Cook on low heat, stirring until sugar dissolves. Cover; cook 1 minute, until sugar on pan sides melts. Uncover. Bring to boil; cook on high heat without stirring until the candy thermometer reaches 235°. Use electric mixer at high speed to beat whites with salt until stiff peaks form. In a thin stream, pour half of the hot syrup over egg whites. Continue beating. Continue cooking remaining syrup until small amount forms hard ball in water or 260° on candy thermometer. Pour into mixture while continuing to beat. Add vanilla and nuts; beat until mixture is stiff enough to hold shape, about 5 minutes. Drop in mounds from spoon.

Mrs. Mark Kapiloff

MILLIONAIRES

Do Ahead

1 lb. Kraft caramels
2 T. water
3 c. pecans

Melt Together:
   1 lb. plain Hershey bars
   ⅛ lb. paraffin

Put caramels and water in top of double boiler and melt. Add whole pecans and drop on waxed paper. Chill overnight. Dip candy in melted chocolate. Place on waxed paper. Store in cool place.

Mrs. Frank Fleitas
Atlanta, Georgia

NONNIE'S PEANUT BRITTLE

Do Ahead

2 c. sugar
2 c. raw peanuts
¾ c. light corn syrup
¼ c. water
pinch salt
2 tsp. soda
1" x 2" paraffin

Combine first 5 ingredients and cook until candy thermometer registers hard crack (290°). Remove from heat and add soda and paraffin, beat vigorously. Spread on a buttered marble slab. As soon as you can handle, pull until thin and break into pieces. (Can use large tray if marble slab not available.)

Mrs. James K. Duffes

PEANUT BON BONS

Easy
Do Ahead

1 box 4X sugar
1 c. crunchy peanut butter
½ c. margarine or butter
1 (12 oz.) pkg. butterscotch
   bits
½ block paraffin

Mix sugar, peanut butter, and butter. Shape in small balls. Chill. Melt butterscotch bits with paraffin. Dip balls until well coated.

Mrs. J. Lamar Wells
Mt. Vernon, Georgia

PEANUT BUTTER CANDY

Do Ahead

2 c. sugar
⅔ c. milk
1 tsp. vanilla
1 (med.) jar crunchy
   peanut butter
1 jar marshmallow whip

Into a large boiler put sugar and milk. Boil to soft ball stage on medium heat. Then add peanut butter and marshmallow whip. Remove from heat and add 1 tsp. vanilla. Mix well. Pour into 12" x 8" pan lined with waxed paper. Spread, cut in squares.

Mrs. William L. Joiner
First President of The Utility Club

POTATO CANDY

Easy

1 med. Irish potato
1 box powdered sugar
peanut butter

Peel and boil potato, mash with fork. While hot, add powdered sugar to a stiff, doughy consistency. Roll on sheet of waxed paper sprinkled with powdered sugar; spread with thin layer of creamy peanut butter. Roll into log (like a jelly roll). Continue rolling with hands until roll is approximately 1" in circumference. Cut into ¼" slices. Candy will have pinwheel look.

Mrs. William T. Johnson

ROCKY ROAD CLUSTERS

Easy
Do Ahead

Yield: 3 dozen

2 c. semi-sweet chocolate
   bits
¾ c. white raisins
16 marshmallows, cut in
   pieces
1½ c. chopped pecans

Melt chocolate bits in top of double boiler over warm water; stir to keep smooth. Add remaining ingredients and when coated, drop by teaspoonfuls onto waxed paper. Let cool. May need to refrigerate.

Mrs. Walker Cook, Jr.

ENGLISH TOFFEE

Do Ahead

1 c. butter
1 c. sugar
2 T. water
1 T. white corn syrup
½ c. chocolate chips
⅔ c. finely chopped nuts

Melt butter over low heat. Add sugar and stir until melted. Add water and syrup. Cook over low heat until syrup becomes brittle (320°). Pour on well greased marble slab or cookie pan (should be thin). Cool. Melt chocolate chips and spread on brittle. Sprinkle pecans on top and mash in. Break into pieces. (Can be put in refrigerator until chocolate hardens.)

Mrs. James B. Dunaway

CANDY DIPPING TIPS

Melt chocolate and paraffin to 110° or less for dipping. Always use double boiler.

Notes

PRESERVES and PICKLES

JAMS AND JELLIES

FREEZER STRAWBERRY JAM

†   Yield: 5 - ½ pint jars

1 qt. strawberries, fully
   ripe
1 box (1¾ oz.) powdered
   fruit pectin
4 c. sugar
¾ c. water

Prepare containers. Stem and crush berries one layer at a time. Measure 2 c. into a large bowl. If necessary, add water for exact amount. Mix sugar into fruit, let stand 10 minutes. Mix water and powdered fruit pectin in a saucepan. Bring to a boil and boil 1 minute, stirring constantly. Stir into fruit. Continue stirring 3 minutes. A few sugar crystals will remain. Ladle into sterilized containers. Cover at once with lids. Set at room temperature. (Takes up to 24 hours.) Store in freezer. If used within 3 weeks, store in refrigerator.

Mrs. Albert B. Coltrane
Stone Mountain, Georgia

MUSCADINE JAM

Yield: 5 pints

5 lbs. fruit
3 lbs. sugar
spices - optional

Pulp grapes (remove hulls) and put pulp to cook in small quantity of water. Cook until broken. Put through coarse strainer to remove seeds. To hulls put sufficient water to boil until tender. Mix the two together, add sugar and cook slowly, stirring often to prevent scorching. Season with spices. Pour into jars and seal.

Mrs. John J. Flynt, Jr.

MICROWAVE APPLE JELLY

Yield: 2 - ½ pints

2 T. sugar
1½ T. liquid fruit pectin
1¼ c. apple juice
1½ c. sugar

In a 3 qt. glass casserole dish, combine the 2 T. sugar and fruit pectin. Stir in the apple juice slowly. Cover and bring to the boiling point - 3 minutes with electronic energy. Add the 1½ c. sugar. Mix well and cover. Bring to the boiling point - 2½ minutes. Stir and cook uncovered for 1 minute or until jelly sheets from a spoon. Allow to stand 1 minute, skim, fill jars. If you prefer different colors, add a drop of food coloring to each glass and stir. Cover with paraffin.

Mrs. William L. Wages

BLACKBERRY JELLY

Yield: 4-5 pints

2 gal. berries
water to cover
skin from 2 tart apples
  or crabapples
sugar

Wash berries. Place with apple skins in large pot and barely cover with water. Bring to boil, cover, and simmer 2 hours. Strain, discard pulp and measure juice. In large pot, put 1 c. juice to 1 c. sugar, but no more than 4 c. juice at a time. Bring to rolling boil, stirring constantly. When mixture is thick enough for 2 drops to come off spoon together, boil 1 more minute. Mixture should sheet from spoon (drop in sheet, not drops). Pour into hot jars and seal.

Mrs. J. Robb Sautter
Highlands, North Carolina

"TIP"

Dip a silver fork into boiling jelly, and if it fills in between the tines of the fork, the jelly is done.

LOW COUNTRY PEPPER JELLY

Yield: 4 pints

¾ c. chopped hot peppers
  (about 20)
¾ c. bell peppers (about 4)
1½ c. vinegar (no more
  than 10% acidity)
6½ c. sugar
1 (6 oz.) bottle liquid
  pectin
red or green food coloring

Wear rubber gloves to remove seeds. Place vinegar and chopped peppers in blender (or Cuisinart) and chop fine. Place in saucepan and bring to boil. Stir in sugar until dissolved. Remove from heat and strain through a mesh sieve. Let set 5 minutes. Add pectin and food coloring. Stir. Cover with hot wax in clean jars.
Serve with cream cheese and crackers.

Mrs. H. Alfred Bolton III

Editor's note: This makes a delicious, but very hot jelly. If you prefer a milder jelly, use ¼ c. hot pepper.

ORANGE MARMALADE

Yield: 9 - ½ pints

4½ c. prepared fruit:
  3 med. sized oranges
  1 sm. grapefruit
  2 med. sized lemons
⅛ tsp. soda
7½ c. sugar
1 (6 oz.) bottle liquid pectin

For prepared fruit:
Remove skins from fruit. Shave off and discard about half of white. Put rind in 2¼ c. of water and grind in blender. Add ⅛ tsp. soda to water and rind mixture. Bring to boil and simmer, covered, 20 minutes stirring occasionally. Remove seeds from peeled fruit. Put in blender on high. Add this pulp and juice to undrained cooked rind. Simmer, covered, 10 minutes. Measure 4½ c. fruit mixture. Mix with sugar, bring to rolling boil. Boil 1 minute. Add pectin and boil 1 minute. Ladle into glasses. Cover with ⅛" hot paraffin.

Mrs. Charles Smith

PEACH BUTTER

Yield: 5 pints

1 peck fresh peaches
1 T. allspice
1 tsp. cinnamon
dash cloves
7½ c. sugar
3 oz. liquid pectin

Wash, peel and cut fruit off pits in chunks.   Add sufficient water to cover bottom of pan.   Boil down until very soft. Mash through a food mill.   Measure 5 c. of the fruit. Add spices and sugar.   Cook until long drop forms off spoon.   Add pectin and bring to rolling boil for 2 minutes. Pour in hot jars and seal. (Can substitute apples for peaches.)

Mrs. Douglas J. Brown

FIG CONSERVES

Yield: 4 to 6 - ½ pints

1 qt. figs
2 oranges
1 c. seedless raisins
3 c. sugar
1 c. nuts (optional, add
    as used)

Peel and mash figs. Seed oranges and grind - rind and all. Chop raisins. Mix all with sugar.   Cook until mixture thickens, stirring almost constantly. Seal while hot.
Good for sandwiches with softened cream cheese.

Mrs. W. Barron Cumming

STRAWBERRY PRESERVES

†

Yield: 2 pints

4 c. sugar
4 heaping c. strawberries,
    chopped
1 c. water

Dissolve sugar in water over medium heat for about 3 minutes.   Add strawberries. Boil vigorously for about 23 minutes, stirring frequently but not constantly.   Remove from heat and skim off white foam from top. Pour into bowl to cool, then into glass jars and refrigerate for use within 2 weeks. Otherwise, freeze in plastic containers or glass freezer jars.

Mrs. Arthur Lesser III

PICKLES

BRANDIED PEACHES

peaches
1 c. sugar per qt. jar
1 c. brandy per qt. jar

Peel firm peaches. Pack in quart jars. (Peel and seal 1 jar at a time.) To each jar add 1 c. sugar and 1 c. brandy. Seal jars and invert. Every 24 hours, reverse position of jars. Check top daily to see if lids need tightening. After 3 weeks, keep jars upright.

Edith D. Phillips
Baton Rouge, Louisiana

BREAD AND BUTTER PICKLES

Yield: 5 - 6 pints

12 lge. cucumbers, sliced
2 c. onions, sliced
½ c. salt
2 c. sugar
1 qt. vinegar
2 tsp. mustard seed
1 tsp. tumeric

Cover the cucumbers and onions with salt and cold water and let set overnight. Drain. Mix sugar, vinegar, mustard seed and tumeric and bring to boil. Add cucumbers and let boil, pack and seal in pints. Makes 5 - 6 pints. This recipe can be doubled or tripled very easily.

Mrs. Alyn R. Jones, Jr.
Zebulon, Georgia

CRISP AS ICE CUCUMBER SLICES

Yield: 7 - 9 pints

4 qts. cucumbers, thinly
  sliced
8 onions, thinly sliced
2 green peppers, seeded and
  cut in strips
½ c. non-iodized salt
1 tray ice cubes
4 c. sugar
1½ tsp. tumeric
½ tsp. cloves
3½ tsp. mustard seed
4½ c. vinegar

Combine vegetables and salt. Put ice cubes in middle of vegetables and cover all with water. Let stand at least 3 hours or overnight. Drain vegetables. Boil sugar, spices and vinegar in large container. Add vegetables and heat to scalding, but do not boil. Pour into sterilized jars and seal.

Mrs. W. Barron Cumming

KOSHER DILL PICKLES

20-25 cucumbers, 4" long

Per jar measurements:
$\frac{1}{8}$ tsp. powdered alum
1 clove garlic, peeled
2 heads fresh dill or
    4 T. dill seed
1 sm. hot red pepper (or 1
    piece red pepper from
    mixed pickling spice box)
4 c. vinegar
1 c. salt (non-iodized)
3 qts. water

Wash fresh cucumbers thoroughly. Drop in cold water and leave 1 hour. Remove and wipe dry. Pack in hot sterilized quart jars. To each jar add $\frac{1}{8}$ tsp. powdered alum, 1 clove garlic, 2 heads fresh dill and 1 small hot pepper. Boil together the vinegar, salt and water. Pour over cucumbers and seal. Do not open for 6 weeks.

Mrs. W. Barron Cumming

PICKLING TIP

Plain (non-iodized) salt will not darken pickles like iodized salt; it will also makes a crisper pickle.

GREEN TOMATO PICKLES

Yield: 4 - 6 quarts

7 lbs. green tomatoes
2 c. lime
2 gals. water
5 lbs. sugar
2 qts. vinegar
1 lb. onions
spices to taste

Slice tomatoes and onions. Soak in lime water overnight. Wash to remove lime. Mix in large pot - sugar, spices, and vinegar. Bring to boil. Add tomatoes and onions. Boil 15 minutes. Pack in hot jars.

Mrs. Ronald Peaden

Editor's note: 7 lbs. cucumbers can be substituted for green tomatoes.

WATERMELON RIND PICKLE

1 watermelon rind
1 vial Lily Lime
1 gal. water (or water to cover)
1 qt. vinegar
5 lbs. sugar
1 oz. stick cinnamon
1 oz. whole cloves

First prepare the watermelon rind. Remove all red and green. Cut up. Soak overnight in water with lime. Drain. DO NOT WASH. Cover with water and cook 2 hours. Drain again and cook slowly for 1 hour in syrup made from vinegar, sugar and spices. (Spices in gauze bag.) Syrup should cover rind. Seal while hot. (If more syrup is needed, add 1 c. vinegar to mixture.)

Mrs. Robert Smalley

ZUCCHINI SQUASH PICKLE

Yield: 6 - 7 pints

4 qts. very thinly sliced zucchini
6 med. onions, very thinly sliced
2 green peppers, seeded and cut in thin strips
½ c. non-iodized salt
4 c. sugar
1½ tsp. celery seed
2 T. mustard seed
3 c. cider vinegar

In large container, mix vegetables with salt. Cover vegetables with ice cubes. Let stand 3 hours. Drain vegetables well. Combine sugar, spices and vinegar and heat to boiling. Pour over drained vegetables. Heat over low heat to scalding. Do not allow to boil. Stir frequently to prevent scorching. Ladle into hot sterilized jars. Seal immediately.

Mrs. W. Barron Cumming

RELISH

CAULIFLOWER RELISH

Yield: 4 pints

½ c. flour
2 T. mustard
1 tsp. tumeric
2½ c. water
1 c. sugar
2 T. salt
1 tsp. pepper
1 tsp. garlic salt
2 T. mustard seed
1½ c. vinegar
8 c. cauliflower (broken
    into flowerettes)
1½ c. onion rings
whole red peppers, or sliced
    red peppers (optional)

Make a paste of flour, mustard, tumeric and water. Add sugar, salt, vinegar, pepper, garlic powder and mustard seed. Cook until sauce thickens. Add cauliflower and onions. Cook approximately 10 minutes. Stir often, add red peppers and stir. Seal in 4 pint jars.

Mrs. Charlie T. Phillips

AUNT SARA'S GREEN TOMATO RELISH

Yield: 14 pints

1 scant peck green
    tomatoes
20 onions
1 med. head cabbage
8 green peppers
8 red peppers
½ c. salt

1½ qts. vinegar
3 c. water
9 c. sugar (½ white,
    ½ brown)
2¼ tsp. tumeric
(Following in cloth bag)
    1½ T. celery seed
    1 T. mustard seed
    1½ oz. whole allspice

Put vegetables through coarse chopper and add ½ c. salt. Let stand overnight and drain. Add vinegar, water, sugar, and spices. Bring to boil. Simmer for 10-15 minutes. Pour into jars and seal.

Mrs. J. Robb Sautter
Highlands, North Carolina

INDIA RELISH

Yield: 4½ pints

2 lbs. cucumbers
2 lbs. green tomatoes
4½ T. salt
1 pt. finely cut celery
or cabbage
1 c. chopped onion
1½ c. chopped green or red
sweet pepper
2 T. finely chopped hot
red pepper
1½ c. sugar
2 c. cider vinegar
2¼ tsp. salt
¼ c. white mustard seed
¼ tsp. tumeric
⅛ tsp. each of ground
mace and cloves

Put tomatoes and cucumbers through food chopper - using coarse blade. Put into a glass or enamel bowl. Add salt, let stand overnight. Place in colander - press out and discard liquid. Add next four vegetables, then remaining ingredients. Simmer 20 to 30 minutes, stirring occasionally. Pour into sterilized jars and seal.

Mrs. J. Lamar Wells
Mt. Vernon, Georgia

PEAR RELISH

Yield: 10-12 pints

1 peck hard pears
(about 15 lbs.)
6 med. onions
1 doz. red bell peppers*
1 doz. green bell peppers
2 - 4 pods hot pepper, seeded
1 bunch celery
6 c. cider vinegar
2 lbs. sugar
1 T. non-iodized salt
1 T. mixed pickling spices
tied in cheesecloth bag

Seed pepper, peel pears and onions. Grind peppers, onions, pears and celery on coarse blade of food grinder. Mix sugar, salt and vinegar. Heat, with spice bag, to boiling. Pour into ground mixture and mix well. Over low heat, cook until mixture is heated thoroughly - takes 20-30 minutes. Stir frequently. Ladle into hot sterilized jars and seal.
*If red pepper is not available, use more celery and green peppers. Then stir in some chopped, canned pimiento just before end of cooking time.

Mrs. W. Barron Cumming

MISS JUDY'S PEPPER RELISH

Yield: 8 pints

24 lge. red pimientos
12 lge. onions
4 hot peppers
2 T. celery salt
2 T. salt
1 qt. vinegar
4 c. sugar

Roast pimientos in slow oven. Cool and peel. Coarsely grind pimientos, onions and hot peppers. Add remaining ingredients and cook slowly. Stir constantly, cooking for about 20 minutes after mixture is thoroughly hot. Pour in jars and seal. This may be doubled easily.

Mrs. R. O. Campbell

Editor's note: A delicious pepper relish. Red and green bell peppers may be substituted for pimientos. Do not roast or peel, merely seed and chop.

MAGGIE'S CHUTNEY

Yield: 1½ quarts

1 lemon
1 clove garlic
1 c. onions
5 c. peeled pears
2½ c. brown sugar
8 oz. raisins
3 oz. ginger (candied
   Australian is best)
1½ tsp. salt
¼ tsp. red pepper
2 c. cider vinegar
4 oz. mustard seed

Coarsely chop lemon, garlic, onions and pears. Add remaining ingredients and cook slowly for 3 hours. Pour in jars and seal.

Mrs. R. O. Campbell

SPICED MUSCADINE SAUCE

5 lbs. fruit
3 lbs. sugar
1 pt. cider vinegar
1 T. cinnamon
1 T. allspice
1 tsp. cloves

Pulp (remove hulls) grapes and put pulp to cook in a small quantity of water. Cook until broken. Put through coarse strainer to remove seeds. To hulls put sufficient water to boil until tender. Mix together, add sugar, vinegar and spices. Cook slowly, stirring often to prevent scorching. Pour into jars and seal.

Mrs. John J. Flynt, Jr.

VEGETABLE SOUP BASE

Yield: 14 pints

12 pods okra
3 bell peppers
8 ears corn
2 c. butter beans
3 hot peppers
1 gal. tomatoes, peeled
    and cut up
3 onions, peeled and
    cut up
1 c. sugar
1 c. vinegar
salt

Slice okra, peppers, and corn off the cob. Shell butter beans and boil 15 minutes. Put into mixture with the remaining ingredients and boil for 30 minutes. Put into hot sterilized jars and put ½ tsp. salt in top of each jar.
A doubled recipe twice a summer lasts the winter.

Mrs. William T. Scott, III

HELPFUL HINTS

SUBSTITUTIONS

For these	You may use these
1 whole egg, for thickening or baking	2 egg yolks. Or 2 tablespoons dried whole egg plus 2½ tablespoons water.
1 cup butter or margarine for shortening	⅞ cup lard, or rendered fat, with ½ teaspoon salt. Or 1 cup hydrogenated fat (cooking fat sold under brand name) with ½ teaspoon salt.
1 square (ounce) chocolate	3 or 4 tablespoons cocoa plus ½ tablespoon fat. For semi-sweet, add 3 tablespoons sugar.
6 ozs. semi-sweet chocolate	2 ozs. unsweetened chocolate, 7 tablespoons sugar and 2 tablespoons fat.
1 teaspoon double-acting baking powder	1½ teaspoons phosphate baking powder. Or 2 teaspoons tartrate baking powder.
sweet milk and baking powder, for baking	Equal amount of sour milk plus ½ teaspoon soda per cup. (Each half teaspoon soda with 1 cup sour milk takes the place of 2 teaspoons baking powder and 1 cup sweet milk.)
1 c. sour milk, for baking	1 cup sweet milk mixed with one of the following: 1 tablespoon vinegar. Or 1 tablespoon lemon juice. Or 1¾ teaspoons cream of tartar.
1 cup whole milk	½ cup evaporated milk plus ½ cup water. Or 4 tablespoons nonfat dry milk plus 2 teaspoons table fat and 1 cup water.
1 cup skim milk	4 tablespoons nonfat dry milk plus 1 cup water.
1 tablespoon flour, for thickening	½ tablespoon cornstarch, potato starch, rice starch, or arrowroot starch. Or 1 tablespoon granulated tapioca.
1 cup cake flour, for baking	⅞ cup all-purpose flour.
1 cup all-purpose flour for baking breads	Up to ½ cup bran, whole-wheat flour, or corn meal plus enough all-purpose flour to fill cup.
1 tablespoon cornstarch	1½ tablespoons flour.
1 cup corn syrup	¾ cup sugar plus ¼ cup water.
1 tablespoon tomato paste	1 tablespoon tomato catsup.
3 tablespoons chopped fresh parsley	1 teaspoon dried parsley flakes.
1 tablespoon prepared mustard	1 teaspoon dry mustard plus 1 tablespoon vinegar.

EQUIVALENTS

3 tsps.	1 T.
4 T.	¼ cup
5⅓ T.	⅓ cup
8 T.	½ cup
10⅔ T.	⅔ cup
12 T.	¾ cup
16 T.	1 cup
½ cup	1 gill
2 cups	1 pt.
4 cups	1 qt.
4 qts.	1 gal.
8 qts.	1 peck
4 pecks	1 bu.
16 ozs.	1 lb.
32 ozs.	1 qt.
8 ozs. liquid	1 cup
1 oz. liquid	2 T.

(For liquid and dry measurements use standard measuring spoons and cups. All measurements are level.)

OVEN TEMPERATURES EXPLAINED

Slow oven	250° to 325°F.
Moderately slow oven	326° to 349°F.
Moderate oven	350° to 374°F.
Quick moderate oven	375° to 399°F.
Hot oven	400° to 449°F.
Quick oven	450° to 500°F.
Very hot oven	501° to 575°F.

FOOD WEIGHTS

Apples
1 lb. = 3 c., sliced

Bananas
1 lb. = 3 c., sliced

Beans, dry
1 lb. - 2⅓ c.

Butter, Lard, Margarine
1 oz. = 2 T.
2 ozs. = ¼ c.
¼ lb. (stick) = ½ c.
½ lb. = 1 c.

Cheese
¼ lb. American or Cheddar = ¾ - 1 c., grated
1 lb. cottage = 2 c.
3 oz. package white cream = 6 T.
½ lb. package white cream = 16 T. (1 c.)

Chocolate, Unsweetened
½ lb. package = 8 squares
1 oz. = 1 square

Cocoa
1 lb. = 4 c.

Coconut, Shredded
1 lb. = 5 c.

Coffee
1 lb. regular grind = 5⅓ c. (80 T.)
1 lb. fine grind = 5 c.

Corn Meal
1 lb. = 3 c.

Cream
½ pt. (8 ozs.) = 1 c. (2 c. whipped)

FOOD WEIGHTS

Eggs
  5-6 whole = 1 c.
  12-14 yolks = 1 c.
  8-10 whites = 1 c.

Flour
  1 lb. all-purpose = 4 c. (sifted)
  1 lb. cake = 4½ c. (sifted)

Honey, Strained
  11 ozs. = 1 c.

Lemons, Medium Size
  1, juice = 2 to 3 T.
  1, rind, lightly grated = 1½ - 3 tsp.

Macaroni, Uncooked
  1 lb. = 5 c.

Marshmallows
  ¼ lb. = 16

Meat, Ground
  1 lb. = 2 c.

Oranges, Medium Size
  1, juice = ⅓ - ½ c.
  1, rind, lightly grated = 1 - 2 T.

Rice, Uncooked
  1 lb. = 2⅓ c.

Shortening, Solid Pack
  1 lb. = 3 c.

Sugar
  1 lb. granulated = 2 c.
  1 lb. brown = 2¼ c. (firmly packed)
  1 lb. confectioners = 3½ c. (sifted)
  1 lb. powdered = 2⅓ c.

Spaghetti, Uncooked
  1 lb. = 5 c.

Tea
  2 ozs. = ⅞ c.
  1 lb. = 6 c.

352

SERVINGS FROM COMMERCIAL CAN SIZE

Can Size	Contents	Servings
No. 0 (Buffet)	1⅓ c.	2
No. 1	1 c.	2
No. 1 (Tall)	2 c.	4
No. 303	2 c.	4
No. 2	2½ c.	4-5
No. 2½	3½ c.	6-7
No. 10	13 c.	25

VOLUME SERVINGS

12 qts. punch	96 punch glasses
1 gallon punch	serves 20
12 lb. ham	serves 20
20 lb. turkey (or chickens)	serves 20 generously
1 gallon ice cream	serves 30 if scoop is used
11" casserole	serves 8 amply
A 4 lb. chicken	yields 4 c. diced chicken

BUYING GUIDE — DRIED FRUITS, NUTS

If You Buy:	You Have:
Almonds, 1 lb. (in shells)	1-1¾ c.
(shelled)	3½ c.
Candied fruits or peels, ½ lb.	1½ c.
Dates, 1 lb. whole	2¼ c.
Figs, 1 lb.	2¾ c.
Peanuts, 1 lb. (in shells)	2¼ c.
(shelled)	3 c.
Pecans, 1 lb. (in shells)	2¼ c.
(shelled)	4 c.
Prunes, 1 lb. whole	2⅓ c.
Raisins (15 oz. package)	3 c.
Walnuts, 1 lb. (in shells)	1⅔ c.
(shelled)	4 c.

BUYING GUIDE — AMOUNTS FOR TWO

Vegetables

Cabbage or carrots	½ lb.
Lima beans or peas, unshelled	1 to 1½ lbs.
Onions	1 lb.
Potatoes to boil or mash	1 lb.
Potatoes, sweet	¾ lb.
String beans	½ - ¾ lb.

Beef

Chopped or ground	¾ lb.
Pot roast	2½ lbs.
Sirloin roast	3 lbs.
Club steak	1 - 1¼ lbs.
Porterhouse steak	1½ lbs.
Round steak	1 lb.
Sirloin or minute steak	1¼ lbs.

Pork

Canadian bacon	¼ lb. per person
Frankfurters or sausage	½ lb.
Ham steak or slice	1 lb.
Roast loin or spareribs	1½ lbs.

Veal

Cutlet or steak	1 lb.
Calf's liver	¾ lb.

Sausage

Bologna, liverwurst, salami	¼ lb.

Fish

Fillets	¾ lb. (approx.)
Steaks	1 lb.
Whole fish	1½ lbs.

BUYING GUIDE FOR CROWDS

PURCHASE TO SERVE:	25	50
Beef:		
Standing rib with bone	9-10 lbs.	17-20 lbs.
Rolled chuck roast	12 lbs.	2 (12 lbs.)
Ground beef (meat loaf)	5-6 lbs. (lean)	10-12 lbs.
Ham:		
Uncooked, ¾ lb. per serving	12-18 lbs.(bone in)	
Fully cooked, ½ - lb. per serving	8½ lbs. bone in or	
	6 lbs. canned boneless	
Chicken:		
Fried, quartered, 2½-3 lbs., uncooked	6-7 birds	14 birds
Fried, halves, 2½-3 lbs., uncooked	13-14 birds	25-30 birds
Salad, 6 lb. hen	2	4
Roast turkey: uncooked	16-20 lbs.	2 (16 lbs.)
Salad:		
Cabbage, slaw	5 lbs.	10 lbs.
Lettuce	4-5 heads	8-10 heads
Tomatoes, sliced	7 lbs.	12-14 lbs.
Vegetable salad	5 qts.	2½ gals.
Vegetables:		
Potatoes, mashed	7½-8 lbs.	16-18 lbs.
Sweet potatoes, fresh	9-10 lbs.	20 lbs.
Sweet potatoes, canned	7-8 No. 303	15-16 No. 303
	or 1 No. 10	or 2 No. 10
Green beans, canned	7-8 No. 303	14-16 No. 303
Asparagus, canned	8-9 No. 303	18-20 No. 303
English peas, canned	6-7 No. 303	14-16 No. 303
English peas, frozen	6 lbs.	12 lbs.
Corn, canned	7 No. 303	14-16 No. 303
Corn, frozen (packages)	10 (10 oz.)	17 (10 oz.)
Rice, regular	2 lbs.	4 lbs.
Rice, instant	8½ c.	17 c.
Other:		
Butter for rolls	¾ lb.	1½ lbs.
Ice cream, 1 full scoop	1½ gals.	3 gals.
Beverages:		
Milk	4½ qts.	2½ gals.
Tea, loose	½ c.	¼ lb.
Coffee, ground	½ - ¾ lb.	1¼ lbs.
Cream for coffee	1½ pts.	1½ qts.
Sugar for coffee	½ lb.	1 lb.

Beef:

Hamburger	30-36 lbs.
Beef	40 lbs.
Meat Loaf	24 lbs.

Pork:

Ham	40 lbs.
Roast Pork	40 lbs.
Weiners	25 lbs.

Vegetables:

Canned	4 No. 10 cans (26 lbs.)
Baked beans	5 gals.
Beets	30 lbs.
Cauliflower	18 lbs.
Cabbage for Slaw	20 lbs.
Carrots	33 lbs.
Potatoes	35 lbs.

Salads:

Potato	12 qts.
Fruit	20 qts.
Vegetable	20 qts.
Lettuce	20 heads
Dressing	3 qts.

Breads:

Rolls	200
Bread	10 loaves
Butter	3 lbs.

Other:

Coffee	3 lbs.
Sugar	3 lbs.
Light Cream	3 qts.
Milk	6 gals.
Fruit Cocktail	2 - ½ gals.
Fruit Juice	4 No. 10 cans (26 lbs.)
Soup	5 gals.
Oysters	18 qts.
Olives	1¾ lbs.
Pickles	2 qts.
Nuts	3 lbs.
Cheese	3 lbs.

Desserts:

Cakes	8
Pies	18
Ice Cream	4 gals.

BUYING GUIDE FOR SHRIMP:

Using green shrimp - 21 to 25 count per pound - buy ⅓ pound per person.

BAR SET-UP

For 25 (2½ hour serving time)

2 - 5ths scotch
1 - qt. bourbon
2 - 5ths vodka
1 - qt. gin

Mixers:
1 soda water (lge.)
2 gingerale
2 tonic water

Cut limes and lemons
1 lb. ice per person

For 50 (2½ hour serving time)

2½ qts. scotch
2 qts. bourbon
2½ qts. vodka
1 qt. gin

Mixers:
2 soda water
4 gingerale
5 tonic water

Cut limes and lemons
1 lb. ice per person

For 75 (2½ hour serving time)

4 qts. scotch
3½ qts. bourbon
4 qts. vodka
2 qts. gin

Mixers:
3 soda water
6 gingerale
7 tonic water

Cut limes and lemons
1 lb. ice per person

Kenneth H. Williams

METRIC CONVERSION TABLES

Liquid Measure:

> 1 tsp. = 5 c.c.
> 1 T. = 15 c.c.
> 1 oz. = 30 milliliters
> 1 c. = about ¼ liter
> 1 qt. = about 1 liter

To determine liquid measure multiply

The number of:	By	To Get
ounces	30	milliliters
pints	0.47	liters
quarts	0.95	liters

Dry Measure:

> 1 oz. = about 28 grams
> 1 lb. = about 454 grams

To determine dry measure multiply

The number of:	By	To Get
ounces	28	grams
pounds	0.45	kilograms

> 4 ozs. = ½ c.
> 8 ozs. = 1 c.

Food Measurements:

Sugar:

> 1 T. = 15 grams
> 1 c. = 240 grams

Flour:

> ¼ c. = 35 grams
> 1 c. = 140 grams

Salt:

> 1 T. = 15 grams

Rice:

> 1 c. = 240 grams

Butter:

> 1 T. = 15 grams
> ½ c. = 125 grams

Notes

362

The Stuffed Griffin
The Utility Club
P.O. Box 711
Griffin, Georgia 30224

Please send _____ copies of THE STUFFED GRIFFIN at $19.95 each plus
$3.00 postage and handling per book. For Georgia delivery add 7% sales tax per
book. Make checks payable to The Utility Club Cookbook.

Name _____

Street _____

City, State _____

Zip _____

The Stuffed Griffin
The Utility Club
P.O. Box 711
Griffin, Georgia 30224

Please send _____ copies of THE STUFFED GRIFFIN at $19.95 each plus
$3.00 postage and handling per book. For Georgia delivery add 7% sales tax per
book. Make checks payable to The Utility Club Cookbook.

Name _____

Street _____

City, State _____

Zip _____

The Stuffed Griffin
The Utility Club
P.O. Box 711
Griffin, Georgia 30224

Please send _____ copies of THE STUFFED GRIFFIN at $19.95 each plus
$3.00 postage and handling per book. For Georgia delivery add 7% sales tax per
book. Make checks payable to The Utility Club Cookbook.

Name _____

Street _____

City, State _____

Zip _____

Names and addresses of bookstores, gift shops, etc. in your area would be appreciated.

_____

_____

_____

_____

_____

_____

_____

- -

Names and addresses of bookstores, gift shops, etc. in your area would be appreciated.

_____

_____

_____

_____

_____

_____

- -

Names and addresses of bookstores, gift shops, etc. in your area would be appreciated.

_____

_____

_____

_____

_____

_____

_____